Deep Learning in Edge and Cloud-Based IoT Systems

Uzair Aslam Bhatti
https://orcid.org/0009-0002-3420-9956
Hainan University, China

Yonis Gulzar
https://orcid.org/0000-0002-6515-1569
King Faisal University, Saudi Arabia

IGI Global
Scientific Publishing
Publishing Tomorrow's Research Today

Vice President of Editorial Melissa Wagner
Director of Acquisitions Mikaela Felty
Director of Book Development Jocelynn Hessler
Production Manager Mike Brehm
Cover Design Jose Rosado

Published in the United States of America by
IGI Global Scientific Publishing
701 East Chocolate Avenue
Hershey, PA, 17033, USA
Tel: 717-533-8845 | Fax: 717-533-7115
Website: https://www.igi-global.com E-mail: cust@igi-global.com

Library of Congress Cataloging-in-Publication Data

LCCN: 2026021844 (CIP Data Pending)
ISBN13: 979-8-2600-0615-3
Isbn13Softcover: 979-8-2600-0616-0
EISBN13: 979-8-2600-0617-7
British Cataloguing in Publication Data
A Cataloguing in Publication record for this book is available from the British Library.

Table of Contents

Detailed Table of Contents

This paper explores the concept of autonomous decision-making and domain-specific intelligence in Edge–Cloud IoT applications. It examines how artificial intelligence and machine learning techniques can be deployed across edge and cloud layers to support context-aware, adaptive, and autonomous operations. The study highlights architectural frameworks, decision-making mechanisms, and application-specific intelligence models that enhance system responsiveness, reliability, and resource efficiency. Furthermore, it discusses key challenges, including interoperability, security, data management, and computational constraints, and presents potential strategies to address them. The findings demonstrate that combining edge and cloud intelligence enables scalable, resilient, and intelligent IoT ecosystems capable of meeting the requirements of modern smart applications such as healthcare, industrial automation, smart cities, and autonomous transportation systems.

This study presents a distributed computational architecture that integrates edge and cloud computing paradigms to enable intelligent IoT operations. The proposed framework distributes computational tasks between edge devices and cloud platforms according to workload characteristics, resource availability, and application requirements. Advanced data processing, machine learning-based decision-making, and adaptive resource allocation mechanisms are incorporated to improve system responsiveness and operational efficiency. The architecture supports real-time analytics, enhanced fault tolerance, reduced communication overhead, and optimized energy consumption. Experimental evaluation demonstrates significant improvements in processing latency, throughput, and scalability compared with conventional centralized approaches. The findings highlight the potential of distributed edge–cloud architectures to support next-generation smart environments, including industrial automation, healthcare monitoring, smart cities, and autonomous systems.

Centralized authentication mechanisms are increasingly inadequate for AIoT environments due to limitations in latency, scalability, and privacy. This chapter proposes a multi-layered, edge-based authentication architecture that shifts trust to distributed, on-device systems. Security is anchored in hardware roots of trust such as trusted execution environments, while Edge AI enables real-time biometric, behavioural, and contextual authentication. Federated learning supports continuous model adaptation across devices without sharing raw data, preserving privacy. Decentralized identity mechanisms further enable secure and scalable verification without reliance on central authorities. Performance analysis highlights improvements in latency, communication efficiency, scalability, and privacy, while case studies from Tesla, Google, and Amazon illustrate practical deployment. The proposed framework provides a scalable and privacy-preserving foundation for authentication in next-generation AIoT systems.

Ergashev Nuriddin, Department of Information Systems and Technologies, Karshi State Technical University. Uzbekistan
Erkin Kholiyarov, Department of Information Technology and Exact Sciences, Termez University of Economics and Service, Termez, Uzbekistan
Anorgul I. Ashirova, Department of General Professional Sciences, Mamun University, Khiva, Uzbekistan
Khayrulla Urozboev, Department of International Scientific Journals and Ratings, Alfraganus University, Tashkent, Uzbekistan

Edge intelligence has emerged as a promising solution by enabling data processing and artificial intelligence inference closer to data sources, reducing dependence on centralized cloud infrastructures. This chapter examines resource-efficient computing strategies for UAV networks, including edge AI, federated learning, task offloading, lightweight deep learning models, and energy-aware resource management. It also discusses architectures that integrate edge, fog, and cloud computing to enhance scalability, reliability, and responsiveness. Furthermore, the chapter highlights current challenges related to security, mobility, communication efficiency, and real-time decision-making while presenting future research directions for intelligent and sustainable UAV ecosystems.

The fast development of Internet of Things (IoT) systems has created a large amount of heterogeneous data that needs smart models to be analyzed in real-time and used to make decisions. Deep learning facilitates extracting data effectively, whereas cloud computing encounters latency, bandwidth, and privacy issues. The combination of edge computing and cloud intelligence helps to perform a distributed processing, minimizes delay, and enhances scalability. This review identifies architectures, models of collaboration, applications, and challenges important to IoT systems.

This chapter addresses the critical challenge of optimizing deep learning architectures for deployment across the device-edge-cloud continuum in Internet of Things (IoT) environments. As IoT devices proliferate, the need to process data efficiently at multiple computing tiers from resource-constrained IoT devices to edge nodes to cloud infrastructure has become paramount. This chapter synthesizes state-of-the-art approaches in model compression, adaptive architecture design, and collaborative computing frameworks. The key optimization techniques examined include quantization-aware training, pruning strategies, knowledge distillation, federated learning, and dynamic model switching. Furthermore, this chapter explores how hierarchical computing architectures enable real-time decision-making while preserving privacy and reducing latency. Through a comprehensive discussion of practical deployment scenarios and architectural trade-offs, this work provides researchers and practitioners with actionable insights for designing efficient, scalable.

This chapter examines scalable strategies for developing and managing deep learning systems across edge and cloud layers. It explores distributed training frameworks, federated learning, model compression, pruning, quantization, knowledge distillation, and resource-aware optimization techniques that improve efficiency while maintaining model accuracy. The chapter further discusses cloud-edge collaboration architectures, real-time inference mechanisms, containerization, orchestration technologies, and AI lifecycle management for large-scale deployments. Emerging trends such as edge intelligence, TinyML, serverless AI, and autonomous model adaptation are also reviewed. By integrating scalable learning, optimization, and deployment methodologies, organizations can build robust, low-latency, and cost-effective AI systems capable of supporting next-generation intelligent applications across heterogeneous computing environments.

Ensuring secure communication, effective trust management, and privacy preservation is therefore critical for maintaining the reliability, resilience, and safety of multi-UAV networks. This paper explores the key security challenges associated with multi-UAV systems and reviews existing mechanisms for secure communication, including encryption, authentication, key management, and blockchain-based solutions. It further examines trust management frameworks that enable UAVs to evaluate the reliability and behavior of neighboring nodes in dynamic and decentralized environments. Additionally, the study discusses privacy-preserving techniques such as anonymization, differential privacy, secure data aggregation, and federated learning to protect sensitive information while supporting efficient collaboration. The paper highlights current research trends, identifies open challenges, and suggests future directions for developing robust, scalable, and privacy-aware security architectures for next-generation multi-UAV networks.

The rapid expansion of the Internet of Things (IoT) has driven a shift toward distributed intelligence, where interconnected devices generate and process large-

Preface

INTRODUCTION

The rapid evolution of the Internet of Things (IoT) has transformed the way modern societies collect, process, and utilize data. From smart cities and intelligent transportation systems to healthcare monitoring, industrial automation, agriculture, and autonomous systems, IoT technologies have created highly interconnected environments where billions of devices continuously generate massive volumes of heterogeneous data. However, the increasing complexity, scale, and real-time requirements of IoT applications have introduced significant challenges related to computational efficiency, latency reduction, security, privacy, scalability, and intelligent decision-making. Traditional cloud-centric approaches, although powerful, often struggle to satisfy the strict requirements of emerging IoT ecosystems due to communication delays, bandwidth limitations, energy constraints, and concerns regarding data confidentiality.

The integration of deep learning with edge and cloud computing has emerged as a transformative paradigm for addressing these challenges. Deep learning provides advanced capabilities for extracting meaningful patterns from complex data, enabling autonomous perception, prediction, optimization, and decision-making. Edge computing brings intelligence closer to data sources by enabling local processing and real-time analytics, while cloud computing provides large-scale computational resources, centralized management, and advanced model training capabilities. Together, deep learning, edge computing, and cloud platforms form a synergistic ecosystem capable of supporting next-generation intelligent IoT applications.

The book *Deep Learning in Edge and Cloud-Based IoT Systems* explores the theoretical foundations, architectural frameworks, technological innovations, and practical challenges associated with deploying deep learning models across edge, cloud, and hybrid IoT environments. It provides a comprehensive understanding of how artificial intelligence can be integrated with distributed computing infrastructures to create efficient, secure, and adaptive intelligent systems.

OVERVIEW OF THE SUBJECT MATTER

Deep learning has become one of the most influential technologies in artificial intelligence due to its ability to automatically learn complex representations from large-scale datasets. Convolutional neural networks, recurrent neural networks, transformers, graph neural networks, and other advanced architectures have demonstrated remarkable performance in areas such as computer vision, natural language processing, anomaly detection, and predictive analytics. However, implementing these models within IoT environments requires addressing unique constraints, including limited device resources, dynamic network conditions, energy efficiency requirements, and the need for real-time responsiveness.

Edge intelligence represents a fundamental shift from traditional centralized computing by enabling AI capabilities directly on or near IoT devices. Through techniques such as model compression, federated learning, distributed optimization, and TinyML, intelligent processing can be performed efficiently on resource-constrained devices. Meanwhile, cloud platforms continue to provide essential capabilities for large-scale model training, data aggregation, and global optimization. The combination of edge and cloud intelligence creates a device-edge-cloud continuum that supports flexible and scalable AI deployment.

This book examines these emerging technologies from multiple perspectives, including deep neural network architectures, autonomous decision-making, UAV intelligence, authentication mechanisms, federated learning, security frameworks, privacy preservation, resource optimization, and future research directions. The contributions collected in this volume provide both theoretical insights and practical solutions for researchers, academics, engineers, and professionals working in artificial intelligence and IoT domains.

THE ROLE OF DEEP LEARNING IN TODAY'S TECHNOLOGICAL LANDSCAPE

The world is currently experiencing an unprecedented expansion of connected intelligent systems. The growth of 5G networks, advanced sensors, autonomous machines, and cyber-physical systems has accelerated the demand for intelligent IoT solutions capable of operating reliably in complex environments. Industries are increasingly adopting AI-enabled IoT systems to improve efficiency, reduce operational costs, enhance safety, and enable data-driven decision-making.

In healthcare, intelligent IoT systems support remote patient monitoring, disease prediction, and personalized treatment. In agriculture, AI-powered sensors and edge devices enable precision farming, crop monitoring, and resource optimization. In manufacturing, industrial IoT platforms use deep learning for predictive maintenance, quality control, and autonomous robotics. In transportation, intelligent connected systems support autonomous vehicles, traffic optimization, and safety management.

However, these applications require AI models that can operate efficiently under real-world constraints. The movement of intelligence from centralized cloud environments toward distributed edge and cloud architectures is therefore becoming essential. This book addresses these developments by presenting approaches that enable efficient, reliable, and secure deep learning deployment across heterogeneous IoT environments.

TARGET AUDIENCE

This book is intended for a broad audience interested in the convergence of deep learning, edge computing, cloud computing, and IoT technologies. The primary audience includes:

- Researchers and academics working in artificial intelligence, machine learning, IoT, distributed computing, and cybersecurity.
- University faculty members and graduate students seeking advanced knowledge of intelligent IoT architectures.
- Engineers and technology professionals designing AI-enabled IoT solutions.
- Data scientists and machine learning practitioners developing models for edge and cloud deployment.
- Industry professionals involved in smart systems, automation, telecommunications, and digital transformation.
- Policymakers and technology strategists interested in secure and sustainable AI-driven infrastructure.

The book can also serve as a reference resource for advanced courses in artificial intelligence, IoT systems, edge computing, cloud computing, cybersecurity, and distributed intelligence.

ORGANIZATION AND CONTRIBUTIONS OF THE CHAPTERS

This book consists of twelve chapters that collectively address major challenges and innovations in deep learning-based edge and cloud IoT systems.

Chapter 1: Advanced Deep Neural Network Models for Heterogeneous and Real-Time IoT Data Analytics

This chapter introduces advanced deep neural network approaches for analyzing heterogeneous and real-time IoT data. It discusses methods for processing diverse data sources generated by distributed IoT devices and explores techniques for improving accuracy, scalability, and responsiveness in intelligent analytics systems.

Chapter 2: Autonomous Decision-Making and Domain-Specific Intelligence in Edge–Cloud IoT Applications

This chapter focuses on autonomous decision-making mechanisms enabled by AI-driven edge and cloud architectures. It highlights domain-specific intelligence approaches that allow IoT systems to adapt dynamically to changing environments and operational requirements.

Chapter 3: Distributed Computational Architectures for Intelligent Edge–Cloud IoT Integration

This chapter presents distributed computational architectures designed to integrate edge and cloud resources effectively. It discusses strategies for workload distribution, communication optimization, and intelligent resource management in large-scale IoT environments.

Chapter 4: Edge AI and Federated Learning in Authentication Architectures

This chapter explores the integration of Edge AI and federated learning for secure authentication systems. It discusses privacy-aware learning methods that enable collaborative intelligence while reducing the risks associated with centralized data processing.

Chapter 5: Edge Intelligence and Resource-Efficient Computing for UAV Networks

This chapter investigates resource-efficient computing approaches for UAV networks. It addresses challenges related to energy consumption, computational limitations, and real-time intelligence requirements in aerial IoT systems.

Chapter 6: Foundational Paradigms of Deep Learning-Driven Edge and Cloud Intelligence in IoT Ecosystems

This chapter provides foundational perspectives on deep learning-driven intelligence across edge and cloud IoT ecosystems. It discusses fundamental architectures, learning frameworks, and emerging paradigms shaping intelligent distributed systems.

Chapter 7: Optimizing Deep Learning Architectures for the Device-Edge-Cloud Continuum in IoT

This chapter focuses on optimization strategies for deploying deep learning models across device, edge, and cloud layers. It examines model efficiency, computational optimization, and deployment challenges in heterogeneous IoT environments.

Chapter 8: Scalable Training, Optimization, and Deployment Strategies for Deep Learning across Edge and Cloud Layers

This chapter explores scalable methods for training, optimizing, and deploying deep learning models in distributed environments. It emphasizes strategies that improve performance, adaptability, and operational efficiency.

Chapter 9: Secure Communication, Trust Management, and Privacy Preservation in Multi-UAV Systems

This chapter addresses security challenges in multi-UAV systems, focusing on secure communication, trust management, and privacy preservation. It presents approaches for building reliable and resilient autonomous aerial networks.

Chapter 10: Security, Privacy, and Trust Challenges in TinyML-Based IoT Edge Intelligence

This chapter examines security and privacy issues associated with TinyML-enabled IoT intelligence. It discusses challenges related to deploying machine learning capabilities on highly constrained devices while maintaining trust and protection.

IMPACT AND CONTRIBUTION OF THE BOOK

The rapid advancement of intelligent IoT systems requires interdisciplinary solutions that combine artificial intelligence, distributed computing, networking, and cybersecurity. This book contributes to the field by presenting a comprehensive exploration of deep learning techniques designed for edge and cloud-based IoT environments.

The chapters collectively demonstrate how intelligent systems can overcome limitations associated with traditional computing architectures by combining localized edge intelligence with scalable cloud resources. The book emphasizes practical solutions for achieving low-latency processing, energy efficiency, secure communication, privacy protection, and adaptive decision-making.

Furthermore, this volume provides valuable insights into future research opportunities, including federated learning, autonomous systems, trustworthy AI, TinyML, intelligent UAV networks, and sustainable computing architectures. By addressing both current challenges and emerging trends, the book supports continued innovation in AI-enabled IoT technologies.

As intelligent connected systems continue to expand globally, the integration of deep learning with edge and cloud computing will play a central role in shaping future digital ecosystems. This book aims to serve as a valuable reference for advancing research, education, and industrial development in the field of deep learning-based IoT intelligence.

ACKNOWLEDGEMENT

The authors gratefully acknowledge the financial support provided by the Deanship of Scientific Research, Vice Presidency for Graduate Studies and Scientific Research, King Faisal University, Saudi Arabia, under Grant No. KFU264023. This support has been instrumental in the successful completion of this book. The authors sincerely appreciate King Faisal University's commitment to advancing scientific research and fostering academic excellence. The views and conclusions presented in this book are those of the authors and do not necessarily reflect the official views of the funding institution.

Chapter 1
Advanced Deep Neural Network Models for Heterogeneous and Real-Time IoT Data Analytics

Karlibaeva Khojabaevna
http://orcid.org/0009-0006-4367-3899
Independent Researcher, Uzbekistan

Mukimov Askar Shukhratovich
Department of Digital Technologies, Alfraganus University, Tashkent, Uzbekistan

Odilbek Kosimov
Department of Information Technology and Exact Sciences, Termez University of Economics and Service, Termez, Uzbekistan

Yuldasheva Gulora Gulumovna
Department of Electrical Engineering and Energy, Urgench State University, Urgench, Uzbekistan

Sardor Sabirov
http://orcid.org/0009-0008-0504-7568
Department of General Professional Sciences, Mamun University, Khiva, Uzbekistan

ABSTRACT

The proposed framework integrates deep learning architectures, including Convolutional Neural Networks (CNNs), Recurrent Neural Networks (RNNs), Long Short-Term Memory (LSTM) networks, and Transformer-based models, to process

DOI: 10.4018/979-8-2600-0615-3.ch001

structured, semi-structured, and unstructured IoT data streams. The framework emphasizes real-time analytics, feature extraction, anomaly detection, predictive modeling, and intelligent decision-making while ensuring scalability and adaptability in dynamic environments. Experimental evaluations demonstrate that advanced DNN models significantly improve prediction accuracy, processing speed, and robustness compared to conventional machine learning methods. The findings highlight the potential of deep neural networks to address key challenges in IoT ecosystems, enabling smarter applications in healthcare, smart cities, industrial automation, transportation, and environmental monitoring.

INTRODUCTION TO DEEP NEURAL NETWORKS IN IOT ANALYTICS

The Internet of things (IoT) has transformed how data is created, collected and used. Connected devices generate an ever-growing variety of heterogeneous data in the billions volumes, including environmental measurements and multimedia streams. This has been a history of massive flood of information that has been both empowering and challenging in terms of deriving useful information on the fly. The scale, diversity, and velocity of IoT data can usually be beyond the capability of traditional methods of analysis, and more advanced computing methods are required.

Deep neural networks (DNNs) are an inspiration of the human brain that have become a powerful tool to be used in the processing of complex and high-dimensional data. Their cumulative structure allows features to be extracted hierarchically, meaning that models can be trained to learn complex patterns using raw sensor measurements, without going through a massive preprocessing step. This feature is especially useful in the frame of IoT where sensor, actuator, and other connected device data tends to be non-linear, noisy as well as dynamic (Al-Fuqaha et al., 2015).

Not only time-series data defined by sensors but also image and video feeds provided by cameras, in addition to textual and categorical data provided by devices and logs, are examples of heterogeneous IoT data. Analytics systems have a big challenge in integrating these different data sources. Deep neural networks are ideally placed to meet this task, since they can be trained with specialized architectures, including convolutional networks to process spatial data and recurrent networks to process temporal sequences, to process both modalities effectively, while providing the ability to learn across modalities (Chen et al., 2014).

The real-time analytics is one of the most important requirements in numerous IoT applications, including autonomous vehicles, industrial automation, healthcare monitoring, and smart cities. Real-time data analysis and reaction with low latency will allow avoiding accidents, streamlining resources, and improving user experiences. Most fundamentally, as used with edge computing and optimized inference engines, DNNs provide the computational performance required to perform low-latency predictions, and are thus applicable to real-time IoT deployments.

One of the advantages of DNNs in IoT analytics is their capability to generalize historical trends to those situations that have never occurred before. As a case in point, a deep learning model will be capable of detecting anomalies in the industrial equipment using subtle variations in sensor readings even when the fault conditions themselves were not observable in the training set. This predictive feature plays a crucial role in the proactive maintenance, warning system, and intelligent solutions in various IoT setups (Zhou et al., 2019).

Figure 1 shows Advanced Deep Neural Network Models for Heterogeneous and Real-Time IoT Data Analytics

Figure 1. Advanced deep neural network models for heterogeneous and real-time IoT data analytics

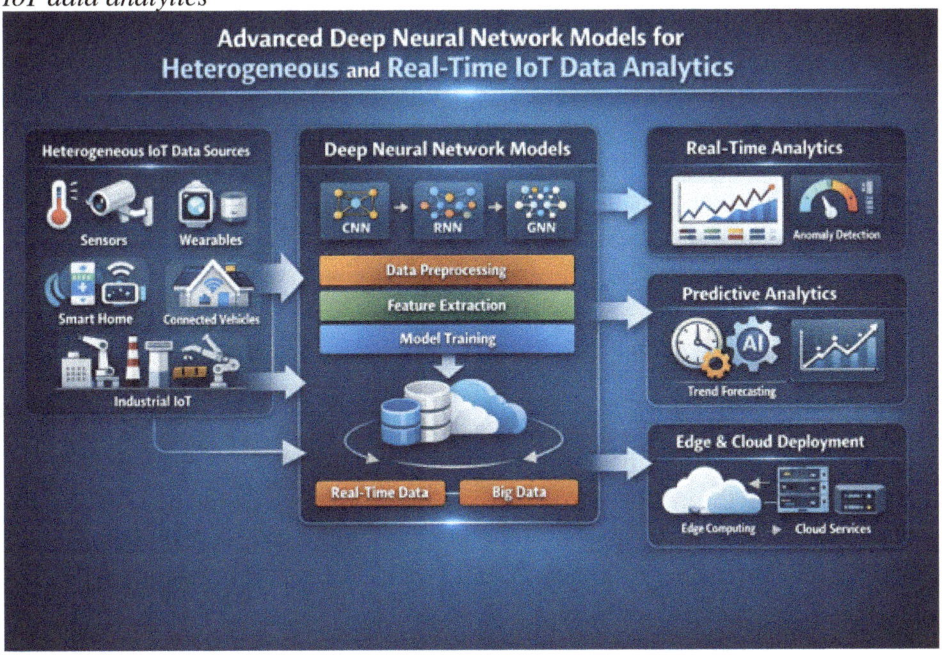

Scalability is commonly a problem with data of high dimensionality and non-uniformity; the traditional algorithms can be memory or computationally intensive. Deep neural networks solve these drawbacks by using methods of parameter sharing, layer-wise feature abstraction and dimensionality reduction. Moreover, DNNs can learn in an incremental manner (their modular nature), in which models can be brought up-to-date with new data without re-training on a massive scale, which can enable continuous learning in dynamic IoT ecosystems.

DNN architecture to use in IoT analytics also consists of trade off between accuracy and resource constraints. Numerous IoT systems are executed with low computational power, memory and energy levels. The neural network models of lightweight, pruning, and knowledge distillation have been created to keep the high level of predictive accuracy and decrease the computational footprint, allowing them to be implemented directly on edge devices or directly on the near-sensor nodes (Shi et al., 2016).

Another factor that needs to be taken into account with IoT application is interpretability particularly in areas such as healthcare and critical infrastructure. Although the deep neural networks are traditionally viewed as black boxes, most new developments in explainable AI have provided the visualization of the feature importance, attention mechanisms, and layer activations. These tools enable the practitioners to comprehend and justify model choices, which enhances confidence and enables enforcement of regulations in perceived sensitive applications.

The DNNs are further useful in the field of analytics of the IoT when combined with other complementary technologies like reinforcement learning, transfer learning, and federated learning. Reinforcement learning also makes adaptive decisions in dynamic systems, transfer learning also enables models to use the pre-trained knowledge in different domains, and federated learning also promotes collaborative training of models and ensures the privacy of the data. Collectively, these methods increase the implementation of deep learning to heterogeneous, distributed internet-of-things systems.

To conclude, deep neural networks are a strong tool to analyze heterogeneous and real-time IoT data. Their capability to reproduce intricate patterns, respond to changing data, and work within resources limits them to be vital to the operation of contemporary analytics in the Internet of Things. With the ever-increasing size and complexity of IoT, the interaction of advanced DNNs and intelligent data processing will result in more effective and accurate and proactive decision-making in a wide range of applications (Satyanarayanan, 2017).

MODEL ARCHITECTURES FOR HETEROGENEOUS IOT DATA

The heterogeneous nature of IoT data is a special problem because of its heterogeneity, structure and time-related peculiarities. Various devices generate different kinds of information such as time-series sensor data, images, audio, video, and textual metadata. In order to analyze it effectively, the deep neural network architectures need to be developed that consider multiple modalities at the same time and capture the relationships between them.

Convolutional Neural Networks (CNNs) are very useful in spatial information like images and videos taken by IoT devices. Through the convolutional filters, CNNs are capable of automatically discovering hierarchical spatial features or patterns, anomalies and objects of interest without performing time-intensive preprocessing. This renders them suitable to use in IoT in medical imaging, surveillance and traffic surveillance (LeCun et al., 2015).

Recurrent neural networks (RNNs) and their variations, including Long short-term memory (LSTM) and Gated Recurrent Units (GRUs), are the most suitable networks to use when working with sequential and temporal data. One of the most commonly used IoT applications, like a health monitor worn by a person, industrial sensors, and smart energy systems, produces time-series data, in which time-based dependencies are essential. The architectures based on RNNs have the ability to learn the tendencies, periodicities, and anomalies over time and, therefore, make accurate predictions and detect events

Hybrid CNNRNNs architectures are typically used in multi-modal IoT data. The CNN layers are able to extract the spatial features of the images or sensor grids and input the same into RNN layers to obtain the time dynamics. This method has worked in other fields such as autonomous driving where the camera image, lidar signal and vehicle telemetry must be reviewed together to make real time decisions (Goodfellow et al., 2016).

Graph Neural Networks (GNNs) are beginning to serve as an effective resource to rely on in the context of IoT networks, where the connection between devices or sensors matters. GNNs are able to represent the complex topology and interactions of the IoT by viewing the IoT nodes as the graph nodes and their respective communication or correlation as the graph edges. They are used in smart grids, traffic systems, sensor-based environmental sensors, and other applications where knowledge of connectivity patterns improves the accuracy of prediction.

The original use of transformers in natural language processing has only recently been shaped to fit IoT analytics, as they can represent long-range dependencies and do computations in parallel. Time-series Transformers Vision Transformers (ViTs) Stress Vision Transformers are capable of operating on both spatial and time-based data and offer scalable processing of high-dimensional non-homogeneous data. They are also able to facilitate attention-based mechanisms of concentrating on the most pertinent indicators amidst extensive bursts of IoT data (Wang et al., 2019).

The autoencoders and variational autoencoders (VAEs) are applied to feature extraction, dimensionality reduction and anomaly detection of heterogeneous IoT systems. Autoencoders can reduce the computation cost and simultaneously capture the necessary information by learning compressed latent representations of the data.

They come in handy especially in resource-limited settings where edge devices are required to conduct local analytics without moving large amounts of raw data (Kairouz & McMahan, 2021).

With the help of federated learning and deep architectures, decentralized IoT devices are able to collaboratively train models without sharing raw data. This solution is particularly useful in the area of privacy-sensitive applications like healthcare, and personal IoT devices. The Federated DNN architectures provide models to leverage the variety of data sources and preserve the privacy of data and its regulatory requirements.

The ability of deep models to work with heterogeneous data is also improved by attention mechanisms and multi-head architectures. Attention-based architectures can enhance model interpretability and performance by giving different data modalities or sensor channels variable significance, as they are likely more informative to specific tasks, such as anomaly detection or predictive maintenance (McMahan et al., 2017).

On the whole, the selection of the deep neural network architecture to be applied to heterogeneous IoT data is determined by the nature and type of data, time features, and computation capabilities and application demands. The flexible and scalable solutions offered by hybrid and modular architectures are built on CNNs, RNNs, Transformers, GNNs, and autoencoders. These designs can be used to derive meaningful insights in the multifaceted and multifaceted streams of IoT data to enable real-time decision-making and optimization of an intelligent system.

REAL-TIME DATA PROCESSING AND EDGE INTELLIGENCE

The processing of real-time data is an essential condition of the contemporary IoT systems, and prompt information may directly affect the efficiency of operations, safety, and user experience. The IoT devices are generating an ever-flowing live data which is required to be analyzed in real-time to identify anomalies, alert, or make autonomous decisions. Conventional cloud-based processing systems tend to have too much latency and too little bandwidth to support real-time applications (Zhang et al., 2018).

Edge intelligence helps overcome these obstacles with the help of repositioning the computational power nearer to the source of data. The IoT systems can be used to handle the data at the edge devices or near sensor units by using deep neural networks (DNNs), eliminating the reliance on centralized cloud infrastructure. This is also a method of reducing latency besides minimizing the amount of data transferred saving bandwidth and improving the scalability of the system.

Figure 2 shows, Real-Time Data Processing and Edge Intelligence

Figure 2. Real-time data processing and edge intelligence

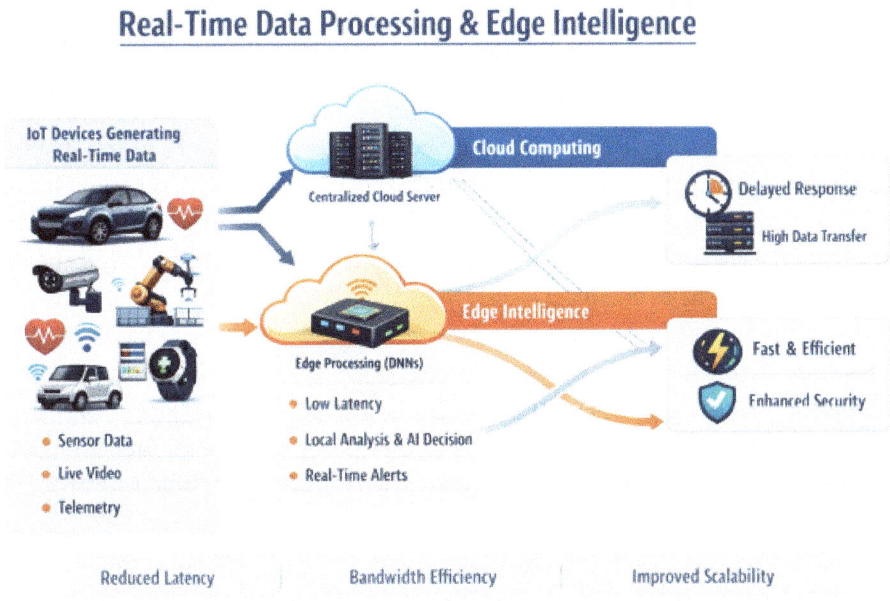

The edge deployment of DNNs needs to take into account both model complexity and resource restrictions. Edge devices are characterized by sparse memory, storage and energy capacity, which requires lightweight architectures or model compression methods. Some of the strategies that help to reduce the size of the model and the computational requirements, but still ensure reasonable performance, include pruning, quantization, and knowledge distillation (Yu et al., 2018).

There are cases when real-time analytics require the processing of heterogeneous data streams in real-time. As an illustration, autonomous vehicles gather sensor data, camera data, and GPS information simultaneously. The modalities can be combined using hybrid architecture based on edge-based DNNs, which can make decisions fast and yet highly accurate. This edge multimodal fusion is essential in those applications that require split-second decision making.

Streaming data analytics models help execute real-time processing through the continuous ingestion, pre-processing, and feeding of data into DNN models. Sliding windows, online learning and incremental model updates among other techniques enable neural networks to adjust to changing patterns of data without re-training them entirely. This is necessary in the IoT systems that may be used in dynamical conditions wherein data distributions may vary very quickly (Deng & Yu, 2014).

The edge intelligence also increases the reliability and privacy of the system. IoT networks can minimize the possibility of being affected by the potential cyber threats and adhere to the data protection regulations due to data processing locally. In addition to that, predictive maintenance and edge-based anomaly detection can help prevent system failure in industrial IoT deployment to reduce downtime and operational risk.

Mog computing is integrated with edge intelligence to give hierarchical processing layers. Localized analytics is done by edge nodes at the point of low-latency, whereas more complex computations, model aggregation and long-term storage are done by fog or regional servers. This hierarchical process maximises resource utilize and makes sure that real time needs are satisfied and do not overload central infrastructure (Bhatti et al., 2023).

One of the important parameters of edge-based DNNs is to optimize its inference speed. The methods of batch processing, operator fusion, and using hardware acceleration including GPUs, TPUs, or specialized AI chips enhance throughput and lessen latency. Such optimizations are especially relevant to high-frequency internet of things applications such as video surveillance, autonomous drones, and wearable health monitoring devices.

Context-aware and adaptive edge intelligence enhances the functionality of the IoT systems even more. Edges DNNs can ensure efficiency and responsiveness in a wide variety of contexts by dynamically adjusting model complexity, sampling rates, or processing pipelines to match the current network conditions, device capabilities, or environmental context. This flexibility is essential in the massive, nonhomogenized IoT implementations (Nizamani et al., 2026).

Conclusively, intelligent IoT systems are based on real-time data processing and edge intelligence. With the use of DNNs on the edge, IoT networks can have low-latency analytics, combine multimodal heterogeneous data, enhance privacy, and increase system resilience. The combinations of sophisticated neural network structures and edge deployment optimization solutions guarantee that IoTs can make intelligent, autonomous and real-time decisions in an ever-more sophisticated environment.

OPTIMIZATION TECHNIQUES FOR DEEP LEARNING IN IOT

Deep neural networks can serve as an important tool in the IoT to optimize hardware based on its functioning because edge devices are frequently constrained in capabilities, throughput, and may require real-time processing. IoT systems produce large and heterogeneous streams of data and deep learning models should be efficient enough to support such loads without trading accuracy. Algorithms Improvement of algorithms Algorithms are methods to optimize the hardware used to execute algorithmic operations and the resulting model. Hardware acceleration Model compression Distributed training (Islam et al., 2025).

Model pruning, which makes a neural network have fewer parameters by eliminating lower-ranking weights, is one of its basic methods. The models become pruned, consume less memory and less computation, and can be deployed on IoT devices that have limited resources. Cautious pruning guarantees that there is little loss of predictive performance but the inference speed is greatly enhanced.

Another optimization method commonly used is quantization. It entails the scaling down of the accuracy of weights and activations of 32-bit floating points to smaller-bit values, like 8-bit integers. Quantized networks have fewer memory requirements and can be executed more quickly, especially with custom hardware such as edge GPUs or AI accelerators, without a critical impact on precision.

In knowledge distillation, a substantially larger and more complex teacher network is used to obtain a smaller student network. The student model trains to imitate the behavior of the teacher, learning relevant patterns at a lightweight that allows them to be deployed to the edge. This approach enables the deep learning models to maintain high performance with low computational requirements (Xu et al., 2025).

Neural network architectures, like MobileNets, SqueezeNet, and ShuffleNet, are special-purpose in terms of their use in an IoT or mobile setting. These architectures use depthwise separable convolutions, grouped convolutions and other structural innovations to minimize the number of parameters and calculations to offer a tradeoff between accuracy and resource usage.

Hardware specific optimization of the edges is also vital. TPUs, AI accelerators and low-power GPUs can accelerate inference and training of IoT devices. The performance of deep learning models in real-time IoT applications can be further improved by optimizing the network operations to take advantage of these hardware capabilities: operator fusion, parallelization, and memory-efficient execution (Tang et al., 2025).

Another way of optimization is through sparse representations and low-rank approximations. Networks can save memory and compute time by storing weight matrices in a sparse representation or decomposing them into low-rank factors at the expense of little predictive power. It is also especially useful in large models that run on edge servers or gateways.

Incremental and online learning methods enable the IoT systems to change continuously with changing data. In place of re-training the whole model each time, incremental updates modify existing weights, requiring less computation and allowing models to keep up with dynamic conditions like industrial monitoring, autonomous vehicles or smart cities.

Other areas where optimization is applied include preprocessing of the data and feature selection. Dimensionality reduction of the inputs, scaling sensor values and filtering of irrelevant data streams can help a lot to reduce model load and enhance convergence speed. Together with lightweight architectures, the techniques can help IoT systems to handle heterogeneous data effectively and in real time (Chen et al., 2020).

Lastly, distributed learning and federated optimization enables different IoT devices or edge nodes to jointly train a model without having to centralize raw data. This method saves on communication overhead, data privacy is maintained, and the collectiveness of computational power in a network of devices is utilized. With gradient compression and adaptive aggregation, fed learn algorithms guarantee model accuracy as well as efficiency.

SECURITY, PRIVACY, AND ROBUSTNESS IN IOT ANALYTICS

The IoT analytics is sensitive as security, privacy, and robustness are paramount issues in this field because the data collected by connected devices is sensitive. IoT networks are distributed services and are heterogeneous in nature which has made them vulnerable to different threats such as unauthorized access, data tampering and cyberattacks. To be able to make deep neural network models work in such an environment reliably, one should carefully design them and should incorporate mechanisms that can be used to ensure security (Liu et al., 2020).

One of the most significant problems of the IoT system is the issue of data privacy, especially when the devices gather personal or sensitive data. The processing can be centralized, and in this case, the raw data is most likely to be sent to cloud servers thereby exposing it to misuse or interception. Federated learning provides a privacy-sensitive alternative, where local model training is performed on devices, and only aggregated model updates are disseminated, thus, keeping raw data localized.

The encryption methods are critical in protecting communication between the IoT devices, the edge nodes, and the cloud servers. End-to-end encryption, secure multi-party computation, and homomorphic encryption enable the data to stay confidential and at the same time make it useful in analytics. Such approaches preserve the privacy without affecting the performance of deep learning models in real-time IoT applications (Sze et al., 2017).

Another important feature of the IoT deep learning is its resilience to adversarial attacks. Neural networks may be fooled by adversarial examples, tiny yet maliciously generated perturbations, into making a false prediction. Adversarial training, defensive distillation, and input preprocessing are some of the methods that can be used to enhance the resilience of the models and guarantee the stability of their performance even in the case of attacks.

Deeply learned anomaly detection and intrusion detection systems serve as an added security measure. Since these systems can always monitor the traffic of the IoT network as well as sensor data, it is possible to identify unusual patterns, possible breach, or ineffective devices. Detecting anomalies in real time is especially relevant in critical infrastructure, healthcare, and industrial IoT settings where the loss of security can lead to the dire outcomes.

Data integrity is also a necessity of sound analytics. The IoT systems should make sure that the received information is genuine and unaltered. Blockchain solutions have been considered to develop irrevocable and verifiable accounts of IoT transactions, which can increase the credibility of collaborative networks and distributed deep learning applications (Li et al., 2019).

Edge intelligence is a part of security and privacy since it minimizes the transmission of raw data over networks. Storage and processing of sensitive data at the edge devices or gateways reduces the vulnerability to cyber attacks. Also, edge nodes are capable of providing real-time monitoring and active security policy to dynamically respond to emerging risks.

The effective management of heterogeneous and noisy IoT data is also a model robustness requirement. The accuracy of deep neural networks can be compromised by sensor errors, missing values and environmental noise. Approaches like data augmentation, regularization, dropout and robust loss functions assist models to be efficient and stable with respect to generalization over both heterogeneous and imperfect datasets.

IoT analytics involve regulatory compliance as a critical factor. Legal acts including GDPR and HIPAA provide stringent stipulations in the protection of data, consent, and auditability. The combination of the privacy-sensitive strategies, secure methods, and transparent AI processes will help to make sure that deep learning models are used in the legal environment and that stakeholders will trust them (Zhang et al., 2021).

Conclusively, security, privacy, and robustness of IoT analytics are the pillars that are independent and depend on each other to ascertain the reliability of deep learning applications. It is possible to use privacy preserving learning, encryption, anomaly detection, edge intelligence and robustness enhancing strategies to provide resilient, robust and trusted analytics within the IoT systems. All these steps are essential in making sure that advanced deep neural network models are safely deployed in actual heterogeneous IoT settings.

CHALLENGES, EMERGING TRENDS, AND FUTURE RESEARCH DIRECTIONS

Despite the significant advancements in deep neural networks for IoT analytics, numerous challenges persist in deploying these models effectively across heterogeneous and real-time environments. The diversity of data types, including time-series, images, videos, and textual information, introduces complexities in feature extraction, model design, and integration. Ensuring consistent performance across these heterogeneous modalities remains a key research focus.

Scalability is a major concern as IoT networks continue to expand with billions of connected devices. Handling large volumes of streaming data without incurring high latency or resource bottlenecks requires innovative solutions in distributed computing, edge intelligence, and hierarchical model deployment. Efficient load balancing and data prioritization strategies are necessary to maintain real-time responsiveness.

Data quality and reliability also pose challenges in IoT environments. Sensor noise, missing readings, and inconsistent sampling rates can significantly impact deep learning performance. Developing robust models that can adapt to imperfect or incomplete data, while still delivering accurate insights, is essential for critical applications such as healthcare, industrial automation, and autonomous systems.

Resource constraints of edge and IoT devices remain a significant hurdle. While model compression, quantization, and pruning provide partial solutions, designing deep neural networks that balance computational efficiency with predictive accuracy continues to be an active research area. Lightweight architectures and energy-efficient inference methods are expected to play a central role in future developments (Hinton et al., 2006).

Security and privacy are ongoing challenges in IoT analytics. Protecting sensitive data while enabling collaborative and distributed learning demands robust encryption, federated learning, and privacy-preserving techniques. Emerging threats, such as adversarial attacks on edge-deployed models, require the development of resilient and adaptive defense mechanisms to maintain trustworthiness in IoT networks.

Interoperability and standardization are critical for widespread adoption of deep learning in heterogeneous IoT systems. Devices from different manufacturers often use proprietary protocols and data formats, complicating model deployment and data integration. Future research should focus on developing universal frameworks and middleware that facilitate seamless cross-device analytics while maintaining efficiency and security.

Explainability and interpretability of deep learning models are gaining importance, especially in safety-critical and regulated industries. Understanding how models make decisions from complex, multimodal IoT data is crucial for gaining trust, ensuring compliance, and enabling informed interventions. Techniques such as attention mechanisms, feature visualization, and post-hoc explainability are likely to see greater adoption.

Emerging trends in deep learning for IoT include the integration of reinforcement learning, self-supervised learning, and graph-based approaches. These techniques can enhance adaptability, reduce reliance on labeled data, and model complex relationships among devices. Combining these approaches with edge intelligence is expected to enable more autonomous, context-aware, and efficient IoT systems.

Another promising direction is the convergence of IoT analytics with 5G/6G networks and cloud-edge orchestration. High-speed, low-latency connectivity enables real-time model updates, collaborative learning, and dynamic resource allocation. Future research will likely explore optimized architectures that exploit these networks to maximize efficiency and responsiveness of deep learning models in IoT ecosystems (Abadi et al., 2016).

In conclusion, the future of heterogeneous and real-time IoT analytics lies in the development of scalable, secure, interpretable, and adaptive deep learning models. Addressing challenges related to data heterogeneity, resource constraints, security, and model robustness will be critical. Emerging trends such as edge intelligence, self-supervised learning, and advanced network integration promise to transform IoT analytics, enabling smarter, faster, and more resilient systems across diverse real-world applications.

CONCLUSION

Highly developed deep neural network models have changed the future of IoT analytics by facilitating smart processing of heterogenous and high-dimensional data. Their capability of automatical extraction of meaningful features of a wide range of modalities, such as time-series sensor measurements, images, and textual information, makes them very well-suited to complex IoT settings. These models are used in predictive, adaptive, and real-time decision-making in a broad field of application.

Incorporation of edge intelligence and real-time processing has also contributed to the expandability of deep learning in the IoT systems. With computation brought nearer to data, latency is minimized, bandwidth is minimized and real-time responses are made possible. This is especially essential in important fields like automobile automation, machine surveillance, and medical systems.

Pruning, quantization, knowledge distillation, and lightweight network design are optimization techniques that allow deploying high-performing models to resource-constrained IoT devices. These methods make sure that there is a balance between execution capacity and predictive power that can make real-time analytics possible without overwhelming edge infrastructure.

The security, privacy, and robustness are still the main factors when implementing deep learning models in the network of IoT. The methods such as federated learning, encryption, anomaly detection, and adversarial defense enhance credibility and safeguard privacy. To assure the safety and effectiveness of the work of IoT systems, it is necessary to make sure that the models are reliable in adversarial or noisy environments.

Even though great progress has been made, scalability, heterogeneity of data, interoperability and interpretability challenges still exist. New tendencies, such as self-supervised learning, graph-based structures, reinforcement learning, and further network integration, can provide new possibilities to solve these problems and make IoT analytics smarter.

To conclude, combination of deep neural network models, edge intelligence and advanced optimization solutions constitute a strong infrastructure of heterogeneous and real-time IoT analytics. Further studies that relate to scalability, security, interpretability and adaptive learning will keep growing the possibilities of intelligent IoT systems and will lead to innovations in the fields of industry, commercial and social matters.

REFERENCES

Abadi, M., Agarwal, A., Barham, P., Brevdo, E., Chen, Z., Citro, C., . . . Zheng, X. (2016). Tensorflow: Large-scale machine learning on heterogeneous distributed systems. *arXiv preprint arXiv:1603.04467.*

Al-Fuqaha, A., Guizani, M., Mohammadi, M., Aledhari, M., & Ayyash, M. (2015). Internet of Things: A survey on enabling technologies, protocols, and applications. *IEEE Communications Surveys and Tutorials*, *17*(4), 2347–2376. DOI: 10.1109/COMST.2015.2444095

Bhatti, U. A., Tang, H., Wu, G., Marjan, S., & Hussain, A. (2023). Deep learning with graph convolutional networks: An overview and latest applications in computational intelligence. *International Journal of Intelligent Systems*, *2023*(1), 8342104. DOI: 10.1155/2023/8342104

Chen, M., Mao, S., & Liu, Y. (2014). Big data: A survey. *Mobile Networks and Applications*, *19*(2), 171–209. DOI: 10.1007/s11036-013-0489-0

Chen, X., Li, J., Li, Q., & Tang, M. (2020). Real-time data analytics in IoT: A survey on deep learning approaches. *Journal of Network and Computer Applications*, *164*, 102689.

Deng, L., & Yu, D. (2014). Deep learning: Methods and applications. *Foundations and Trends in Signal Processing*, *7*(3–4), 197–387. DOI: 10.1561/2000000039

Goodfellow, I., Bengio, Y., & Courville, A. (2016). *Deep learning*. MIT Press.

Hinton, G. E., Osindero, S., & Teh, Y. W. (2006). A fast learning algorithm for deep belief nets. *Neural Computation*, *18*(7), 1527–1554. DOI: 10.1162/neco.2006.18.7.1527 PMID: 16764513

Islam, T., Akter, A., Islam, M. N., Zafir, E. I., Hasib, S. A., Sarker, S. K., & Bhatti, U. A. (2025). A novel explainable deep generative model-aided transfer learning CNN for pelvis fracture detection. *Biomedical Signal Processing and Control*, *110*, 107987. DOI: 10.1016/j.bspc.2025.107987

Kairouz, P., & McMahan, H. B. (2021). Advances and open problems in federated learning. *Foundations and Trends in Machine Learning*, *14*(1-2), 1–210. DOI: 10.1561/2200000083

LeCun, Y., Bengio, Y., & Hinton, G. (2015). Deep learning. *Nature*, *521*(7553), 436–444. DOI: 10.1038/nature14539 PMID: 26017442

Li, X., Li, H., Li, H., & Li, K. C. (2019). Real-time anomaly detection for IoT networks based on deep learning. *IEEE Access : Practical Innovations, Open Solutions*, *7*, 127961–127970.

Liu, Y., Chen, M., Zhang, Y., & Dou, W. (2020). Real-time IoT analytics: Edge-based deep learning models and applications. *Future Generation Computer Systems*, *108*, 102–117.

McMahan, B., Moore, E., Ramage, D., Hampson, S., & Arcas, B. A. (2017, April). Communication-efficient learning of deep networks from decentralized data. In *Artificial intelligence and statistics* (pp. 1273–1282). Pmlr.

Nizamani, A. H., Chen, Z., & Bhatti, U. A. (2026). Deep-Fusion: A lightweight feature fusion model with Cross-Stream Attention and Attention Prediction Head for brain tumor diagnosis. *Biomedical Signal Processing and Control*, *111*, 108305. DOI: 10.1016/j.bspc.2025.108305

Satyanarayanan, M. (2017). The emergence of edge computing. *Computer*, *50*(1), 30–39. DOI: 10.1109/MC.2017.9

Shi, W., Cao, J., Zhang, Q., Li, Y., & Xu, L. (2016). Edge computing: Vision and challenges. *IEEE Internet of Things Journal*, *3*(5), 637–646. DOI: 10.1109/JIOT.2016.2579198

Sze, V., Chen, Y. H., Yang, T. J., & Emer, J. S. (2017). Efficient processing of deep neural networks: A tutorial and survey. *Proceedings of the IEEE*, *105*(12), 2295–2329. DOI: 10.1109/JPROC.2017.2761740

Tang, H., Cheng, M., Bhatti, U. A., Xu, B., Zhou, N., Guo, R., & Wei, B. (2025). Digital twin-driven reinforcement learning-based operational management for customized manufacturing. *Engineering Applications of Artificial Intelligence*, *159*, 111754. DOI: 10.1016/j.engappai.2025.111754

Wang, S., Tuor, T., Salonidis, T., Leung, K. K., Makaya, C., He, T., & Chan, K. (2019). Adaptive federated learning in resource-constrained edge computing systems. *IEEE Journal on Selected Areas in Communications*, *37*(6), 1205–1221. DOI: 10.1109/JSAC.2019.2904348

Xu, B., Wang, S., Bhatti, U. A., Zhang, X., & Tang, H. (2025). Explainability Analysis Based on Attribution Features for Optimizing Automatic Modulation Classification. *Computer Networks*, *272*, 111696. DOI: 10.1016/j.comnet.2025.111696

Yu, W., Liang, F., He, X., Hatcher, W. G., Lu, C., Lin, J., & Yang, X. (2018). A survey on the edge computing for the Internet of Things. *IEEE Access : Practical Innovations, Open Solutions*, *6*, 6900–6919. DOI: 10.1109/ACCESS.2017.2778504

Zhang, Q., Chen, M., Yang, L. T., & Zhang, Z. (2018). Deep learning for sensor-based activity recognition: A survey. *IEEE Communications Surveys and Tutorials*, *21*(1), 1–31.

Zhang, Y., Zhang, W., & Zhao, K. (2021). Heterogeneous IoT data analytics with deep learning: Techniques and applications. *Sensors (Basel)*, *21*(8), 2765. PMID: 33919861

Zhou, Z., Chen, X., Li, E., Zeng, L., Luo, K., & Zhang, J. (2019). Edge intelligence: Paving the last mile of artificial intelligence with edge computing. *Proceedings of the IEEE*, *107*(8), 1738–1762. DOI: 10.1109/JPROC.2019.2918951

Chapter 2
Autonomous Decision-Making and Domain-Specific Intelligence in Edge-Cloud IoT Applications

Anum Mehmood
http://orcid.org/0009-0004-8105-1690
College of Food Science and Engineering, Hainan University, Haikou City, China

Akbar Toyirov
Department of Information Technology and Exact Sciences, Termez University of Economics and Service, Termez, Uzbekistan

Babayev Shavkat
Department of Taxation and Taxation, Tashkent State University of Economics, Tashkent, Uzbekistan

Mukhammad Khabibullaev
Department of Computer Science, Urgench State University, Urgench, Uzbekistan

Mamatkhujaev Otabek
Department of International Scientific Journals and Ratings, Alfraganus University, Tashkent, Uzbekistan

Sardor Sabirov
http://orcid.org/0009-0008-0504-7568
Department of General Professional Sciences, Mamun University, Khiva, Uzbekistan

ABSTRACT

This paper explores the concept of autonomous decision-making and domain-specific intelligence in Edge–Cloud IoT applications. It examines how artificial intelligence and machine learning techniques can be deployed across edge and cloud layers to support context-aware, adaptive, and autonomous operations. The study highlights

DOI: 10.4018/979-8-2600-0615-3.ch002

architectural frameworks, decision-making mechanisms, and application-specific intelligence models that enhance system responsiveness, reliability, and resource efficiency. Furthermore, it discusses key challenges, including interoperability, security, data management, and computational constraints, and presents potential strategies to address them. The findings demonstrate that combining edge and cloud intelligence enables scalable, resilient, and intelligent IoT ecosystems capable of meeting the requirements of modern smart applications such as healthcare, industrial automation, smart cities, and autonomous transportation systems.

INTRODUCTION TO AUTONOMOUS DECISION-MAKING IN EDGE–CLOUD IOT SYSTEMS

The increased pace of the Internet of Things development has disrupted the digital landscape with the integration of devices, sensors, machines, and services in a variety of environments. The interrelated systems are producing data in large amounts that are in constant need of being processed and intelligently interpreted. Due to the complexity of the IoT application, the necessity in systems able to make independent and context-specific decisions has gained even greater significance. Independent decision-making has consequently become a major strength in contemporary edge clouds IoT systems (Zhou et al., 2019).

Autonomous decision making can be described as the capability of a system to interpret the data received, to consider the available actions, and to take the necessary steps without having to be supervised by a human. The capability is necessary in such an IoT environment since various applications run under dynamic and time-sensitive environments. As an example, a healthcare tracking device, a robot in the industrial field, or a smart traffic controller will be required to respond to the altering conditions in real time quite frequently. Late decision making can minimize the efficiency of the systems and in certain instances generation of severe operational risks (Shi et al., 2016).

The combination of edge and cloud computing has provided an effective platform on which autonomous intelligence can be supported in IoT systems. With edge computing, data processing can be done near its origin point, which makes it responsive and has a lower latency. Cloud computing, on the other hand, provides a massive computing power, centralized analytics and long-term data storage. These layers combined create a collaborative environment, such that local decisions can be made fast at the edge and larger learning, coordination, and optimization are done in the cloud.

High scale of the devices is one of the primary factors that make autonomous decision-making in edge cloud IoT systems important. Since the number of sensors and smart objects keeps growing, it is not feasible to have all decisions being handled centrally. There may be bottlenecks in communication, overloading of bandwidth and slower response time in the event that a centralized approach is implemented. Through the implementation of intelligence throughout the edge and cloud, the IoTs will be able to function more effectively and make quicker decisions relying on local and global data (Satyanarayanan, 2017).

The core feature of these distributed systems to facilitate autonomous decision-making is artificial intelligence and machine learning. Through these technologies, IoT platforms can recognize patterns, anticipate events, categorize conditions, and make appropriate decisions. Lightweight models can be deployed on the edge to perform quick inferences to provide quick responses. The more advanced models can be trained with bigger datasets in the cloud and pushed back to the edge nodes. Such a constant interaction enhances local autonomy and system-wide intelligence.

The other requirement of autonomous operation in the IoT systems is context awareness. In the real environment, decisions may rely not just on sensor reading but also on other factors in the environment that include location, time, user behaviour, environmental conditions, and priorities in operation. Systems based on edge-cloud IoT should thus be set to decipher situations internally and change their responses. This renders autonomous intelligence more precise, applicable, and valid in various fields of use (Chiang & Zhang, 2016).

Autonomous systems have a particular concern with the edge with regard to latency-sensitive applications. The milliseconds time frame is quickly required in making decisions in smart transportation, industrial control, medical monitoring, and surveillance. The possibility of sending all data to cloud to analyze it can create intolerable delays. Edge computing resolves the issue by enabling a real-time data filtering process, local analytics, and real-time actuation. This is an important feature that can enhance the responsiveness and resilience of the IoT systems.

Meanwhile, the cloud is needed when it comes to functions that must have a bigger view and more computing power. The cloud has the ability to consolidate information across various edge devices, determine long-term trends, optimize models, and make decisions in support of the global policy. It is also able to coordinate across distributed IoT networks, making sure that autonomous behaviours on the edge can be coordinated with the overall system goals. Through this, the cloud does not take over edge autonomy but enhances it (Li et al., 2018).

There are also a number of challenges, even though it has potential, with autonomous decision-making under edge cloud IoT systems. They are dealing with the heterogeneity of handling devices, limited edge resource management, secure communication, sensitive data protection, and trust in automated decisions. Real-world settings are further complicated and this makes it necessary to have strong, explainable and adaptive decision structures. The following issues are crucial to the formation of reliable and scalable autonomous solutions of the IoT.

In general, autonomous decision-making is a significant leap in the history of edge-cloud IoT systems development. It enables interconnected settings to embrace a stage of gone beyond data gathering to smart and self-managed functioning. The closer proximity of edge computing to the cloud and its processing capabilities, based on their analytical power, allows contemporary IoT designs to make quicker, smarter, and more context-beautiful decisions. This base is determining the future of intelligent applications in very diverse fields (Gubbi et al., 2013).

DOMAIN-SPECIFIC INTELLIGENCE FOR SMART IOT APPLICATIONS

Domain-specific intelligence is the capacity of the IoT systems to execute specialized knowledge, decision rules, and analytical models, which are specific to the application domain. In contrast to general-purpose intelligence, domain-specific intelligence is intended to perceive the special circumstances, limitations and goals of a particular discipline like healthcare, agriculture, transportation, manufacturing, or smart energy. This domain-specific intelligence can be applied to edge-based IoT systems to make factual and pertinent decisions more effectively, considering the circumstances of the context where the systems are operating.

The increased sophistication of smart IoT applications has rendered domain-specific intelligence to be more significant. The IoT devices produce high amounts of heterogeneous data, which cannot be used as raw data to make meaningful decisions. The systems should have the capability of interpreting data in a manner that is reflective of domain knowledge and operational priorities. Indicatively, a single reading in the environment can possess various interpretations in a hospital, farm or factory. Domain-specific intelligence offers the interpretation layer which is used to convert sensor inputs to actionable intelligence (Yu et al., 2018).

Domain-specific intelligence is used in smart agriculture to enable IoT systems to optimize farming practices depending on the environmental and crop conditions. Sensors are able to record soil moisture, temperature, humidity, crop development, and pest activities and the intelligent models process this data in order to regulate irrigation, fertilization, and disease control. The edge devices enable real-time local actions at the field, whereas cloud platforms process past and regional data to enhance future agricultural policies. This synergistic mix is more productive and sustainable.

Domain-specific intelligence also is of great value to transportation and mobility systems. IoT systems in smart traffic network and autonomous mobility applications have to know road conditions, vehicle behaviour, and traffic movement, and safety requirements. Real-time decisions have to be made frequently to prevent congestion, control routes or respond to incidents. Domain specific intelligence allows the system to focus on the mobility efficiency and public safety as it adjusts to dynamic traffic condition (Wang et al., 2019).

The domain-specific intelligence is applied in the industrial IoT to enhance operational efficiency, predictive maintenance, and process automation. Information on equipment performance, energy consumption, quality production and environment are gathered by machines and sensors. Smart models have the ability to discover failures, forecast failures, and streamline processes according to the needs of the industry. Since manufacturing systems are frequently subject to severe timing and reliability factors, edge-cloud collaboration is particularly useful in facilitating prompt and well-informed decisions.

Smart energy and environmental monitoring systems are domain-specific intelligence based the fact that they use intelligence to manage resources and ensure sustainability. IoT can be used in this field to track the use of electricity, production of renewable energy, pollution, and other factors related to climate conditions. Smart decision systems are useful in balancing supply and demand, in identifying anomalies and facilitating effective resource distribution. Domain knowledge is critical to comprehending the consequences of altered environmental and energy situations as well as to making the most effective choices (Kairouz & McMahan, 2021).

The main benefit of domain-specific intelligence is that it enhances accuracy and reliability of autonomous decision making. By constructing IoT systems with an understanding of the desired domain, they become capable of minimizing irrelevant behaviors and give results that are far more closely matched with real-world objectives. This is especially critical in the sensitive applications like healthcare, transportation and industrial control where mistakes made may have severe implications. Domain adaptation also enhances the reliability of the systems in dissimilar working environments.

The creation of the domain-specific intelligence demands that data-driven learning is combined with expert knowledge and contextual knowledge. Patterns can only be identified by machine learning models, but domain knowledge assists in making sure that the patterns are decoded in the right way and applied accordingly. Artificial intelligence techniques are typically used together with rule-based systems, ontologies, knowledge graphs, and contextual models to design more robust and understandable IoT solutions. This is a hybrid strategy that enhances performance and transparency (McMahan et al., 2017).

In general, domain-specific intelligence is one of the core aspects of smart IoT applications in edge cloud. It allows systems to escape generic automation and move to intelligent behavior that is responsive to the unique requirements of any application domain. Integrating domain expertise with distributed computing and real-time analytics, domain-specific intelligence augments the utility and versatility of the contemporary IoT systems in a vast spectrum of real-life situations.

EDGE–CLOUD COLLABORATIVE ARCHITECTURES FOR INTELLIGENT DECISION SUPPORT

Edge-cloud collaborative architectures have gained a critical role in supporting intelligent decisions in current IoT-based applications. These architectures bring together the low-latency processing of edge devices and large-scale processing and storage of the cloud. Through intelligence dissemination in these layers, they allow IoT systems to analyze and react promptly to local occurrences and assist with more analytical capabilities. This team-based model is particularly essential in those settings where they are supposed to make decisions in a timely manner and in a manner that is sensitive to the situation at hand.

Figure 1 shows Edge–Cloud Collaborative Architectures

Figure 1. Edge–cloud collaborative architectures for intelligent decision support

The edge layer in intelligent decision support systems is mainly used to perform local inference and immediate data processing. The image of sensors, gateways, mobile devices, and embedded processors will be able to collect and analyze the data near the source urging the necessity to send all information to big servers. Not just this reduces delays in communication but in addition it increases system responsiveness. In scenarios like healthcare monitoring, traffic control, industrial automation, etc. local decision support at the edge could provide a great performance and reliability (Chen et al., 2014).

Cloud layer is a complementary service of edge operations as it offers high-performance computing, massive data storage, and long-term learning services. It is also highly adapted to training complicated machine learning models, merging information across several assets, and finding more extensive patterns that might not be apparent at a localized scale. Centralized policy control and updated models can also be supported by the cloud which guarantees that edge devices are run with better knowledge and uniform decision logic. This forms a powerful connection between local autonomy and global intelligence.

Sharing of tasks based on the requirements of the system is one of the distinguishing features of edge-cloud collaborative architectures. Processing tasks that are time sensitive and light weight are often performed at the edge whereas cloud based processing tasks that are resource-intensive are performed at the cloud. This division of tasks helps to work more efficiently and make sure that every layer works in accordance to its strengths. This balanced allocation of responsibilities throughout the architecture is very critical to intelligent decision support (Abadi et al., 2016).

Data filtering and preprocessing are one of the processes that are usually done at the edge and then the information is sent to the cloud. This minimizes the amount of information sent out and only information that is relevant or summarised can be shared. This is especially applicable in large scale IoT implementations where either bandwidth is scarce or expensive. Collaborative architectures reduce the needless communication, thereby accelerating the decision process and the optimal use of resources.

Edge cloud deployment is also based on a collaborative approach to model deployment. The lightweight models could be used on edge devices to make quick local decisions, and more sophisticated models could be on the cloud to deep analyze and retraint. In other scenarios, model partitioning is employed wherein a part of the decision-making process is done at the edge and the rest of it is done in the cloud. Such a stratified deployment enables the systems to be responsive and analytical (Zaharia et al., 2010).

Intelligent decision support requires effective communication and coordination between edge and cloud layers. Coordinated architectures rely on the availability of quality data interchange, model synchronization, and standard policy implementation. Change in network conditions, system loads and application priorities are often necessitated by adaptive communication strategies. Coherency at the edge and cloud allows the edge and cloud components to coordinate effectively as opposed to them being independent units.

Another issue in edge-cloud collaborative decision systems is security and privacy. Since the data can be transmitted between various devices and platforms, there is a chance of unauthorized access, information leakage, or interference on decision making. Collaborative architectures then need to have secured communication protocols, authentication schemes and privacy sensitive approaches in data handling. Edge computing is also used to preserve privacy in most instances by making sensitive data to be handled locally as opposed to being sent to the cloud (Bhatti et al., 2023).

The other significant advantage of these architectures is that they are scalable. With the continued growth in the field of IoT networks, the centralized systems might not be able to handle the growing number of connected devices and real-time streams of data. Edge cloud collaboration can be used to promote scalability by decentralizing a portion of the processing load without reducing centralized control where it is required. This allows the intelligent decision support systems to perform well in a small and large deployment environment.

Altogether, edge-cloud collaborative architectures offer an effective and efficient model of intelligent decision support of IoT applications. They integrate the power of local processing and centralized intelligence to be able to make decisions faster, smarter and more adaptive. The architectures contribute to the development of autonomous and domain-aware IoT systems by facilitating effective allocation of tasks, real-time analytics, secure communication, and scalable operations (Xu et al., 2024).

MACHINE LEARNING AND CONTEXT-AWARE ANALYTICS IN IOT ENVIRONMENTS

Intelligent IoT environments now consist of machine learning and context-aware analytics. With the ever-gathering of information of both the physical environment, users, and running systems, the coordination of IoT gadgets, the necessity to convert information into valuable choices and adaptable behavior increases. Machine learning offers the ability to detect patterns, make predictions and optimize the performance of the system over time, whereas context-aware analytics allows interpreting information based on certain environmental, temporal, and situational aspects. These strategies, combined, enable smarter and more responsive IoT systems on edge and cloud layers.

Figure 2 shows Machine Learning and Context-Aware Analytics in IoT Environments

Figure 2. Machine learning and context-aware analytics in IoT environments

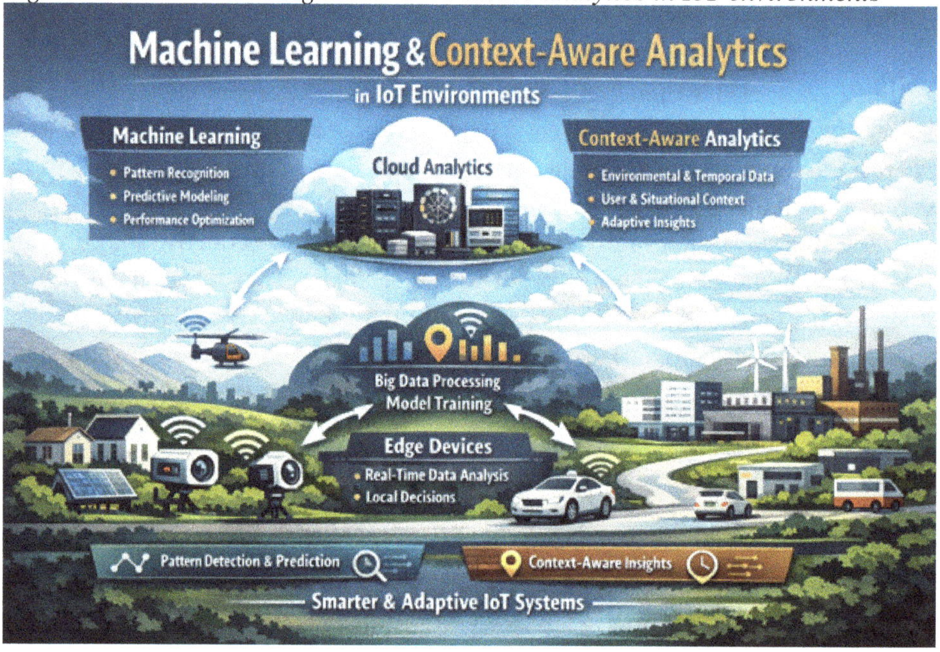

Machine learning is applied in IoT settings to handle high volumes of heterogeneous sensor, device, and network-related data. Such data streams usually contain data on temperature, movement, position, pressure, power usage and health factors as well as user activities. Machine learning models, based on learning using such data, can be used to classify events, detect anomalies, predict future states and aids autonomous decision-making. This necessitates machine learning in controlling the complexity and dynamism of the IoT ecosystems (Zhang et al., 2024).

The context-aware analytics plays the role of making sure that the information is interpreted based on the context under which it is produced. In most IoT systems, the same data value can be interpreted differently in different places, at different times, when used by different people, in different environmental conditions, or even on different operational purposes. Context-aware systems thus transcend abstraction by taking the situational information into analysis and decisions. This is what enables the IoT platforms to be smarter and offer more actions that are closer to the actual world circumstances.

Both edge and cloud computing play a role in machine learning and context-aware analytics complementary to each other. On the edge, there can be deployed lightweight models that are able to perform quick inference and local adaptation so that the systems can respond instantly to changing conditions. Tasks with a higher level of computational demand like training of models, massive data aggregation, and long-term analytics can be run effectively in the cloud. The edge-cloud interface facilitates real-time responsiveness and enhanced learning with IoT systems.

All of the supervised, unsupervised, and reinforcement learning methods are applicable to the IoT. Supervised learning is typically applicable in classification and prediction whereby historical data is labeled and unsupervised learning is applied to identify patterns, clusters, and anomalies in unlabeled data. Reinforcement learning is also applicable particularly in systems that require learning optimal actions by interacting with dynamic environments. These learning paradigms enable the IoT applications to change their behavior with respect to the domain requirements and operational objectives (Bhatti et al., 2024).

Context-sensitive analytics comes in especially handy in applications that do not have regular environmental and user-conditions. Contextual factors like patient movement, time of the day and medical history of patient in healthcare IoT determine how physiological data are interpreted. Weather, soils, and crop development phases influence the decision-making process in smart agriculture. Road conditions, traffic density, and the routes that are used by users are the determinants of how data should be analyzed in the transport systems. With such context, the IoT systems will be more correct, topical, and efficient.

Machine learning and context-aware analytics are also enhanced in order to make personalization and adaptability better. IoT systems have the ability to understand the preferences of users, trends in their behavior, and interactions with the environment to more personalized services. Indicatively, smart homes can program lighting, heating and security systems depending on occupancy levels and day-to-day activities. Likewise, industrial IoT systems have the ability to optimize the operations, depending on the behavior of the machines, production timetables, and maintenance records. The capabilities improve the user experience and system performance (Huang et al., 2018).

Regardless of its benefits, applying machine learning and context-driven analytics to IoT-based settings is associated with a number of challenges. Limiting deployable model complexity by resources at the edge can limit the complexity of deployable models and heterogeneous data sources may complicate the integration and interpretation of models. Moreover, context information can also be incomplete, noisy, and dynamic and hence it is hard to have consistent decision-making. The security, privacy and explainability are also significant issues, especially when automated decisions are involved in critical services or sensitive personal information.

To cope with these issues, scholars are considering lightweight learning models, federated learning, transfer learning, and hybrid context models combining data-driven and knowledge-based methods. The strategies are supposed to enhance the efficacy, scalability, and resilience of smart IoT systems. The difficulty in deploying machine learning solutions in real-time and resource-constrained environments is also becoming easier due to the advancement of edge AI hardware and adaptive analytics frameworks. These advancements are enhancing the utility of context-conscious intelligence in a distributed IoT system (LeCun et al., 2015).

On the whole, the progress of autonomous and intelligent IoT environments is related to machine learning and context-aware analytics. They enable interrelated systems to proceed beyond mere sensing and communicating to adaptive reasoning and decision-making. IoT applications can provide more efficient, personalized and domain-aware services by using predictive learning with contextual understanding. This integration is defining the future of intelligent systems in the fields of health-care, agriculture, transportation, industry and most other applications.

CHALLENGES IN REAL-TIME AUTONOMY, SECURITY, AND SCALABILITY

The most significant issues in the development of intelligent edge-cloud IoT systems are real-time autonomy, security, and scalability. With more autonomy and being used in a wider variety of domains, these systems should be able to make fast and dependable decisions with their operation subject to severe resource and communication limitations. Distributed intelligence, heterogeneous devices, and dynamic environments provide a complicated environment where stabilizing and reliable performance is still a major issue (Goodfellow et al., 2016).

Latency is one of the greatest challenges of real-time autonomy. IoT can be used in many applications where quick responses to rapidly changing conditions are necessary, including autonomous vehicles, industrial automation, healthcare monitoring, and smart surveillance. Minor delays in sensing, processing, communication, or actuation may decrease the effectiveness of the system and cause critical failures in some instances. Despite the fact that edge computing minimizes latency through bringing processing closer to the data sources, the need to maintain low response times in distributed systems is a challenging undertaking.

The other problem is low computational ability of edge devices. Autonomous operation in real time usually necessitates machine learning models which consume a lot of processing power, memory and energy. Not all IoT devices have plenty of hardware, however, and simple intelligence can be difficult to implement on-the-edge. This incurs a trade-off between accuracy and efficiency of executing a model, and must be optimized carefully to ensure that performance is tolerable in resource limited environments (He et al., 2016).

The real-time autonomy is also complicated by the presence of dynamic and unpredictable operating conditions. IoT systems operate in conditions where the quality of the network, the reliability of sensors, the load of the work, and environmental factors may fluctuate quickly. Due to this, decision-making mechanisms should be dynamic and hardy. An effective model in one setting cannot be equally effective in another setting. This brings out the significance of powerful learning techniques and understanding dependent approaches that would ensure a consistent functioning under uncertainty.

Another significant issue in edge cloud IoT architectures is security. Since such systems include a number of interconnected devices, communication networks and processing layers, they provide a wide attack surface of cyber threats. Illegal access, data corruption, denial-of-service intrusions, and tricky undesired model manipulation can undermine the functionality of the system and user confidence. Intelligent IoT environments are therefore vulnerable and need robust device, network, edge, and cloud security mechanisms (Hinton et al., 2006).

Close to the concept of security is data privacy, especially when personal and medical information, industrial or location information is being used. Self-driven IoT systems tend to be based on the constant data collection and analysis, which provokes the question of the protection of sensitive information, its storage, transmission, and usage. Although edge computing can minimize the risks of privacy, as local processing of data alleviates the risk, privacy-preserving learning and secure communication schemes are necessary to avoid information leakage and abuse at distributed layers.

Scalability is also another significant issue because the number of linked devices and streams of data will only keep increasing. Extensive IoT infrastructures are required to facilitate communication, coordination and decision making among a potentially thousands or millions of nodes. Handling this scale cannot be done with just centralized systems and even the decentralized systems will add complexity to the issues of synchronization, management, and interoperability. One of the key research and engineering concerns is to design architectures that become efficient as deployments scale.

Scalability and system reliability are also influenced by interoperability and heterogeneity. IoT systems usually have devices that are made by various manufacturers, with varying protocols, data formats, and differing hardware compatibility. Co-ordination between these various parts into a single intelligent system is not easy particularly when real time coordination is needed. To facilitate smooth interaction between heterogeneous edge and cloud ecosystems, standardization, flexible middleware, and adaptive orchestration mechanisms are required.

The reasonableness and reliability of autonomous decisions is another issue. In other areas of life like critical areas like healthcare, transportation and industrial control, a system needs to do more than make a fast decision, the decision must be explainable, defendable and must be in line with operational objectives. Black-box models can be very precise, but they lack in terms of confidence when the users or the operators are not in a position to understand how the decisions are made. Enhancing explainability is thus very necessary in enhancing the safe and responsible implementation of autonomous IoT systems (Zhang et al., 2021).

In general, the issues of real-time autonomy, security, and scalability are significantly interrelated in edge -cloud IoT application. The need to deal with one issue will lead to others, which need to be dealt with in a balanced and integrated manner. The future developments in this area will rely on the developments of lightweight intelligence, secure distributed architectures, adaptive communication, privacy-preserving learning, and scalable orchestration. These obstacles need to be overcome, and then it is possible to create intelligent IoT systems that are high-speed, secure, reliable, and fit to be deployed in the real world.

FUTURE TRENDS AND RESEARCH DIRECTIONS IN EDGE–CLOUD IOT INTELLIGENCE

Future trends in edge–cloud IoT intelligence are being shaped by the growing demand for systems that are more autonomous, adaptive, secure, and domain-aware. As IoT applications continue to expand across healthcare, agriculture, transportation, industry, and smart cities, the need for intelligent architectures that can process data efficiently and make timely decisions is becoming increasingly important. Edge–cloud collaboration is expected to move beyond simple task distribution toward more integrated and self-managing forms of intelligence that can respond effectively to complex and dynamic environments.

One of the most important future directions is the development of more advanced autonomous decision-making frameworks. Current systems are often limited by predefined rules or narrow task-specific models, but future IoT intelligence will require greater flexibility and self-adaptation. Research is likely to focus on systems that can learn continuously from changing environments, update their strategies in real time, and coordinate decisions across multiple layers of distributed infrastructure. This will improve the ability of IoT systems to operate independently in uncertain and rapidly evolving conditions.

Another major trend is the increasing use of federated and collaborative learning in edge–cloud environments. Rather than relying solely on centralized data collection, future systems will place greater emphasis on distributed learning models that allow devices to train collaboratively while keeping sensitive data local. This approach can improve privacy, reduce communication costs, and support scalable intelligence across large device networks. Continued research will aim to make federated learning more efficient, robust, and suitable for heterogeneous IoT settings.

Context-aware and domain-specific intelligence is also expected to become more sophisticated. Future IoT systems will need to understand not only raw sensor data but also the broader context in which that data is generated. This includes environmental conditions, user behavior, operational priorities, and domain knowledge. Research in this area will likely explore hybrid intelligence models that combine machine learning with knowledge graphs, ontologies, and rule-based reasoning to create more explainable and reliable decision systems.

Edge intelligence hardware and lightweight AI models will continue to play a central role in future developments. As more intelligence is pushed closer to the data source, there will be increasing demand for models that can perform effectively on devices with limited memory, power, and processing capabilities. Research will focus on efficient neural network architectures, model compression, adaptive inference, and hardware acceleration. These innovations will make it possible to deploy more powerful decision-support mechanisms directly on edge devices.

Another significant research direction involves intelligent orchestration across edge and cloud layers. Future edge–cloud IoT systems will require automated mechanisms for resource allocation, workload balancing, model placement, and service coordination. Rather than relying on static deployment strategies, upcoming architectures are expected to use artificial intelligence to manage the system itself. This form of self-orchestration will help optimize performance, energy efficiency, and service reliability under changing network and workload conditions.

Security and privacy will remain central priorities in future IoT intelligence research. As autonomous systems gain more control over critical decisions, the consequences of cyberattacks, data breaches, or adversarial manipulation become more serious. Future research is expected to focus on secure communication protocols, privacy-preserving learning methods, trust management frameworks, and resilient decision systems that can operate safely even in hostile environments. These efforts will be essential for ensuring confidence in intelligent edge–cloud infrastructures (Li et al., 2019).

Explainability and trustworthiness are also emerging as major future concerns. Many advanced learning models offer strong predictive performance but remain difficult to interpret. In real-world IoT applications, especially in healthcare, transportation, and industrial control, users and operators need to understand why decisions are made. Research will therefore increasingly address explainable artificial intelligence, transparent decision models, and human-centered design approaches that make autonomous systems more accountable and acceptable.

The integration of digital twins and real-time simulation is another promising trend in edge–cloud IoT intelligence. Digital twins can create virtual representations of physical systems, allowing intelligent platforms to monitor, predict, and optimize operations more effectively. When combined with edge–cloud computing, digital twins can support real-time analysis and control in domains such as manufacturing, logistics, energy systems, and smart infrastructure. This area is likely to grow as intelligent systems become more complex and interconnected.

Future research will also emphasize sustainability and energy-aware intelligence. As IoT deployments become larger and more widespread, their environmental and energy impacts will become increasingly important. Researchers are expected to explore methods for reducing computation costs, improving power efficiency, and designing greener edge–cloud architectures. Sustainable intelligence will involve not only efficient hardware and software but also intelligent policies for managing workloads and communication in energy-constrained environments.

Overall, the future of edge–cloud IoT intelligence lies in the creation of systems that are more distributed, collaborative, adaptive, and trustworthy. Advances in autonomous learning, context-aware reasoning, secure orchestration, efficient edge intelligence, and domain-specific decision support will define the next generation of smart IoT applications. These trends will push IoT systems beyond simple connectivity and automation toward truly intelligent environments capable of supporting complex real-world operations with greater efficiency, safety, and resilience.

CONCLUSION

The advancement of edge–cloud IoT intelligence has significantly reshaped the design and operation of modern intelligent systems. By combining autonomous decision-making with domain-specific intelligence, these systems are becoming more capable of handling complex, dynamic, and real-time application requirements across diverse sectors. The integration of edge computing and cloud computing provides a balanced framework in which low-latency local processing and large-scale centralized analytics work together to support efficient, adaptive, and context-aware operations.

This review has highlighted the importance of autonomous decision-making, specialized intelligence, collaborative architectures, and machine learning-driven analytics in enabling smart IoT applications. These components collectively strengthen the ability of IoT systems to interpret data, respond to environmental changes, and deliver intelligent services tailored to the needs of specific domains. The role of edge–cloud collaboration is especially critical in ensuring that decision support remains both responsive and scalable, even in highly distributed environments.

At the same time, the development of such systems is accompanied by major challenges related to real-time performance, security, privacy, interoperability, and large-scale deployment. Addressing these concerns requires continuous innovation in lightweight intelligence, secure communication, context-aware reasoning, and adaptive orchestration. Future research must focus on building systems that are not only technically efficient but also trustworthy, explainable, and resilient under real-world conditions.

In conclusion, edge–cloud IoT intelligence represents a powerful direction for the future of connected systems. As autonomous capabilities and domain-specific models continue to evolve, IoT applications will become increasingly intelligent, self-managing, and effective in solving complex problems. This emerging paradigm has the potential to transform a wide range of application domains by enabling smarter decision-making, improved operational efficiency, and more reliable interaction between digital and physical environments.

REFERENCES

Abadi, M., Barham, P., Chen, J., Chen, Z., Davis, A., Dean, J., & Zheng, X. (2016). {TensorFlow}: a system for {Large-Scale} machine learning. In *12th USENIX symposium on operating systems design and implementation (OSDI 16)* (pp. 265-283).

Bhatti, M. A., Song, Z., Bhatti, U. A., & Syam, S. M. S. (2024). AIoT-driven multi-source sensor emission monitoring and forecasting using multi-source sensor integration with reduced noise series decomposition. *Journal of Cloud Computing (Heidelberg, Germany), 13*(1), 65. DOI: 10.1186/s13677-024-00598-9

Bhatti, U. A., Tang, H., Wu, G., Marjan, S., & Hussain, A. (2023). Deep learning with graph convolutional networks: An overview and latest applications in computational intelligence. *International Journal of Intelligent Systems, 2023*(1), 8342104. DOI: 10.1155/2023/8342104

Chen, M., Mao, S., & Liu, Y. (2014). Big data: A survey. *Mobile Networks and Applications, 19*(2), 171–209. DOI: 10.1007/s11036-013-0489-0

Chiang, M., & Zhang, T. (2016). Fog and IoT: An overview of research opportunities. *IEEE Internet of Things Journal, 3*(6), 854–864. DOI: 10.1109/JIOT.2016.2584538

Goodfellow, I., Bengio, Y., & Courville, A. (2016). *Deep learning*. MIT Press.

Gubbi, J., Buyya, R., Marusic, S., & Palaniswami, M. (2013). Internet of Things (IoT): A vision, architectural elements, and future directions. *Future Generation Computer Systems, 29*(7), 1645–1660. DOI: 10.1016/j.future.2013.01.010

He, K., Zhang, X., Ren, S., & Sun, J. (2016). Deep residual learning for image recognition. *Proceedings of the IEEE Conference on Computer Vision and Pattern Recognition*, 770–778.

Hinton, G. E., Osindero, S., & Teh, Y. W. (2006). A fast learning algorithm for deep belief nets. *Neural Computation, 18*(7), 1527–1554. DOI: 10.1162/neco.2006.18.7.1527 PMID: 16764513

Huang, M., Han, H., Wang, H., Li, L., Zhang, Y., & Bhatti, U. A. (2018). A clinical decision support framework for heterogeneous data sources. *IEEE Journal of Biomedical and Health Informatics, 22*(6), 1824–1833. DOI: 10.1109/JBHI.2018.2846626 PMID: 29994279

Kairouz, P., & McMahan, H. B. (2021). Advances and open problems in federated learning. *Foundations and Trends in Machine Learning, 14*(1-2), 1–210. DOI: 10.1561/2200000083

LeCun, Y., Bengio, Y., & Hinton, G. (2015). Deep learning. *Nature, 521*(7553), 436–444. DOI: 10.1038/nature14539 PMID: 26017442

Li, S., Xu, L. D., & Zhao, S. (2018). The internet of things: A survey. *Information Systems Frontiers, 17*(2), 243–259. DOI: 10.1007/s10796-014-9492-7

Li, X., Li, H., Li, H., & Li, K. C. (2019). Real-time anomaly detection for IoT networks based on deep learning. *IEEE Access : Practical Innovations, Open Solutions, 7*, 127961–127970.

McMahan, B., Moore, E., Ramage, D., Hampson, S., & Arcas, B. A. (2017, April). Communication-efficient learning of deep networks from decentralized data. In *Artificial intelligence and statistics* (pp. 1273–1282). Pmlr.

Satyanarayanan, M. (2017). The emergence of edge computing. *Computer, 50*(1), 30–39. DOI: 10.1109/MC.2017.9

Shi, W., Cao, J., Zhang, Q., Li, Y., & Xu, L. (2016). Edge computing: Vision and challenges. *IEEE Internet of Things Journal, 3*(5), 637–646. DOI: 10.1109/JIOT.2016.2579198

Wang, S., Tuor, T., Salonidis, T., Leung, K. K., Makaya, C., He, T., & Chan, K. (2019). Adaptive federated learning in resource-constrained edge computing systems. *IEEE Journal on Selected Areas in Communications, 37*(6), 1205–1221. DOI: 10.1109/JSAC.2019.2904348

Xu, B., Bhatti, U. A., Tang, H., Yan, J., Wu, S., Sarhan, N., Awwad, E. M., Syam, S. M. S., & Ghadi, Y. Y. (2024). Towards explainability for AI-based edge wireless signal automatic modulation classification. *Journal of Cloud Computing (Heidelberg, Germany), 13*(1), 10. DOI: 10.1186/s13677-024-00590-3

Yu, W., Liang, F., He, X., Hatcher, W. G., Lu, C., Lin, J., & Yang, X. (2018). A survey on the edge computing for the Internet of Things. *IEEE Access : Practical Innovations, Open Solutions, 6*, 6900–6919. DOI: 10.1109/ACCESS.2017.2778504

Zaharia, M., Chowdhury, M., Franklin, M. J., Shenker, S., & Stoica, I. (2010). Spark: Cluster computing with working sets. *Proceedings of the USENIX Conference on Hot Topics in Cloud Computing.*

Zhang, C., Aamir, M., Guan, Y., Al-Razgan, M., Awwad, E. M., Ullah, R., Bhatti, U. A., & Ghadi, Y. Y. (2024). Enhancing lung cancer diagnosis with data fusion and mobile edge computing using DenseNet and CNN. *Journal of Cloud Computing (Heidelberg, Germany), 13*(1), 91. DOI: 10.1186/s13677-024-00597-w

Zhang, Y., Zhang, W., & Zhao, K. (2021). Heterogeneous IoT data analytics with deep learning: Techniques and applications. *Sensors (Basel), 21*(8), 2765. PMID: 33919861

Zhou, Z., Chen, X., Li, E., Zeng, L., Luo, K., & Zhang, J. (2019). Edge intelligence: Paving the last mile of artificial intelligence with edge computing. *Proceedings of the IEEE, 107*(8), 1738–1762. DOI: 10.1109/JPROC.2019.2918951

Chapter 3
Distributed Computational Architectures for Intelligent Edge-Cloud IoT Integration

Karlibaeva Khojabaevna
http://orcid.org/0009-0006-4367-3899
Independent Researcher, Uzbekistan

Rayxanov Ulugmurod Aliyevich
Pendidikan International Joint Degree Faculty, Tashkent State University of Economics, Tashkent, Uzbekistan

Rayxanov Ulugmurod Aliyevich
Department of Finance, Alfraganus University, Tashkent, Uzbekistan

Ismatulla Khayrullayev
Department of Information Technology and Exact Sciences, Termez University of Economics and Service, Termez, Uzbekistan

Yuldasheva Gulora Gulumovna
Department of Electrical Engineering and Energy, Urgench State University, Urgench, Uzbekistan

Anorgul Ashirova
http://orcid.org/0009-0006-7271-3634
Department of General Professional Sciences, Mamun University, Khiva, Uzbekistan

ABSTRACT

This study presents a distributed computational architecture that integrates edge and cloud computing paradigms to enable intelligent IoT operations. The proposed framework distributes computational tasks between edge devices and cloud platforms according to workload characteristics, resource availability, and application

DOI: 10.4018/979-8-2600-0615-3.ch003

requirements. Advanced data processing, machine learning-based decision-making, and adaptive resource allocation mechanisms are incorporated to improve system responsiveness and operational efficiency. The architecture supports real-time analytics, enhanced fault tolerance, reduced communication overhead, and optimized energy consumption. Experimental evaluation demonstrates significant improvements in processing latency, throughput, and scalability compared with conventional centralized approaches. The findings highlight the potential of distributed edge–cloud architectures to support next-generation smart environments, including industrial automation, healthcare monitoring, smart cities, and autonomous systems.

INTRODUCTION TO EDGE–CLOUD IOT INTEGRATION

Internet of Things (IoT) has become one of the major shifts in the current technology that links billions of appliances in various locations to offer intelligent surveillance, control, and decision-making. These devices produce huge quantities of heterogenous data, sensor measurements and images, video streams and environmental readings. The traditional centralized computing systems do not support such a deluge of information due to the bandwidth, latency and computing resources constraint. It has contributed to the edge and cloud computing integration becoming one of the primary methods of addressing the computational and operational needs of the large-scale IoT systems.

Edge-cloud IoT integration: This is an allotment of edge-based localized processing with cloud computing resources of high-scale and high-performance computing at the cloud. The edge devices, such as gateways, microcontrollers and embedded systems are deployed close to the data origin and are used to perform initial processing, filtering and analysis. This closeness minimizes latency and network congestion as well as real-time decision-making of applications where real-time responsiveness is crucial, like autonomous vehicles, industrial automation, and healthcare monitoring (Bhatti et al., 2023).

Cloud computing is an enhancement to edge intelligence because of its centralized data storage, large-scale computing resources, and state-of-the-art analytics tools. The cloud runs complicated processes, such as the training of deep learning models, global pattern recognition, and predictive analytics on a large scale. The cloud also facilitates aggregation of distributed data of large numbers of edge nodes, and enables systemwide optimization and holistic views not feasible with localized processing.

The hierarchical distribution of computational tasks can be considered one of the main benefits of edge–cloud integration. Tasks with low resources, including data preprocessing, feature extraction, and simple inferences, are executed on the edge, whereas resources-demanding tasks, such as model training and large-scale analytics, are offloaded to the cloud. Such a hierarchical model is efficient on using computational resources, minimizing latency, and load balancing between edge and cloud layers and enables greater responsiveness and scalability of IoT systems (Bhatti et al., 2024).

Figure 1 shows Distributed Computational Architectures

Figure 1. Distributed computational architectures

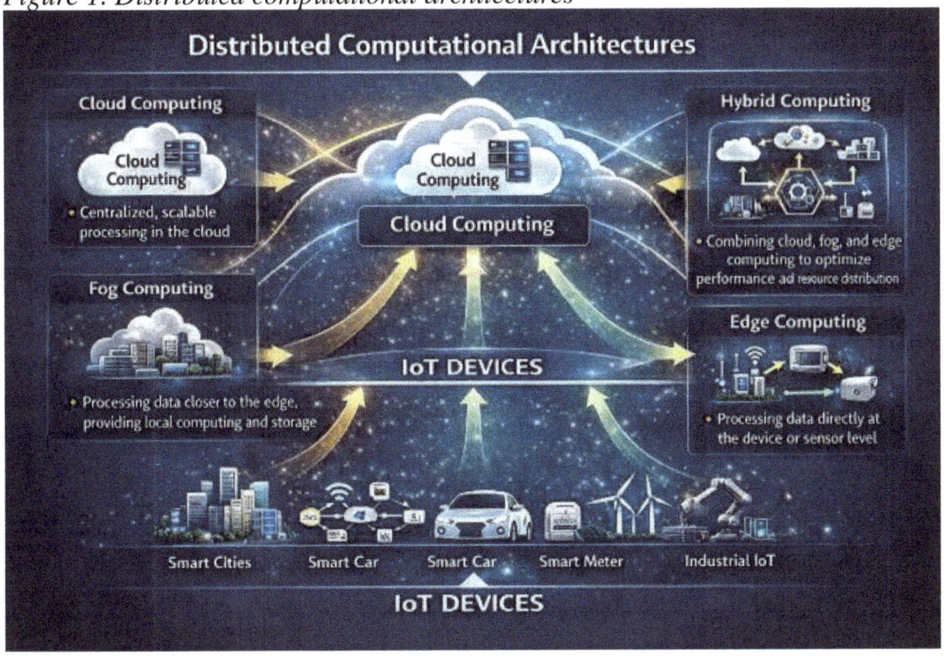

In edge-cloud IoT integration, interoperability and standardization are crucial factors to be considered. Iot ecosystems consist of heterogeneous devices, data format, communications protocols. It is very important to design architectures that would effectively combine such a variety of components to allow free flow of activities, data sharing as well as maintain uniform performance in the network. Standardization also makes it easier to achieve cross-platform compatibility and make systems deployment and maintenance less complex.

The most important issues with integrated edge-cloud systems are security and privacy. The IoT devices usually handle sensitive data, such as personal health data, industrial operational metrics, or place-based data. Edge computing is a method that reduces some of the risks by computing the sensitive data on-premises, eliminating the necessity to transmit raw data to the cloud. However, to enforce the integrity and privacy of data throughout the architecture, there is a need to implement secure communication protocols, encryption, authentication and privacy preserving methodologies like federated learning (Xu et al., 2024).

Another important issue when it comes to edge-cloud IoT integration is energy efficiency. Edge devices are usually resource limited, have a short battery life, and limited processing capability. To extend the life of the device and to maintain the sustainability of the work of the IoT networks, particularly large-scale and long-distance ones, it is necessary to allocate the tasks between the edge and cloud layers efficiently, to deploy the models with optimality, and energy-aware computing strategies.

Edge-cloud cooperation is especially valuable to latency-sensitive applications, including industrial automation, autonomous navigation, etc. When critical computations are done at the edge, the systems have the capacity to act immediately when the environment or activities change. The cloud is also expanding these systems by allowing continuous learning, historical data analysis and global coordination to ensure that the edge devices are running with the latest intelligence and reducing delays.

The management of data in edge-cloud IoT systems is complicated with the sheer amount, type, and speed of data generated. Effective data aggregation, storage, and retrieval plans are very important to ensure that the system functioning remains intact. Long term storage, large-scale analysis and model training is done in the cloud, whereas data summarization and filtering is done on edge nodes. Such a collaborative method guarantees that the applicable insights are mined in an efficient manner without putting an undue burden on network and computation capabilities.

The edge-cloud integration has been critical when developing intelligent, adaptable, and resilient networks, as the world of IoT is continually expanding. Distributed computational architectures allow one to create responsive and efficient IoT applications by integrating local processing in real-time with a scalable cloud-based analytics. The paradigm encompasses a wide range of applications, including smart cities and industrial internet of things, medical surveillance and sensor networks, and is the foundation of the new era of autonomous and intelligent IoT platforms (Bhatti et al., 2022).

ARCHITECTURAL MODELS FOR DISTRIBUTED EDGE–CLOUD COMPUTING

Distributed edge-cloud computing architectures, which are scalable, efficient and smart data processing, have been at the heart of existing Internet of Things (IoT) ecosystems. These architectures are aimed at dividing the computational workload between edge devices and centralized cloud-based systems, with the emphasis on the tasks with latency causes on the edge, and on the larger analytics and large-scale data processing tasks being performed in the cloud. The edge-cloud architecture can make its systems responsive, reduce network congestion, and utilize resources optimally in broad application in the IoT by distributing calculations across the hierarchical layers (Bhatti et al., 2021).

One of the commonest models that have been widely used in distributed edge-cloud computing is hierarchical architectures. According to this model, the lowest-layer IoT gadgets collect and transmit the information to the middle edge nodes capable of making first-level processing and local decision-making. The uppermost layer is the cloud layer which undertakes high order analytics, model training and coordination. Such a tiered design enables tasks to be delegated effectively to ensure that time sensitive tasks are handled as near to the source of data as possible and resource intensive calculations are made using the cloud.

Fog computing architectures are based on the hierarchical model but with additional levels of intermediate between the edge devices and the cloud. The nodes of these mogs offer local storage services, computation services, and networking service, which enables a quicker processing of data and lowering latency. The fog architectures can specifically be beneficial in the use of smart cities, industrial automation, and vehicle networks, where data needs to be processed quickly and real-time decisions need to be made. The distributed nature of the fog nodes is also an enhancement to fault tolerance and system reliability.

Another variant is the peer to peer edge architecture where edge devices have the capability to communicate directly with each other to share data, resources and knowledge. This decentralized approach will minimize reliance on the cloud to do real-time tasks and enable joint processing of devices. P2P architectures are used in swarm robotics, sensor networks, emergency response systems, or any other scenario where distributed decision making and recovery of a system in the event of network failures is required (Bhatti et al., 2020).

The hybrid edge-cloud architecture bridges the capabilities of the centralized cloud computing and the localized edge processing. These models are dynamic and distribute the workloads between the edge and the cloud depending on the requirements of the computations, latencies, and the network conditions. Hybrid architectures are conducive to adaptive processing that enables the IoT systems to optimize performance conditions with different environmental conditions, traffic, and application requirements. This solution improves the flexibility, scalability and power efficiency of spread-out IoT networks.

The complexity of the distributed IoT systems is turning to microservice-based architectures. The microservice architecture allows the application to be scaled, maintained more easily, and updated independently through break-even services, providing scalability and robustness to service-based applications. Various microservices can be deployed on edge nodes and cloud platforms, enabling data preprocessing and model inference, analytics and storage to be distributed efficiently. The modular design is also interoperable and integrates with heterogeneous IoT devices.

Distributed edge computation frameworks have become a topology that is viable through serverless computing model. Under this method, the cloud and edge resources are utilized to carry out event-driven functionality without necessarily involving constant resource allocation. Dynamic scaling of IoT systems Serverless architectures enable dynamically scaling IoT systems according to workload needs, lowering the operational expenses of the systems and enhancing resource utilization. This model is specifically useful when there are sporadic or bursty loads within the smart home systems, industry monitoring, and other environmental sensing networks (Bhatti et al., 2023).

Graph-based architecture is utilized in a distributed edge-cloud framework to represent the complex relationships and dependencies of the IoT devices and sensors and networks. Graph structures facilitate effective routing, resource allocation and cooperation among the devices and nodes. Graph-based architectures can be used to capture patterns of connectivity and dependency, which can be used to perform intelligent data aggregation, anomaly detection, and predictive analytics and make IoT networks more intelligent and coordinated.

Security oriented architectures apply encryption, authentication and intrusion detection functionality to distributed edge-cloud architecture. Such architectures guarantee data security, confidentiality, and resistance to cybercrime. To protect sensitive IoT information without impacting the performance of the system, security-conscious designs typically integrate edge-based monitoring and threat analysis in the cloud to detect and respond to attacks in real-time (Bhatti et al., 2023).

The choice and design of suitable distributed edge -cloud architectural models are important as IOT ecosystems become more and more intense and large-scale. Hierarchical, fog, peer-to-peer, hybrid, microservice-based, serverless, graph-based, and security-focused architectures have their own benefits that can be used based on the needs of the application, the limitations of latency, computing needs, and network settings. Using such architecture models, smart IoT systems have the potential to work on a scale, reliably, and efficiently in a wide range of environments, only to enable further developments in the field of edge-cloud integrated computing.

EDGE INTELLIGENCE: LOCAL PROCESSING AND REAL-TIME ANALYTICS

Another building block of distributed IoT systems is edge intelligence that enables real-time processing and decentralized decision-making. Edge intelligence accelerates the latency, reduces network jamming and allows IoT devices to respond to the dynamic environment, by moving the computation closer to the sources of data. This will be necessary in autonomous vehicles, industrial automation, monitoring in healthcare, and smart city management, among other applications, where real-time insights and actions are the most important in performance and safety (Bhatti et al., 2023).

The fundamental ideology of edge intelligence is to perform data processing, filtering, and initial analytics near or on the IoT devices. Instead of sending raw data to centralized cloud computing nodes, edge nodes carry out simple operations such as feature extraction, anomaly detection, or other simple inference tasks. This local processing will ensure that time-sensitive operations will not be delayed because of network transmissions or cloud computing and will help to make the system more responsive and reliable.

Figure 2 shows Distributed Computational Architectures

Figure 2. Deep learning methods comparisons

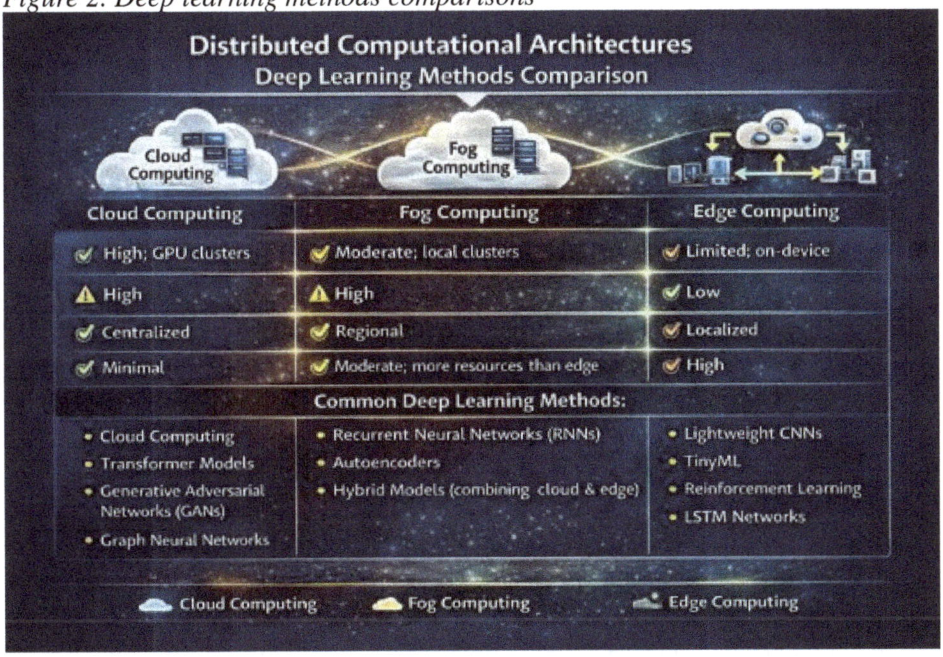

Specialized hardware is becoming more and more common on edge devices, such as GPUs, TPUs, and FPGA accelerators, in order to be able to perform advanced tasks of deep learning inference. The hardware additions allow running convolutional neural networks, recurrent networks, and other AI models at the edge without using cloud resources. Using these capabilities, the IoT systems will be able to conduct image recognitions, sensor fusions, predictive analytics, and other computationally demanding functions in real time (Bhatti et al., 2023).

Edge intelligence is very important and made possible by model optimization techniques. The models of deep learning tend to be computationally expensive and memory-intensive, and are hard to implement on the resource-surpassed edge devices. Such methods as model pruning, quantization, knowledge distillation, and lightweight architecture (MobileNet or TinyML) can be used to balance high-accuracy models with low computational and energy requirements to enable real-time analytics to be deployed at the edge.

Edge intelligence has found its application especially in applications with latency requirements. As an example, in autonomous cars, the sensor data can be analyzed on the roadside to make decisions within a second on how to navigate and avoid obstacles at the edge nodes. Industrial IoT The machinery is fitted with edge-enabled sensors that can detect faults or anomalies in real time and initiate preventive maintenance to prevent downtime. Wearable sensors to check vital signs can also be used in healthcare, where an immediate notification to medical staff is given in case unusual trends are observed, thus the implementation of prompt interventions.

Another new paradigm is collaboration between edge nodes that also enhances real-time analytics even more. With distributed edge intelligence, a plethora of devices can communicate, synchronize, and achieve collaborative processing without fully relying on the cloud. This peer-to-peer collaboration is also essential to applications like swarm robotics, distributed sensor networks and cooperative vehicular systems, where immediate and coordinated responses are essential (Fang et al., 2022)

The edge intelligence is also energy efficient since most of the IoT devices have minimal power limitations. Optimization of computation, Selective processing of data, event-based analytics, and adaptive distribution of workloads can facilitate the minimization of energy consumption, and without harming processing performance. Dynamic voltage and frequency scaling, sleep scheduling, and selective activation of model layers are some of the techniques that help in increasing the lifespan of edge devices.

Privacy-preserving analytics also works with edge intelligence. The processing of sensitive data on the local level and forwarding of aggregated information or encrypted data to the cloud will decrease the likelihood of data breach, as well as ensure compliance with privacy regulations, at a cost of IoT systems. This would be especially significant where personal health data, financial information would be used or in secure industrial operatives (Nawaz et al., 2023).

Combining edge intelligence with cloud computing can improve capabilities of local and global systems. Whereas edge nodes are concerned with real time, immediate analytics, cloud servers are concerned with computationally intensive processes (model training, trend analysis, global optimization). The cloud-to-edge periodic updates of models need to be used to provide continuous learning and system improvement and to combine the benefits of real-time responsiveness with large-scale intelligence.

With the rise of the IoT ecosystems, the edge intelligence will probably become a more dominant component of making autonomous, adaptable, and efficient functions possible. Edge intelligence enables intelligent IoT systems responding to dynamic environments in real-time, with local processing, real-time analytics, collaboration via edge networks, and connection to cloud resources by providing the basis of the wide range of applications supported by smart cities and industrial automation, as well as by healthcare and environmental monitoring (Zeng et al., 2024).

CLOUD INTELLIGENCE: SCALABLE ANALYTICS AND GLOBAL COORDINATION

Cloud intelligence is a key element of distributed IoT systems providing a centralized processing unit, scalable storage, and advanced analytics solutions. Unlike edge intelligence, which is optimized to assist with real time and latency-sensitive processing, cloud providers can assist with large-scale data aggregation, complex model training and system coordination globally. Through cloud smarts, IoT systems can process large volumes of heterogeneous data, sent by devices spread over geographical regions, derive insights capable of being acted upon and aid strategic decision-making in a variety of fields, such as smart cities, industrial processes, and healthcare.

The primary advantage of cloud intelligence is that it is able to perform analytics of the large-scale datasets generated by IoT. Models of deep learning can be effectively executed in cloud servers with terabytes or even petabytes of data. Such a centralization, in its turn, enables the IoT networks to find patterns, detect abnormalities and anticipate future occurrences at a global level, and provide a more global image that local edge nodes will not be able to generate.

The training of advanced models on the applications of deep learning is also cloud-compatible. Some of the most elaborate neural networks are convolutional networks, recursive networks and transformers which require a lot of computing resources and memory bandwidth to be trained. High-performance GPUs, TPUs, and distributed computing clusters that are offered by the cloud can be used to train these models using large-scale IoT data. The re-deployed trained models can be sent to edge devices to do real-time inference to complete the edge collaboration cycle with clouds (Yang et al., 2024)

Cloud intelligence is also elastic and scalable, which is another benefit. The dynamically allocated cloud resources can be increased or decreased to meet the changes in workloads to ensure the IoT systems are responsive even with the increase in data volumes. Scalability is particularly applicable to large scale applications, such as national sensor systems, industry surveillance systems and smart cities where the volume of incoming data can vary significantly over time.

Data aggregation and integration are some important functions that are enabled by cloud intelligence. The IoT devices produce heterogeneous data including sensor data, video, images and text. The cloud can harmonise these diverse datasets and normalise them besides performing comprehensive analytics. Other advantages of centralized data management are long term storage and historical analysis to aid trend identification, policy creation and resource optimization and entire IoT ecosystems (Han et al., 2024)

Cloud intelligence boosts predictive and prescriptive analytics. Cloud-based systems can predict future events, optimize operations based on historical and live data, and prescribe actions by analyzing the historical and real-time information. Cloud analytics can forecast equipment breakdowns, optimize production cycles, and lower the cost of operations in industrial IoT, e.g. Smart cities can be predicted at the cloud level to foresee the traffic congestion, the energy demand, and the environmental changes to effectively manage and plan them ahead.

Cloud intelligence frameworks are associated with security and privacy management. Cloud systems have strong authentication, encryption, and access control measures to secure sensitive IoT data. They also extend monitoring and audit tools so as to have adherence to the standards of regulation. It is through centralized security management that cloud systems are able to identify anomalies, react to possible threats and other policies applied uniformly across distributed IoT networks (Zhang et al., 2024).

When paired with edge intelligence, one can form an integrated computing environment that makes tasks optimally allocate between localized and centralized layers. Edge nodes are used to deal with immediate and latency-sensitive operations, and cloud platforms are dealing with computationally intensive operations, global coordination, and continuous learning. Such a combination is a guarantee of the low-latency reaction of the real-time applications and the ability to enjoy the global insights and the power of the cloud.

Federated and collaborative learning is also supported by cloud intelligence. The distributed edge devices have the capability to train local models and only to transmit model parameters to the cloud without compromising on privacy but allowing global model enhancement. The cloud synthesizes these updates, optimizes models and republishes them to the edge devices so that the IoT systems can learn perpetually based on distributed information without the transmission of raw information that is sensitive (Fahim et al., 2023).

With the ever-growing scope of the IoT ecosystems, cloud intelligence will still be required to address complexity, offer large-scale analytics, or bring about intelligent coordination to the distributed networks. Incorporation of edge intelligence is complemented by cloud platforms, which make the IoT systems responsive and able to make strategic, data-driven decisions. The bundled solution will enable the introduction of resilient, scalable, and adaptable IoT solutions across sectors, such as healthcare and transportation as well as environmental surveillance and industrial automation.

COMMUNICATION AND DATA MANAGEMENT IN DISTRIBUTED ARCHITECTURES

Distributed edge-cloud IoT architecture depends on effective communication and data management. Having billions of devices in the network and creating enormous amounts of heterogeneous data, it is crucial to have an effective system of transmission, storage, and processing to make the system work reliably. The communication protocols and data management systems should be able to operate with the large amounts of real-time data with reduced latency, bandwidth, and energy consumption, with both the edge devices and cloud servers operating effectively within a distributed environment (Cheng et al., 2023).

The edge-cloud IoT systems use hierarchical communication channels in order to handle the flow of data. Edge devices receive raw sensor data and do primary processing and sends the corresponding information to the intermediate nodes or the cloud directly. The hierarchical model minimizes network congestions, makes optimal use of the bandwidth and only significant data is transferred in order to be further processed by offloading centralized servers.

Distributed IoT architectures are utilized with different communication protocols to match various requirements. Lightweight protocols such as CoAP and MQTT are designed to be used on low-power, constrained devices, and can be used to transmit messages efficiently with minimal overhead. In cases of more significant throughput applications, protocols like HTTP/ HTTPS, WebSockets, and AMQP give strong options of making reliable and secure communication between cloud systems and edge nodes. The choice of the proper protocol is essential in the pursuit of the best performance depending on the ability of the device and the requirements of the task.

Aggregation of data is an important role in the distributed architecture in which edge nodes will aggregate the data of a set of sensors or devices and send it to the cloud. Aggregation leads to less data being sent, better use of bandwidth, and preliminary analysis, including averaging, filtering or detection of anomalies. This makes sure that relevant data is provided to the cloud in structured format to be used in advanced analytics and global coordination.

IoT protection of data in a distributed network is very crucial through secure communication. Access control policies, secure authentication, and encryption protocols are applied to avoid data breach and unauthorized access. Local encryption and anonymization of sensitive information before transmission can also be done using edge devices, which improves privacy and preserves the integrity of the information during the communication chain (Dong et al., 2023).

The storage of data is essential in distributed edge-cloud systems in order to handle a local and a global dataset. The edge devices normally store transient or short time data to aid real time analytics, whereas the cloud platform is involved in long term storage, historical analysis and backup. Cloud databases and distributed file systems enable scalable, resilient and fault tolerant storage solutions where data can be accessed and remain consistent throughout the network.

The distributed IoT network requires a quality of service (QoS) management to achieve stability in performance. The edge-cloud systems put in place ways of prioritizing essential data, dealing with traffic congestion and minimizing latency time of time), sensitive applications. Adaptive bandwidth, congestion control and dynamic routing are used to ensure that high priority tasks get the required resources to continue operating without interruption (Li et al., 2022).

The second notable aspect of distributed architectures is that data is synchronized between the edge nodes and the cloud. Synchronization will ensure that the models and analytics algorithms are processing the most up-to-date available datasets, which will enable them to make accurate predictions and act in unison. There are different methods being employed to provide consistency of distributed components such as incremental updates, event based synchronization and version control without saturating the network.

To handle data properly, heterogeneous IoTs need standardization and interoperability of data formats. Devices of other manufacturers might give information in different formats, and it may need to be translated or normalized before being aggregated. The need to ensure smooth integration is enabled by standardized data schemas, APIs, and middleware solutions that make sure that different devices can communicate with each other and add to an integrated IoT analytics framework (Yi et al., 2020).

As the use of the IoT ecosystems continues expanding, appropriate communication and data management methods will be at the heart of the performance, scalability, and reliability of the distributed edge-cloud architectures. Intelligent IoT systems can be robust, efficient and adaptable to work effectively and efficient in a wide range of applications including automated industrial processes and smart cities, and in medical monitoring and environmental sensing with smart communication protocols, hierarchical aggregation, safe transmission, scalable storage and standardized data management.

CHALLENGES, SECURITY CONSIDERATIONS, AND FUTURE RESEARCH DIRECTIONS

The possibilities of smart, real time and scalable systems, which are offered in the intelligent edge-cloud IoT models are staggering but the challenges are many and will need to be tackled to ensure efficiency, reliability and security. The major issue is dealing with the computational and energy resources of edge devices. Numerous IoT devices have low power consumption and limited processing and memory resources, thus, it is not easy to execute complicated deep learning models on them. The secrets behind defying these limitations include effective model optimization, lightweight architectures and workload distribution that is adaptive.

In the distributed architecture, data security and privacy are given the first priority. Edge devices typically contain sensitive information, including personal health information, industrial process information and geographic information. Transmission of such information on networks or storing it on the cloud exposes it to risk of breach or unauthorized access. Such risks can be addressed through the use of efficient encryption, authentication, and privacy-appropriate approaches like federated learning and still reap the benefits of distributed analytics.

The other major issue of edge–cloud IoT systems is scalability. With the increase in the number of connected devices, the amount of data generated each time is growing exponentially and the computational and storage resources must be allocated dynamically. The scaling effect of the large datasets provided by cloud platforms requires the network bandwidth and edge device capabilities, as well as system coordination to scale as well. There is a need to have scalable resource management and load-balancing mechanisms to ensure that the system works effectively at all times (Nawaz et al., 2023).

Still impediments are standardization and interoperability. IoT systems are quite heterogeneous and a specific device can be compatible with various protocols, data formats and communication standards. Devices in various vendors are incompatible and unless there are standardized interfaces, and middleware solutions, it is a complex task to integrate devices between vendors. Future studies must aim at coming up with open standards and structures which will lead to easy communication of devices and data integration.

Applications that are time sensitive are very sensitive to latency and network reliability. Even though the use of edge computing reduces the dependency of centralized cloud servers, the network disconnect, delays, or low bandwidth could still affect the responsiveness of the system. The design of fault-tolerant architecture, adaptive routing protocols, and local fallback mechanisms can aid in the ongoing operation under the circumstances when the connectivity is not assured.

The explainability and interpretability of models are vital to the development of trust in intelligent IoT systems. Deep learning models tend to be black boxes and hence decisions are not easily understood on how they are arrived at. Such critical applications of explainable AI methods are needed in healthcare, autonomous transportation, and industry automation to offer transparency, accountability, and user confidence in edge to cloud decision making.

Heterogeneity of data and its quality is also a challenge. Sensors can be noisy, incomplete or inconsistent, which will impact the quality and reliability of analytics. Preprocessing of data and anomaly detection as well as powerful learning algorithms are very imperative in making sure that high-performance models are achieved. The data fusion studies, transfer learning, and multimodal learning can be applied in order to improve the system further in different environments of IoT (Bhatti, 2025).

Security threats to distributed architectures are adversarial attacks, tampering of data, and hijacking of devices. Attackers may take advantage of edge or cloud layers vulnerabilities to fail results, disrupt workflow, or steal sensitive information. The IoT infrastructures should be secured against new threats using such tools as the development of powerful models, intrusion detection systems, and secure communication protocols.

Adaptive and self learning architectures were also stressed as the future research directions. IoT environments are dynamic and data dynamics, user dynamics and environmental dynamics vary. Continuous learning, online adaptation and reinforcement learning techniques can be used to augment systems to the level of high accuracy and high operational efficiency on a long term basis without necessarily involving human intervention.

Edge-cloud IoT systems are becoming more concerned with sustainability. Large-scale implementations need power-efficient algorithms, power-efficient hardware, and power-efficient communication plans to reduce the environmental impact of large-scale implementations. The tradeoff between computational performance, security and energy consumption will also play a significant role in ensuring resilient and scalable as well as sustainable IoT networks that will be able to support the increasing demand of intelligent and autonomous applications (Bhatti, 2025).

CONCLUSION

Edge and cloud intelligence-based distributed computational architectures offer radical structures to contemporary IoT ecosystems. These architectures can be used to help provide real time decisions, efficient use of resources and powerful data analytics by combining edge-localized processing with cloud-scale computation and storage. This combination will guarantee that the latency-sensitive tasks will be processed instantly at the edge, and the computationally heavy and large-scale workloads will be provided with the centralized power of cloud services, resulting in a well-balanced and adaptive system.

This paradigm relies on edge intelligence, enabling devices to do local data processing, initial analytics, and inferences without necessarily being dependent on the cloud. The ability increases responsiveness of the system, minimizes the network congestion, and serves applications that demand real-time response, like autonomous vehicles, industrial automation, and healthcare monitoring. Intelligent edge devices, even with limited resources, can be engaged in intelligent decision-making due to the implementation of optimized deep learning models and lightweight architectures.

Cloud intelligence is used to supplement edge computing by delivering high-performance computing, high data aggregation, and sophisticated analytics. The centralized cloud platforms enable deep learning models training, historical data analysis, and predictive modeling among devices that are geographically distributed. Cloud and edge intelligence together make IoT ecosystems run effectively at scale, avoiding actionable insights but with high reliability and responsiveness.

The seamless functionality of distributed architectures necessitates communication and data management strategies. Efficient flow of information between edge nodes and cloud platforms is made possible by optimized protocols, hierarchical data aggregation, secure transmission and standardized data formats. Good data management assists in proper analytics, less latency, better interoperability, and integrity and privacy of sensitive data across the system.

Although these benefits exist, issues like security threats, privacy issues, scalability, interoperability, and energy constraints need to be overcome in order to achieve the best of edge cloud IoT architectures. Studies on resilient models, secure communication, adaptive learning, and energy-efficient algorithms play a crucial role in overcoming such issues and making distributed IoT systems robust, sustainable, and trustworthy.

To summarize, intelligent edge–cloud IoT integration in the form of distributed computational architectures is a cornerstone to the future generation of autonomous, adaptive, and scalable systems. Using both advantages of edge and cloud computing, the IoT networks will be able to attain real-time analytics, predictive information and effective resource usage. These architectures build the path to new applications in smart cities, industrial automation, healthcare and environmental monitoring and other applications, creating a robust and smart base of future IoT ecosystems.

REFERENCES

Bhatti, U. A. (Ed.). (2025). *Deep Learning for Multimedia Processing Applications: Volume One: Image Security and Intelligent Systems for Multimedia Processing*. Taylor & Francis Ltd.

Bhatti, U. A., Tang, H., Ku, C. S., Bazai, S. U., Hussain, S., Fakhar, S., & Yee, P. L. (2023). Deep learning-based trees disease recognition and classification using hyperspectral data. *Computers, Materials & Continua*, *77*(1), 681–697. DOI: 10.32604/cmc.2023.037958

Bhatti, U. A., Yu, Z., Chanussot, J., Zeeshan, Z., Yuan, L., Luo, W., Nawaz, S. A., Bhatti, M. A., Ain, Q., & Mehmood, A. (2022). Local similarity-based spatial–spectral fusion hyperspectral image classification with deep CNN and Gabor filtering. *IEEE Transactions on Geoscience and Remote Sensing*, *60*, 1–15. DOI: 10.1109/TGRS.2021.3090410

Bhatti, U. A., Yu, Z., Yuan, L., Zeeshan, Z., Nawaz, S. A., Bhatti, M. A., Mehmood, A., Ain, Q., & Luo, W. (2020). Geometric algebra applications in geospatial artificial intelligence and remote sensing image processing. *IEEE Access : Practical Innovations, Open Solutions*, *8*, 155783–155796. DOI: 10.1109/ACCESS.2020.3018544

Bhatti, U. A., Yuan, L., Yu, Z., Nawaz, S. A., Mehmood, A., Bhatti, M. A., Ain, Q., Nizamani, M. M., Zeeshan, Z., & Xiao, S. J. (2021). Predictive data modeling using sp-kNN for risk factor evaluation in urban demographical healthcare data. *Journal of Medical Imaging and Health Informatics*, *11*(1), 7–14. DOI: 10.1166/jmihi.2021.3313

Bhatti, U. A., Zhang, C., Guan, Y., Al-Razgan, M., Awwad, E., Ullah, R., & Ghadi, Y. Y. (2024). Enhancing lung cancer diagnosis with data fusion and mobile edge computing using DenseNet and CNN. *Journal of Cloud Computing (Heidelberg, Germany).*

Cheng, M., Li, D., Zhou, N., Tang, H., Wang, G., Li, S., Bhatti, U. A., & Khan, M. K. (2023). Artificial intelligence-driven medical image analysis for healthcare systems. *IEEE Transactions on Instrumentation and Measurement.*

Dong, S., Li, J., Bhatti, U. A., Ma, J., Dong, F., & Li, Y. (2023). Robust zero-watermarking algorithm for medical images based on GFTT-KAZE and DCT. *SNPD Conference Proceedings,* 290–297. DOI: 10.1109/SNPD-Winter57765.2023.10223753

Fahim, A., Tan, Q., Bhatti, U. A., Nizamani, M. M., & Nawaz, S. A. (2023). Machine learning approaches for multimedia data processing and analysis. *Multimedia Tools and Applications.*

Fang, Y., Liu, J., Li, J., Cheng, J., Hu, J., Yi, D., Xiao, X., & Bhatti, U. A. (2022). Robust zero-watermarking algorithm for medical images based on SIFT and bandelet-DCT. *Multimedia Tools and Applications, 81*(12), 16863–16879. DOI: 10.1007/s11042-022-12592-x

Han, H., Zeeshan, Z., Talpur, B. A., Sadiq, T., Bhatti, U. A., Awwad, E., & Al-Razgan, M. (2024). *Deep learning techniques for intelligent environmental monitoring systems.* Applied Environmental and Oceanography Research.

Li, Y., Li, J., Shao, C., Bhatti, U. A., & Ma, J. (2022). Intelligent multimedia security using deep feature extraction. *International Conference on Cyber Security Proceedings.*

Nawaz, S. A., Li, J., Shoukat, M. U., Bhatti, U. A., & Ahmad, M. R. (2023). Hybrid watermarking framework for secure medical image management. *Computers & Electrical Engineering.*

Xu, B., Bhatti, U. A., Tang, H., Yan, J., Wu, S., Sarhan, N., & Ghadi, Y. Y. (2024). Towards explainability for AI-based edge wireless signal automatic modulation classification. *Journal of Cloud Computing (Heidelberg, Germany), 13*(1), 10. DOI: 10.1186/s13677-024-00590-3

. Yang, J., Sadiq, T., Xiong, J., Awais, M., Bhatti, U. A., Alizadehsani, R., & Górriz, J. M. (2024). Myocarditis detection combining deep reinforcement learning and differential evolution algorithm. *Journal of Artificial Intelligence in Healthcare.*

Yi, D., Liu, J., Li, J., Zhou, J., Bhatti, U. A., Fang, Y., & Nawaz, S. A. (2020). Multimedia security framework based on machine learning techniques. *International Conference on Computer Security Proceedings.*

. Zeng, C., Liu, J., Li, J., Cheng, J., Zhou, J., Nawaz, S. A., Xiao, X., & Bhatti, U. A. (2024). Artificial intelligence-based disease detection using medical image processing. *Journal of Artificial Intelligence in Healthcare.*

Zhang, C., Aamir, M., Guan, Y., Al-Razgan, M., Awwad, E., Ullah, R., Bhatti, U. A., & Ghadi, Y. Y. (2024). Intelligent cloud-based systems for geospatial analytics. *Journal of Cloud Computing (Heidelberg, Germany).*

Chapter 4
Edge AI and Federated Learning in Authentication Architectures

Khush Siddharth Bothra
http://orcid.org/0009-0005-9039-2910
Vishwakarma Institute of Information Technology, India

Gitanjali Shinde
http://orcid.org/0000-0001-6623-8722
Vishwakarma Institute of Technology, India

Grishma Bobhate
http://orcid.org/0009-0007-7351-8723
Vishwakarma Institute of Technology, India

Sonal Fatangare
Vishwakarma Institute of Technology, India

Jyoti Deshmukh
http://orcid.org/0000-0003-0644-2136
Marathwada Mitramandal's Institute of Technology, India

ABSTRACT

Centralized authentication mechanisms are increasingly inadequate for AIoT environments due to limitations in latency, scalability, and privacy. This chapter proposes a multi-layered, edge-based authentication architecture that shifts trust to distributed, on-device systems. Security is anchored in hardware roots of trust

DOI: 10.4018/979-8-2600-0615-3.ch004

such as trusted execution environments, while Edge AI enables real-time biometric, behavioural, and contextual authentication. Federated learning supports continuous model adaptation across devices without sharing raw data, preserving privacy. Decentralized identity mechanisms further enable secure and scalable verification without reliance on central authorities. Performance analysis highlights improvements in latency, communication efficiency, scalability, and privacy, while case studies from Tesla, Google, and Amazon illustrate practical deployment. The proposed framework provides a scalable and privacy-preserving foundation for authentication in next-generation AIoT systems.

EDGE AI AND FEDERATED LEARNING IN AUTHENTICATION ARCHITECTURES

The rapid convergence of digital, physical, and biological systems has led to the emergence of Artificial Intelligence of Things (AIoT), where interconnected devices are not only capable of sensing and communication but also autonomous decision-making. From autonomous vehicles coordinating in real time to smart industrial systems optimizing production processes and wearable devices monitoring human health, AIoT environments are characterized by large-scale, latency-sensitive, and data-intensive interactions(Al-Garadi et al., 2020).

This transformation places significant demands on underlying security mechanisms, particularly authentication systems that verify the identity of users and devices. Traditional authentication approaches, which rely on centralized cloud-based verification, were designed for static environments with limited scale and lower real-time requirements. In AIoT settings, however, these models introduce critical limitations, including increased latency, excessive communication overhead, scalability bottlenecks, and heightened privacy risks(Yu et al., 2017).

As AIoT systems continue to expand, authentication can no longer be treated as a discrete, one-time verification step. Instead, it must evolve into a continuous and adaptive process that operates close to the data source. This shift requires rethinking authentication architectures to support real-time decision-making, decentralized trust management, and privacy-preserving learning(T. Li et al., 2020).

This chapter addresses these challenges by examining the limitations of centralized authentication systems and proposing a layered, edge-based authentication architecture that integrates Edge AI, Federated Learning, decentralized identity frameworks, and hardware-based roots of trust. The following sections analyze the fundamental shortcomings of existing approaches and motivate the need for decentralized authentication in AIoT environments.

The Problem of Latency

Latency, defined as the delay between an action and its corresponding response, remains a critical limitation of centralized authentication systems. While delays of a few hundred milliseconds may be acceptable in traditional web-based applications, they become increasingly problematic in AIoT environments where real-time decision-making is essential.

Consider autonomous vehicles operating in dynamic traffic conditions. These systems rely on rapid communication with surrounding entities, including other vehicles and infrastructure, to ensure safe and coordinated operation. When a vehicle broadcasts a critical event, such as sudden braking, the receiving system must first authenticate the message before acting on it. In centralized architectures, this verification depends on communication with remote servers, introducing delays due to both network transmission and processing overhead.

These delays are fundamentally constrained by network latency and the physical limits of signal propagation. In time-critical scenarios, even small delays can reduce system responsiveness and affect overall reliability. As a result, centralized authentication mechanisms are not well suited for applications that require near-instantaneous verification(Yu et al., 2017).

Similar constraints can be observed in other AIoT domains, including industrial automation and real-time healthcare systems, where delayed authentication may disrupt operations or reduce system effectiveness. This requirement for low-latency operation becomes even more critical as networks evolve toward 6G, where ultra-reliable low-latency communication (URLLC) is a fundamental pillar that must balance stringent timing requirements with the security overhead of emerging post-quantum cryptographic protocols. Taken together, these challenges highlight the need for authentication mechanisms that operate closer to the data source, enabling low-latency and real-time decision-making(Turnip et al., 2026).

The Overload of Data and the Bandwidth Bottleneck

AIoT environments are characterized by large-scale data generation, with billions of devices continuously producing and exchanging information. In many cases, authentication mechanisms extend beyond simple credentials and rely on data-intensive inputs such as biometric signals, voice patterns, and contextual information(Al-Garadi et al., 2020).

In centralized authentication systems, this data must be transmitted to remote servers for verification, leading to substantial bandwidth consumption. As the number of connected devices grows, the volume of authentication-related data can place increasing strain on network infrastructure, resulting in congestion and reduced system efficiency.

This issue becomes more pronounced in environments with limited or unreliable connectivity, such as remote deployments or mobile networks. Under such conditions, the continuous transmission of high-dimensional authentication data not only increases communication costs but also contributes to higher energy consumption, particularly for resource-constrained devices(Yu et al., 2017). Recent research indicates that Federated Learning (FL) provides a viable architectural solution to these challenges by enabling decentralized, collaborative model training, which keeps raw data local and significantly reduces the necessity for large-scale data transmission to central servers(Vashisth & Goyal, 2025).

Consequently, centralized authentication introduces performance bottlenecks and may contribute to network congestion, affecting the efficiency of the systems it is intended to secure. These limitations reinforce the need for distributed approaches that reduce data transfer and support local processing.

The Fragility of a Single Point of Failure

Centralized authentication systems inherently introduce a single point of failure, as all authentication requests depend on the availability and integrity of a central server. This architectural dependency limits system resilience and increases vulnerability to both technical failures and malicious attacks.

This fragility can manifest in several ways:

- **Technical Outage:** Failures such as software bugs, hardware malfunctions, or database corruption at the central server can disrupt authentication services across the entire network. In such situations, even fully functional devices may be unable to operate due to the unavailability of the central authority.
- **Cyberattack**: Central authentication servers represent high-value targets for attackers. Distributed Denial of Service (DDoS) attacks or targeted intrusions can overwhelm or compromise these systems, potentially disabling authentication services across large-scale deployments.
- **Physical or Geopolitical Events:** External disruptions, including power outages, natural disasters, or regional network restrictions, can impact access to centralized infrastructure. This may result in widespread service unavailability, regardless of the operational status of individual devices.

These factors collectively highlight the inherent risks of centralized architectures, where the failure or compromise of a single component can have system-wide consequences. Decentralized approaches, in contrast, distribute trust and reduce reliance on a single point of control, thereby improving overall system resilience(Al-Garadi et al., 2020).

The Huge Privacy Risk of Centralized Systems

Centralized authentication systems introduce significant privacy risks due to the aggregation of sensitive user data at a single location. To support authentication processes, central servers often store extremely sensitive information, including passwords, cryptographic keys, biometric identifiers, and behavioral data. This concentration of data creates an attractive target for potential attackers.

In the event of a security breach, large volumes of sensitive information may be exposed, potentially affecting a substantial number of users. Such incidents can lead to identity compromise, financial loss, and a decline in user trust. In AIoT environments, the implications can be even more significant, as authentication data may include information related to location, health, device usage, and personal behavior.

Beyond security concerns, centralized data storage also raises challenges in complying with modern data protection regulations. Frameworks such as the General Data Protection Regulation (GDPR) and the California Consumer Privacy Act (CCPA) impose strict requirements on data collection, storage, and cross-border transfer. Centralized architectures, which depend on large-scale data aggregation, can complicate adherence to these regulatory requirements.

Taken together, these limitations emphasize the need for authentication systems that minimize data exposure, support local processing, and align with privacy-preserving principles by design(Khraisat et al., 2024; Papernot et al., 2017).

The Way Forward: Moving Security to the Edge

The limitations of centralized authentication systems necessitate a shift toward decentralized approaches that bring computation and decision-making closer to the data source. In AIoT environments, this transition enables authentication mechanisms that are not only more responsive, but also more scalable and privacy-aware(Yu et al., 2017).

Two key technologies underpin this shift:

- **Edge AI:** Edge AI enables authentication decisions to be performed locally on devices or nearby edge nodes. By processing data at or near its source, such systems reduce latency, minimize communication overhead, and support real-time operation even under constrained or intermittent connectivity.
- **Federated Learning (FL):** Federated learning facilitates collaborative model training across distributed devices without requiring the transfer of raw

data. Instead, devices train local models and share only model updates, allowing systems to improve collectively while preserving user privacy(McMahan et al., 2017).

Taken together, these technologies enable a new class of authentication systems that are decentralized, adaptive, and privacy-preserving by design. The following sections build on this foundation by presenting a layered authentication architecture, analyzing its performance characteristics, and examining its application in real-world scenarios.

Research Gap

While Edge AI and Federated Learning have emerged as promising paradigms for decentralized intelligence and privacy-preserving learning, their application to authentication architectures remains fragmented and insufficiently explored. Existing authentication systems continue to rely heavily on centralized or partially distributed models, which are often unable to meet the stringent requirements of AIoT environments in terms of latency, scalability, and privacy.

Several key limitations can be observed in current research. First, there is a lack of unified architectural frameworks that integrate hardware-based roots of trust, on-device AI inference, and federated model training into a cohesive authentication pipeline. Most existing approaches treat these components in isolation rather than as interdependent layers within a secure system. Second, although Federated Learning has been extensively studied in general machine learning contexts, its application to continuous authentication scenarios—where models must evolve dynamically based on behavioral and contextual data—remains relatively underdeveloped.

In addition, existing approaches often do not sufficiently address security challenges specific to decentralized learning environments, such as adversarial clients, model poisoning, and privacy leakage through gradients. There is also limited consideration of system-level constraints, including energy consumption, communication overhead, and real-time decision requirements on resource-constrained edge devices. Moreover, the absence of formal threat models and clearly defined security assumptions reduces the rigor of many proposed solutions.

Finally, there remains a gap in translating conceptual architecture into actionable design principles. While industry implementations demonstrate the feasibility of distributed intelligence, there is still a lack of generalized frameworks that can guide the development of secure, scalable, and regulation-compliant authentication systems across diverse AIoT applications.

These gaps collectively highlight the need for a comprehensive, layered authentication architecture that systematically integrates Edge AI, Federated Learning, and hardware-based trust mechanisms, while addressing both security and system-level challenges.

Contributions

To address the limitations identified above, this chapter proposes a structured and integrated approach to authentication in AIoT systems. The key contributions are summarized as follows:

- **Layered Edge Authentication Architecture**: We propose a multi-layer authentication framework that spans from hardware roots of trust (e.g., Trusted Execution Environments and secure enclaves) to on-device Edge AI models and Federated Learning-based adaptation, enabling decentralized and continuous authentication.
- **Integration of Federated Learning for Continuous Adaptation**: The chapter demonstrates how Federated Learning can be applied specifically to authentication systems to enable continuous model updates based on user behavior, without exposing sensitive data. This approach enhances both security and privacy.
- **System-Level Design Considerations**: We analyze critical factors such as latency, bandwidth efficiency, scalability, and energy constraints, providing insights into how decentralized authentication architectures can outperform traditional centralized approaches in AIoT environments.
- **Security and Threat Awareness**: The proposed framework incorporates a security-first perspective by outlining potential threat vectors in decentralized systems and emphasizing the importance of robust trust assumptions and mitigation strategies.
- **Practical Insights from Real-World Systems**: Through case studies of large-scale deployments, we extract generalizable design principles that can guide the implementation of distributed authentication systems beyond specific industry examples.
- **Regulatory and Privacy Alignment**: The chapter discusses how decentralized authentication aligns with modern privacy regulations by minimizing data exposure and enabling on-device processing.

Together, these contributions provide a comprehensive foundation for designing next-generation authentication systems that are secure, scalable, and inherently privacy-preserving in the AIoT era.

EDGE-BASED AUTHENTICATION ARCHITECTURE

Having established the limitations of centralized authentication, the logical progression is toward a decentralized approach in which authentication decisions are performed closer to where data is generated(Yu et al., 2017). This section presents a structured, multi-layer authentication architecture designed for AIoT environments, integrating edge intelligence, federated learning, identity management, and hardware-based trust.

Unlike traditional systems that rely on a single centralized authority, the proposed architecture distributes trust across multiple functional layers. Authentication is primarily performed at the edge, while learning, identity verification, and trust anchoring operate as supporting mechanisms that enhance security, scalability, and privacy.

Device Layer: Data Acquisition and Interaction

The device layer represents the point of interaction between users and the system. It includes IoT devices such as smartphones, vehicles, industrial sensors, and wearable devices that continuously generate data.

These devices function as both data sources and authentication subjects. Inputs such as biometric signals, behavioral patterns, and environmental context originate at this layer and are processed locally or at nearby edge nodes. The effectiveness of the overall architecture depends on the integrity and reliability of data generated at this level.

Edge Authentication Layer: Real-Time Identity Verification

The edge authentication layer is the core of the proposed architecture, where authentication decisions are made in real time. By processing data locally or at nearby edge nodes, this layer eliminates the latency associated with centralized verification.

Authentication at this layer is multi-modal and includes:

- **Biometric Authentication:** Verification using fingerprints, facial recognition, or voice patterns processed within secure device environments.
- **Behavioral Authentication:** Continuous authentication based on user interaction patterns such as typing dynamics, gait, and device usage behavior.
- **Contextual Authentication:** Use of environmental signals such as location, network context, and device state to enhance trust decisions.

A key feature of this layer is continuous authentication. Instead of a single login event, the system maintains a dynamic trust score based on ongoing user behavior.

When anomalies are detected, additional verification mechanisms are triggered(Yu et al., 2017).

Federated Learning Layer: Adaptive Intelligence and Privacy Preservation

The federated learning layer enables continuous improvement of authentication models without requiring centralized data collection. Instead of transmitting raw user data, devices train local models and share only model updates(McMahan et al., 2017).

This approach provides several advantages:

- **Privacy Preservation:** Sensitive biometric and behavioral data remain on-device.
- **Scalability:** Learning occurs across distributed devices without overloading central infrastructure.
- **Adaptability:** Models evolve continuously to detect new behavioral patterns and emerging threats.

However, federated learning introduces challenges such as client drift, data heterogeneity, and potential adversarial updates, which must be addressed through secure aggregation and robust training mechanisms(Bagdasaryan et al., 2020; Karimireddy et al., 2020).

In this architecture, federated learning acts as a supporting intelligence layer that enhances authentication accuracy over time rather than directly performing authentication decisions.

Identity Layer: Decentralized Trust Management

The identity layer manages how devices and users establish and verify identity in a decentralized environment. Instead of relying on centralized identity providers, this layer utilizes decentralized identifiers (DIDs) and verifiable credentials(Consortium, 2022).

In this model:

- Devices possess cryptographically signed credentials issued by trusted authorities.
- Identity verification is performed locally by validating these credentials.
- Trust relationships are established peer-to-peer without requiring constant communication with a central server.

This approach enables fast and scalable identity verification while reducing dependency on centralized infrastructure.

Trust Anchor Layer: Hardware-Based Security Foundation

At the foundation of the architecture lies the hardware root of trust, which ensures that all higher-level authentication processes are anchored in secure and tamper-resistant components.

Technologies in this layer include:

- **Trusted Execution Environments (TEE):** Isolated environments for secure computation and key storage(Sabt et al., 2015).
- **Trusted Platform Modules (TPM):** Dedicated hardware modules for cryptographic operations.
- **Physical Unclonable Functions (PUFs):** Hardware-based unique identifiers that cannot be replicated(Shamsoshoara et al., 2020).

This layer guarantees device authenticity and protects sensitive operations from software-level attacks, forming the basis for secure edge authentication.

Architectural Overview

The proposed edge-based authentication architecture is structured as a multi-layer system that integrates device-level data acquisition, edge-based decision-making, federated learning, decentralized identity management, and hardware-based trust anchors. As illustrated in Figure 1, the architecture defines the interaction between these layers and the flow of data, model updates, and trust verification across the system.

At the device layer, IoT devices generate authentication-relevant inputs, including biometric, behavioral, and contextual data. As shown in Figure 1, this data is transmitted to the edge authentication layer, where real-time processing and identity verification are performed. By localizing computation at the edge, the system minimizes latency and reduces dependency on centralized infrastructure(Yu et al., 2017).

The edge authentication layer serves as the central decision-making component of the architecture. It processes incoming data, performs inference using locally available models, and initiates identity verification when required. As depicted in Figure 1, the edge layer interacts with the federated learning layer through a bidirectional communication loop. Locally trained model updates are sent to the federated learning layer, where they are aggregated to form a global model. This updated model is then redistributed to edge nodes, enabling continuous system adaptation without exposing raw data(Karimireddy et al., 2020).

Identity verification is managed through interaction with the decentralized identity layer. When authentication requires credential validation, the edge layer sends a verification request to the identity layer. As shown in Figure 1, the identity layer manages decentralized identifiers and verifiable credentials, ensuring that identity information is validated without reliance on centralized authorities(Consortium, 2022).

To establish trust in device integrity and execution environments, the identity layer further interacts with the hardware root of trust. This involves issuing attestation requests to hardware components such as Trusted Execution Environments (TEEs) or Trusted Platform Modules (TPMs). The hardware layer responds with attestation results, which are interpreted by the identity layer to determine the authenticity and integrity of the requesting entity. As illustrated in Figure 1, the identity layer then returns a verification decision to the edge authentication layer.

These interactions define three primary flows within the architecture. First, data flows from IoT devices to the edge layer for real-time authentication. Second, a learning loop operates between the edge and federated learning layers, enabling collaborative model training and continuous improvement. Third, a trust verification cycle connects the edge, identity, and hardware layers, ensuring secure and reliable identity validation, as shown in Figure 1.

By combining localized processing, collaborative learning, decentralized identity management, and hardware-backed trust, the architecture achieves low-latency, scalable, and privacy-preserving authentication suitable for dynamic AIoT environments.

Figure 1. Layered architecture of edge-based authentication with Edge AI, federated learning, decentralized identity, and hardware root of trust

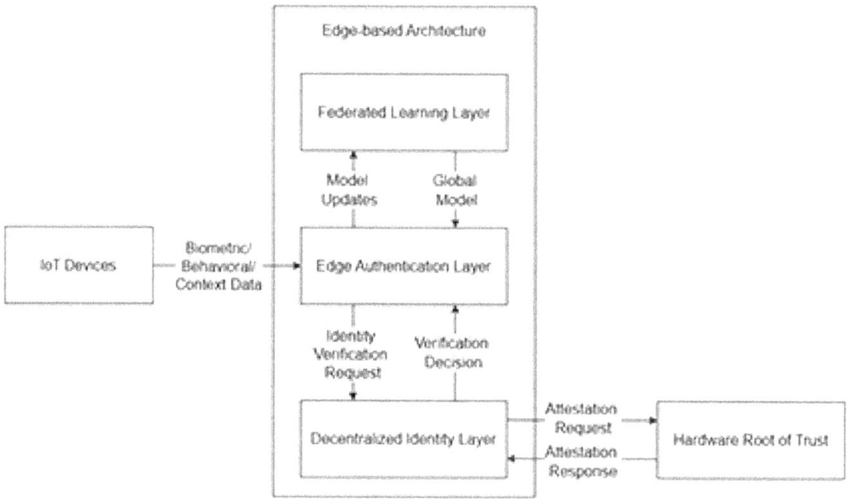

Threat Model and Security Assumptions

To evaluate the security of the proposed edge-based authentication architecture, it is necessary to define a clear threat model outlining the capabilities of potential adversaries, the assumptions made about the system, and the security guarantees provided.

Adversary Model. We consider a powerful adversary operating in a distributed AIoT environment with the following capabilities:

- **Device Compromise:** An attacker may gain control over one or more IoT devices through malware, physical access, or software vulnerabilities.
- **Communication Interception:** The adversary can eavesdrop on or manipulate communication channels between devices, edge nodes, and federated learning participants (man-in-the-middle attacks).
- **Impersonation and Spoofing:** Malicious entities may attempt to impersonate legitimate devices or users to gain unauthorized access.
- **Model Poisoning Attacks:** In the federated learning process, adversarial clients may submit manipulated model updates to corrupt the global model(Bagdasaryan et al., 2020).

- **Inference and Data Leakage Attacks:** Attackers may attempt to extract sensitive information from model updates or gradients shared during federated learning(Papernot et al., 2017).

System Assumptions. The proposed architecture operates under the following assumptions:

- Devices are equipped with hardware-based trust anchors such as Trusted Execution Environments (TEE), Trusted Platform Modules (TPM), or Physical Unclonable Functions (PUFs).
- Communication channels between entities are secured using standard cryptographic protocols (e.g., TLS).
- A subset of participating devices may be untrusted or compromised, but the majority behave honestly.
- Federated learning aggregation is performed using secure aggregation techniques to limit exposure of individual updates(Karimireddy et al., 2020).

Security Guarantees. Under the defined threat model and assumptions, the architecture provides the following security properties:

- **Device Authenticity:** Hardware roots of trust ensure that each device possesses a unique, verifiable identity that cannot be easily cloned.
- **Data Privacy:** Sensitive biometric and behavioral data remain on-device, minimizing exposure and reducing the risk of centralized data breaches.
- **Resilience to Centralized Failures:** Decentralization eliminates single points of failure, improving system availability under attack conditions(Bonawitz et al., 2019).
- **Adaptive Threat Detection:** Federated learning enables continuous model updates, allowing the system to adapt to evolving attack patterns and anomalous behaviors.
- **Layered Defense:** Security is enforced across multiple layers, ensuring that compromise at one level does not immediately lead to total system failure.

Limitations. Despite these protections, certain challenges remain. Federated learning systems are inherently vulnerable to issues such as client drift, data heterogeneity, and adversarial updates, which can affect convergence and model reliability. Additionally, resource constraints on edge devices may limit the complexity of security mechanisms that can be deployed.

These limitations highlight the need for robust aggregation techniques, anomaly detection mechanisms, and efficient model designs in real-world deployments.

Authentication Workflow

To operationalize the proposed architecture, the authentication process follows a structured workflow that integrates hardware trust, edge intelligence, and federated learning. The workflow is designed to enable real-time, continuous, and privacy-preserving authentication in AIoT environments.

Step 1: Device Initialization and Trust Establishment. When a device joins the network, it first establishes its identity using the hardware root of trust. Secure components such as Trusted Execution Environments (TEE), Trusted Platform Modules (TPM), or Physical Unclonable Functions (PUFs) generate and protect cryptographic keys.

This process ensures that each device possesses a unique, verifiable identity anchored in hardware, preventing cloning and unauthorized replication.

Step 2: Local Data Acquisition. The device continuously collects input data relevant to authentication, including:

- Biometric data (e.g., fingerprint, facial features)
- Behavioral patterns (e.g., typing dynamics, motion patterns)
- Contextual signals (e.g., location, network environment)

All data acquisition occurs locally, ensuring that sensitive information does not leave the device.

Step 3: Edge-Based Authentication. On-device or nearby edge AI models process the collected data to perform real-time authentication. The system evaluates the input against learned user profiles and computes an authentication or trust score.

If the computed score exceeds a predefined threshold, access is granted. Otherwise, additional verification steps—such as biometric re-authentication—are triggered.

This step enables low-latency decision-making without reliance on centralized servers(Yu et al., 2017).

Step 4: Continuous Authentication and Monitoring. Unlike traditional systems that authenticate only at login, the proposed architecture continuously monitors user behavior. The trust score is dynamically updated based on ongoing interactions.

If anomalous behavior is detected, the system can:

- Reduce trust score
- Request additional authentication
- Restrict or terminate access

This ensures resilience against session hijacking and unauthorized access after initial authentication.

Step 5: Federated Model Update. To improve authentication accuracy over time, the device periodically trains local models using newly observed data. Instead of transmitting raw data, only model updates are shared with the federated learning layer.

These updates are securely aggregated to produce a global model, which is then redistributed to participating devices.

This process enables continuous learning while preserving user privacy(McMahan et al., 2017).

Step 6: Decentralized Identity Verification. When interaction between devices or systems is required, identity verification is performed using decentralized identifiers and verifiable credentials.

Devices exchange signed credentials and verify them locally without contacting a central authority. This enables fast and secure peer-to-peer authentication(Consortium, 2022).

Step 7: Feedback and Adaptation. The system continuously refines authentication models and trust thresholds based on new data and aggregated learning outcomes. This feedback loop ensures that the system adapts to evolving user behavior and emerging threats.

Algorithmic Representation. The authentication workflow can be summarized as follows:

- Input: Device D, input data X
- Output: Authentication decision A

1. Verify hardware identity of D
2. Acquire biometric, behavioral, and contextual data X
3. Compute authentication score S using edge model
4. If S $\geq$ threshold:

   A $\leftarrow$ Accept

   Else:

   Request additional verification or reject

5. Update local model using X
6. Send model updates for federated aggregation
7. Receive updated global model

This workflow demonstrates how the proposed architecture enables decentralized, adaptive, and secure authentication by combining real-time edge processing with collaborative learning mechanisms.

PERFORMANCE ANALYSIS OF EDGE-BASED AUTHENTICATION ARCHITECTURES

To evaluate the effectiveness of the proposed edge-based authentication architecture, it is essential to compare its performance against traditional centralized authentication systems. This section analyses key system-level metrics, including latency, communication overhead, bandwidth usage, scalability, and security robustness.

Latency Reduction

Centralized authentication systems rely on cloud-based verification, requiring each authentication request to traverse network layers, including local networks, internet backbones, and data centers. This introduces significant delays, particularly in time-sensitive AIoT applications(Yu et al., 2017).

In contrast, the proposed architecture performs authentication at the edge, enabling real-time decision-making. By eliminating the need for cloud round-trips, edge-based systems significantly reduce latency and enable near-instantaneous responses, which are critical in applications such as autonomous systems and industrial automation.

Communication Overhead

Centralized authentication requires continuous transmission of authentication data to a central server, resulting in high communication overhead. This becomes increasingly inefficient as the number of connected devices grows.

Federated learning addresses this limitation by transmitting only model updates instead of raw data. This design reduces communication frequency and volume, making the system more efficient and scalable. The reduction in communication overhead is a fundamental advantage of federated learning-based systems, which are specifically designed to address distributed training constraints(Konečný et al., 2017).

Bandwidth Efficiency

AIoT environments often operate under constrained bandwidth conditions, particularly in remote or mobile deployments. Centralized systems exacerbate this issue by requiring continuous transmission of high-dimensional data, such as biometric inputs and contextual signals.

The proposed architecture significantly reduces bandwidth usage by performing data processing locally and sharing only compressed model updates. This aligns with the requirements of IoT systems, where limited network capacity and resource constraints must be carefully managed(McMahan et al., 2017).

Scalability

Centralized authentication systems are inherently limited by the capacity of the central server and network infrastructure. As the number of devices increases, these systems experience bottlenecks that degrade performance and reliability.

In contrast, the proposed architecture distributes computation across edge devices, enabling horizontal scalability. Each device contributes to both authentication and learning processes, reducing dependency on centralized infrastructure, and allowing the system to scale efficiently with the growth of AIoT networks(Q. Li et al., 2023).

Privacy and Security Advantages

Centralized systems require aggregation of sensitive user data at a single location, increasing the risk of data breaches and unauthorized access. This creates a high-value target for attackers.

The edge-based architecture mitigates this risk by ensuring that sensitive data remains on-device. Federated learning further enhances privacy by allowing collaborative model training without exposing raw data. This decentralized approach reduces the risk of large-scale data compromise and aligns with modern privacy requirements(Papernot et al., 2017).

Energy and Resource Efficiency

Communication is often more energy-intensive than computation in IoT systems. Centralized authentication requires frequent data transmission, which increases energy consumption and reduces device lifespan.

By minimizing communication and leveraging local computation, the proposed architecture improves energy efficiency. This is particularly important for battery-powered devices operating in resource-constrained environments, where efficient energy utilization is critical(Konečný et al., 2017; Yu et al., 2017).

Comparative Summary

Table 1 summarizes the key differences between centralized authentication and the proposed edge-based architecture across multiple performance dimensions.

Table 1. Comparison of centralized and edge-based authentication architectures

Metric	Centralized Authentication	Edge AI + Federated Architecture	Analysis
Latency	High due to cloud round-trip and server processing delays	Significantly reduced due to local edge inference	Edge computing eliminates long-distance communication delays, enabling near real-time authentication decisions
Communication Overhead	High, with frequent data transmission to central servers	Reduced through periodic model updates instead of continuous data transfer	Federated learning minimizes communication by sharing model parameters rather than raw data
Bandwidth Usage	High due to transmission of biometric and contextual data	Lower, as only compressed model updates are transmitted	Reduces network congestion and improves efficiency in bandwidth-constrained IoT environments
Scalability	Limited by central server capacity and network bottlenecks	Highly scalable through distributed computation across devices	Load is distributed across edge nodes, avoiding central bottlenecks
Privacy Exposure	High due to centralized storage of sensitive data	Low, as data remains on-device	Federated learning ensures raw data never leaves the device
Security Robustness	Vulnerable to single point of failure and centralized attacks	Improved resilience due to distributed architecture	Decentralization reduces the impact of targeted attacks
Energy Consumption	High due to continuous communication overhead	Moderate, balancing local computation and reduced communication	Communication is more energy-intensive than local computation in IoT systems
Adaptability	Limited; requires centralized retraining cycles	Continuous adaptation through federated updates	Models evolve based on distributed user behavior patterns
Reliability	Dependent on network connectivity and cloud availability	Operates under intermittent connectivity	Edge-based decisions can function even with limited network access
Attack Surface	Centralized high-value target	Distributed attack surface	Reduces risk of catastrophic system-wide failure

Overall, the proposed architecture demonstrates clear advantages in latency, communication efficiency, scalability, and privacy preservation. These improvements are consistent with findings in edge computing and federated learning research, which show that localized processing reduces latency and communication overhead, while distributed model training improves scalability and bandwidth efficiency(Yu et al., 2017). Additionally, the privacy-preserving nature of federated learning, where sensitive data remains on-device, further supports these advantages. While challenges such as model convergence and device heterogeneity remain, the architectural shift from centralized to edge-based authentication provides a strong foundation for secure and scalable AIoT systems(McMahan et al., 2017; Papernot et al., 2017).

Design Trade-offs in Edge-Based Authentication

While the proposed edge-based authentication architecture offers significant advantages in terms of latency, scalability, and privacy, these benefits are accompanied by several design trade-offs that must be carefully considered.

Latency vs. Resource Utilization. Performing authentication at the edge reduces network latency by eliminating reliance on centralized servers. However, this shift increases computational demands on edge devices, which may have limited processing power and memory. As a result, system designers must balance real-time responsiveness with the resource constraints of edge environments.

Privacy vs. Model Performance. Federated learning enhances privacy by ensuring that raw user data remains on-device. However, the decentralized nature of training can lead to challenges such as data heterogeneity and uneven data distribution across clients. These factors may impact model convergence and overall performance compared to centrally trained models(Karimireddy et al., 2020).

Decentralization vs. Coordination Complexity. Removing centralized control improves system resilience and eliminates single points of failure. At the same time, decentralized systems require more complex coordination mechanisms, particularly for model aggregation, identity management, and trust verification. Ensuring consistency and reliability across distributed components introduces additional system complexity.

Security vs. Communication Overhead Mechanisms such as secure aggregation, attestation protocols, and encrypted communication enhance system security. However, these mechanisms can introduce additional communication overhead and processing delays, especially in large-scale deployments with frequent authentication requests(Bagdasaryan et al., 2020).

Adaptability vs. Stability Continuous learning enables authentication systems to adapt to evolving user behavior and environmental conditions. However, frequent model updates can introduce instability, including model drift or inconsistent decision boundaries across devices. Maintaining a balance between adaptability and stability is essential for reliable authentication(Karimireddy et al., 2020).

These trade-offs highlight that while edge-based authentication architectures address key limitations of centralized systems, they introduce new challenges that must be managed through careful system design. Understanding and balancing these trade-offs is critical for deploying robust and efficient authentication systems in real-world AIoT environments.

Evaluation Metrics for Edge-Based Authentication

The effectiveness of edge-based authentication systems in AIoT environments must be evaluated using a combination of performance, security, and resource-related metrics. Unlike traditional centralized systems, where evaluation is often limited to accuracy and latency, distributed architectures require a broader set of criteria that reflect real-time operation, privacy preservation, and system scalability.

Authentication Accuracy. Authentication systems must reliably distinguish between legitimate and illegitimate entities. This is commonly evaluated using metrics such as False Acceptance Rate (FAR) and False Rejection Rate (FRR), which measure the likelihood of incorrectly granting or denying access. In continuous authentication settings, maintaining low error rates is critical to ensure both security and usability.

Latency. Latency represents the time required to process authentication data and produce a verification decision. In AIoT applications, this metric is particularly important, as delays directly impact system responsiveness. Edge-based architectures aim to minimize latency by performing computations closer to the data source, enabling near real-time authentication.

Communication Overhead. Communication overhead refers to the volume of data exchanged between system components during authentication and model updates. In federated learning systems, this includes the transmission of model parameters rather than raw data. Efficient systems aim to reduce communication frequency and payload size to optimize network utilization(Konečný et al., 2017).

Energy Consumption. Energy efficiency is a key consideration for edge devices, many of which operate under constrained power conditions. Authentication processes, including model inference and communication, must be optimized to minimize energy usage while maintaining performance(Yu et al., 2017).

Scalability. Scalability evaluates the system's ability to maintain performance as the number of devices increases. In large-scale AIoT environments, authentication mechanisms must handle high volumes of concurrent requests without degradation in latency or accuracy(Q. Li et al., 2023).

Security Robustness. Robustness measures the system's ability to withstand adversarial conditions, including spoofing attacks, model poisoning, and compromised devices. Evaluation in this context involves assessing the resilience of authentication mechanisms under various threat scenarios.

Adaptability and Model Stability. In systems that employ continuous learning, adaptability refers to the ability to update authentication models in response to evolving user behavior and environmental changes. At the same time, model stability must be maintained to prevent performance degradation due to excessive updates or data inconsistencies(Karimireddy et al., 2020).

These metrics collectively provide a comprehensive framework for evaluating edge-based authentication systems. By considering not only accuracy and latency but also communication efficiency, energy consumption, and robustness, the proposed architecture can be assessed in a manner that reflects the practical constraints and requirements of real-world AIoT deployments.

FEDERATED LEARNING IN AUTHENTICATION ARCHITECTURES

Edge-based authentication systems—particularly those relying on behavioral and contextual AI—must continuously adapt to evolving user patterns and emerging threats. Static models rapidly degrade in effectiveness, yet centralizing user data for retraining reintroduces the very privacy, latency, and scalability issues that decentralized architectures aim to eliminate.

Federated Learning (FL) addresses this challenge by enabling collaborative model training across distributed devices while keeping raw data local. Instead of transferring sensitive behavioral data such as keystrokes, biometrics, or usage patterns to a central server, FL distributes the training process itself, allowing models to learn directly from edge environments. This paradigm aligns naturally with authentication systems, where privacy preservation and personalization are critical(McMahan et al., 2017; Papernot et al., 2017).

At its core, FL follows an iterative process. A central coordinator distributes the current global model to selected edge devices. Each device then performs local training using authentication-relevant data, such as behavioral biometrics or contextual signals. Instead of sending raw data, devices return only model updates. These updates are aggregated at the server, typically using algorithms such as Federated Averaging, to produce an improved global model. This process repeats continuously, allowing authentication systems to evolve without exposing sensitive user data(McMahan et al., 2017).

Role of Federated Learning in Authentication

In authentication architectures, federated learning plays a critical role in enabling adaptive and privacy-preserving identity verification.

First, it supports continuous personalization. Authentication models must adapt to gradual behavioral drift, such as changes in typing patterns or device usage habits. FL allows models to be refined locally on each device without exposing user data.

Second, it enables collective intelligence without data sharing. By aggregating knowledge across multiple devices, FL improves detection of anomalous behavior and strengthens resistance to impersonation attacks.

Third, it ensures privacy-preserving model evolution. Since authentication data is inherently sensitive, FL minimizes exposure by keeping raw data on-device while still enabling global learning. This aligns with the broader principle of performing computation close to data sources in distributed IoT systems(Q. Li et al., 2023).

Security Challenges in Federated Authentication Systems

While federated learning enhances privacy, it introduces new security challenges that are particularly significant in authentication contexts.

One major concern is gradient leakage, where model updates can unintentionally reveal sensitive information about user behavior. Even without direct data sharing, adversaries may reconstruct inputs from gradients.

Another challenge is the presence of malicious or Byzantine clients. Compromised devices can inject poisoned updates into the training process, potentially degrading model performance or enabling unauthorized access.

Data heterogeneity also poses a problem. Since user behavior varies significantly across devices, federated systems often face non-IID data distributions, leading to client drift and unstable model convergence.

Additionally, federated systems operate under communication constraints, including limited bandwidth and intermittent connectivity, which can impact update frequency and model synchronization.

Finally, model drift and decision errors are particularly critical in authentication scenarios. Small deviations in model behavior can lead to false positives or false negatives, directly affecting both security and usability.

To mitigate these risks, federated authentication systems incorporate several mechanisms. Secure aggregation prevents the server from accessing individual updates. Differential privacy introduces controlled noise to protect user-specific information. Robust aggregation techniques help defend against adversarial clients. Adaptive optimization methods, such as SCAFFOLD, reduce client drift, and improve convergence stability(Bagdasaryan et al., 2020; Karimireddy et al., 2020; Papernot et al., 2017).

Frameworks for Federated Authentication Deployment

Several frameworks support the deployment of federated learning systems, each suited to different authentication scenarios.

TensorFlow Federated (TFF) is primarily designed for research and large-scale experimentation. It provides both high-level APIs and low-level control, making it suitable for prototyping authentication models and studying optimization strategies.

PySyft, developed within the OpenMined ecosystem, focuses on privacy-preserving machine learning. It integrates techniques such as Secure Multi-Party Computation and Differential Privacy, making it well-suited for authentication systems in sensitive domains such as healthcare and finance.

Flower offers a lightweight and framework-agnostic approach, enabling integration with multiple machine learning libraries. Its flexibility and simplicity make it particularly suitable for real-world deployment across heterogeneous edge environments(Beutel et al., 2022).

Table 2. Comparison of federated learning frameworks for authentication deployment

Framework	Strength	Best Fit for Authentication
TensorFlow Federated	Research and simulation capabilities	Model design and experimentation
PySyft	Strong privacy guarantees	High-sensitivity authentication
Flower	Flexibility and scalability	Production-grade deployment

Table 2 presents a comparison of commonly used federated learning frameworks in the context of authentication deployment, highlighting their respective strengths and suitable use cases. In practice, production authentication systems tend to favor lightweight and scalable frameworks such as Flower, while privacy-critical applications may leverage PySyft's advanced cryptographic capabilities. TensorFlow Federated remains valuable for experimentation and algorithm development rather than direct deployment(Q. Li et al., 2023).

CORE CHALLENGES IN FEDERATED EDGE AUTHENTICATION SYSTEMS

While edge-based authentication combined with federated learning offers significant advantages in terms of privacy, scalability, and latency, its practical deployment introduces several fundamental challenges. These challenges arise from the inherently distributed, heterogeneous, and adversarial nature of AIoT environments(Oteafy & Hassanein, 2017).

Data Heterogeneity and Client Drift

In federated authentication systems, data is inherently distributed across users and devices, leading to non-identically distributed (non-IID) data. Behavioral patterns such as typing dynamics, device usage, and biometric signals vary significantly across individuals, environments, and time.

This heterogeneity introduces challenges in model convergence and stability. Local models may become highly specialized to individual users, resulting in client drift, where updates from different devices conflict during aggregation. Over time, this can degrade the performance of the global authentication model and introduce bias toward dominant user patterns(Karimireddy et al., 2020).

System Heterogeneity and Device Constraints

AIoT environments consist of highly diverse devices, ranging from powerful edge servers to resource-constrained sensors and wearables. These devices differ in computational capacity, battery life, and network connectivity.

Such variability affects participation in federated training. Slower or intermittently connected devices may fail to complete training rounds, leading to inconsistent updates and reduced system efficiency. This heterogeneity complicates synchronization and requires adaptive participation strategies to maintain system performance.

Communication Efficiency and Scalability

Although federated learning reduces the need to transmit raw data, model updates themselves can be large, particularly for deep learning models with millions of parameters. Frequent communication between devices and aggregation servers can strain network resources, especially in bandwidth-constrained environments.

As the number of participating devices increases, communication overhead becomes a key bottleneck. Efficient update mechanisms and communication-aware training strategies are therefore essential for scaling federated authentication systems(Konečný et al., 2017).

Security and Adversarial Threats

The decentralized nature of federated systems introduces new attack vectors. Malicious or compromised devices may attempt to manipulate the global model through poisoned updates, potentially enabling unauthorized access or degrading authentication accuracy.

In addition, inference attacks may exploit model updates to extract sensitive information about user behavior. These risks are particularly critical in authentication systems, where model integrity directly impacts security decisions(Bagdasaryan et al., 2020; Papernot et al., 2017).

Model Drift and Decision Reliability

Authentication systems require high reliability, as even minor deviations in model behavior can result in false positives or false negatives. In federated settings, continuous updates and heterogeneous data can lead to model drift over time.

This creates a trade-off between adaptability and stability. While models must evolve to reflect changing user behavior, excessive drift can reduce consistency and trust in authentication outcomes.

Overall, these challenges highlight that while federated edge authentication architectures offer strong theoretical advantages, their real-world deployment requires careful system design to balance efficiency, security, and reliability.

Deployment Considerations in Real-World Environments

While edge-based authentication architectures offer significant advantages, their practical deployment in real-world AIoT environments introduces several operational considerations that extend beyond theoretical design.

Device Heterogeneity: AIoT ecosystems consist of a wide range of devices with varying computational capabilities, memory constraints, and energy resources. Designing authentication systems that operate consistently across such heterogeneous environments requires adaptive models and flexible deployment strategies.

Network Variability: Edge devices often operate under fluctuating network conditions, including intermittent connectivity and limited bandwidth. Authentication mechanisms must therefore be resilient to network disruptions, ensuring that critical operations can continue even in offline or degraded communication scenarios(Yu et al., 2017).

Model Update Management: In federated learning systems, determining the frequency and scale of model updates is a key challenge. Frequent updates improve adaptability but increase communication overhead, while infrequent updates may reduce system responsiveness to changing conditions. Balancing this trade-off is essential for efficient deployment(Konečný et al., 2017).

Integration with Existing Infrastructure: Real-world systems must often integrate with legacy authentication frameworks and organizational security policies.

Ensuring compatibility with existing infrastructure, while introducing decentralized and edge-based components, requires careful system design and standardization.

Operational Reliability and Maintenance: Maintaining consistent performance across distributed systems involves monitoring device health, detecting anomalies, and managing software updates. Automated mechanisms for fault detection and recovery are essential to ensure long-term reliability.

These considerations highlight that successful deployment of edge-based authentication systems requires not only robust architectural design but also careful attention to operational constraints and system integration challenges.

CASE STUDIES

To validate the proposed edge-based authentication architecture, this section examines three distinct real-world case studies: autonomous vehicles, mass-scale mobile platforms, and edge-centric smart environments. These case studies illustrate how large-scale deployments address the systems and statistical challenges outlined in this chapter by systematically leveraging edge intelligence, federated learning, and hardware-based roots of trust.

Case Study 1: Real-Time Edge Authentication in Autonomous Vehicles

Autonomous vehicular platforms operate in highly dynamic and safety-critical environments where authentication decisions must be made with minimal latency and without guaranteed network connectivity. As a result, authentication is performed locally within the vehicle.

These platforms employ a multi-layered edge-based approach. Proximity-based verification systems use cryptographic challenge-response mechanisms over short-range communication channels, such as Bluetooth Low Energy (BLE), to authenticate users without relying on cloud infrastructure. Additionally, onboard AI systems process sensor data locally to detect anomalies and potential security threats in real time.

This architecture directly addresses latency and connectivity constraints, enabling authentication decisions to be made instantaneously. At the same time, the system leverages fleet-wide learning through federated mechanisms. Vehicles share abstracted and anonymized updates derived from observed events, allowing the system to evolve collectively without exposing sensitive user data.

Key Insights:

- Edge-based authentication eliminates latency constraints in safety-critical systems
- Local AI enables continuous and context-aware security monitoring
- Federated learning enables rapid adaptation to emerging threats across distributed devices

Design Implications. The autonomous transportation case highlights the necessity of fully localized authentication mechanisms in latency-critical environments. Systems operating under real-time constraints must prioritize edge-based decision-making to eliminate dependency on cloud verification. Additionally, fleet-level learning demonstrates the effectiveness of distributed intelligence, where collective adaptation can be achieved without centralizing sensitive data. This suggests that future authentication architectures should tightly couple edge inference with collaborative learning to balance responsiveness and adaptability(Khezri et al., 2022).

Case Study 2: Scalable and Privacy-Preserving Authentication on Mass-Scale Mobile Platforms

Mass-scale mobile ecosystems present a fundamentally different challenge: authentication must scale across billions of heterogeneous devices while maintaining usability and privacy.

To address this, modern mobile architectures integrate authentication directly into edge devices through hardware-backed security mechanisms such as Trusted Execution Environments (TEE) and dedicated security chips. These components ensure that sensitive data, including biometric information, is processed and stored locally, never leaving the device.

On-device intelligence further enhances authentication through contextual signals, such as device usage patterns and environmental factors, enabling adaptive and low-friction user verification. Federated learning is used to improve model performance across the ecosystem by aggregating anonymized updates from devices, allowing models to generalize across diverse user behaviors without centralizing raw data.

This approach directly addresses system heterogeneity, scalability, and privacy challenges in large-scale deployments.

Key Insights:

- Hardware roots of trust ensure secure and verifiable authentication at scale
- On-device intelligence balances security with usability in high-frequency authentication scenarios
- Federated learning enables global model improvement while preserving user privacy

Design Implications. This approach illustrates the importance of integrating hardware-backed security with on-device intelligence to achieve both scalability and privacy. In large-scale heterogeneous environments, authentication systems must be designed to operate reliably across diverse device capabilities while maintaining consistent security guarantees. The use of federated learning further indicates that personalization and global model improvement can coexist without compromising user data. This reinforces the need for architectures that combine secure hardware, adaptive models, and decentralized learning(Sabt et al., 2015).

Case Study 3: Context-Aware Authentication in Smart Home Environments

Smart home ecosystems introduce a different set of challenges, including continuous sensing, privacy concerns, and unreliable network conditions.

To address these, modern smart home devices perform significant processing at the edge. Smart cameras and voice assistants use on-device AI models to detect events such as human presence, unusual sounds, or environmental anomalies. Instead of continuously streaming data, devices operate in event-driven modes, transmitting only relevant information when necessary.

This design reduces bandwidth usage and enhances privacy by minimizing exposure of raw audio and video data. Additionally, local processing ensures that core functionality remains operational even under network disruptions.

Federated learning further enhances system performance by enabling models to improve across diverse home environments. Devices contribute anonymized updates based on local observations, allowing the system to adapt to varying conditions such as lighting, noise, and user behavior.

Key Insights:

- Edge processing minimizes bandwidth usage and enhances privacy in continuous sensing environments
- Event-driven architectures improve efficiency and reduce unnecessary data transmission
- Federated learning enables adaptation to highly diverse and dynamic real-world conditions

Design Implications. The context-aware authentication case emphasizes the role of context-aware and event-driven authentication in continuous sensing environments. Systems that operate on high-frequency data streams must minimize unnecessary data transmission while maintaining responsiveness. Edge processing combined with selective communication enables efficient operation under bandwidth and privacy constraints. This suggests that authentication frameworks should incorporate adaptive triggering mechanisms and local intelligence to balance efficiency, privacy, and reliability in dynamic environments(Konečný et al., 2017).

Cross-Case Analysis

Across all three case studies, several consistent patterns emerge. First, authentication decisions are increasingly performed at the edge to meet latency and reliability requirements. Second, hardware-based trust mechanisms play a critical role in securing sensitive operations. Third, federated learning enables continuous system improvement without compromising privacy.

These observations support the practical feasibility and effectiveness of the proposed architecture, demonstrating that its core principles are already being applied in large-scale real-world systems(McMahan et al., 2017; Yu et al., 2017).

Generalized Design Principles. First, authentication decisions must be performed at or near the data source to meet latency and reliability requirements. Second, hardware-based trust mechanisms are essential for securing sensitive operations and establishing device authenticity. Third, federated learning enables continuous system improvement without centralizing user data, supporting both scalability and privacy. Finally, effective authentication systems must balance adaptability with stability, ensuring that continuous learning does not compromise decision reliability. These principles provide a foundation for designing robust, distributed authentication architectures in AIoT environments.

REGULATORY AND PRIVACY CONSIDERATIONS

The deployment of authentication systems in AIoT environments involves the processing of extremely sensitive data, including biometric, behavioral, and contextual information. As a result, such systems must comply with modern data protection regulations, particularly frameworks such as the General Data Protection Regulation (GDPR) and the California Consumer Privacy Act (CCPA). Rather than treating compliance as an external requirement, the proposed architecture inherently aligns with key regulatory principles through its decentralized and privacy-preserving design(Papernot et al., 2017; Yao, 1982).

Table 3 presents a mapping between core regulatory requirements and the corresponding architectural components that enable compliance.

Table 3. Regulatory compliance mapping

Requirement	Description	Architectural Component	Compliance Mechanism
Data Minimization	Only necessary data should be collected and processed	Edge Authentication Layer	Data is processed locally on-device, reducing unnecessary data transmission
Purpose Limitation	Data should be used only for specified authentication purposes	Federated Learning Layer	Model training occurs without exposing raw data, limiting secondary usage
Storage Limitation	Data should not be retained longer than necessary	Edge + Device Layer	Sensitive data remains on-device and can be periodically deleted or updated
User Privacy Protection	Personal data must be protected from unauthorized access	Hardware Trust Anchor Layer	TEE, TPM, and secure enclaves protect data during processing and storage
Secure Processing	Data must be processed in a secure environment	Hardware + Edge Layers	Isolated execution environments ensure secure computation
Transparency and Control	Users should have visibility and control over their data	Identity Layer	Decentralized identifiers and verifiable credentials enable user-controlled identity management
Right to Access and Deletion	Users should be able to access or delete their data	Edge + Identity Layers	Local data storage enables direct user control without dependency on centralized servers
Cross-Border Data Transfer Restrictions	Data transfer across regions must comply with legal constraints	Federated Learning Layer	Raw data is not transferred across regions; only model updates are shared

The mapping demonstrates that compliance is not an added feature but a direct consequence of the architectural design. By minimizing centralized data collection, leveraging on-device processing, and enabling decentralized identity management, the proposed system aligns with core regulatory requirements by default.

Furthermore, the use of federated learning reduces risks associated with cross-border data transfer and large-scale data breaches, while hardware-based trust mechanisms ensure that sensitive operations remain protected even in adversarial environments. This integration of privacy-preserving techniques and secure computation establishes a strong foundation for deploying authentication systems that are both technically robust and legally compliant(Baig et al., 2023).

Overall, regulatory alignment reinforces the practicality of the proposed architecture, ensuring that it can be adopted in real-world applications without conflicting with evolving data protection standards.

FUTURE TRENDS IN DISTRIBUTED AUTHENTICATION

The transition from centralized to decentralized authentication is not only a response to current limitations but also a foundation for future security paradigms. As AIoT ecosystems continue to evolve, authentication mechanisms are expected to become more adaptive, context-aware, and inherently distributed. The proposed edge-based architecture aligns with several emerging trends that are likely to define the next generation of authentication systems.

- **AIoT Zero-Trust Architectures:** Zero-Trust principles, based on the notion of "never trust, always verify," are expected to become standard in distributed environments. In such systems, no device or entity is inherently trusted, and continuous verification is required for every interaction. This directly complements the proposed architecture, where authentication is performed continuously at the edge and supported by hardware-backed trust anchors and decentralized identity mechanisms(Konsta et al., 2023).
- **Predictive Continuous Authentication:** Future authentication systems will move beyond reactive verification toward predictive security. By leveraging on-device intelligence and behavioral modelling, systems will anticipate potential threats based on deviations from established patterns. This reinforces the role of continuous authentication in the proposed framework, where trust is dynamically updated rather than determined through a single verification event(Al-Garadi et al., 2020).
- **Swarm Intelligence and Collaborative Defense:** Distributed devices are expected to operate collaboratively, sharing security-relevant insights to detect and respond to threats in real time. Such swarm-based approaches align with federated learning mechanisms, where knowledge is aggregated across devices without exposing raw data. This enables collective defense strategies while preserving privacy(Yu et al., 2017).
- **Hardware-Accelerated and Neuromorphic Security:** The increasing complexity of on-device AI models will drive the adoption of specialized hardware, such as Neural Processing Units (NPUs) and neuromorphic chips. These technologies enable efficient, low-power execution of security algorithms at the edge, strengthening the feasibility of real-time authentication and continuous monitoring within resource-constrained environments(Sabt et al., 2015).
- **Decentralized Identity and Self-Sovereign Trust:** The shift toward decentralized identity frameworks allows users and devices to maintain control over their credentials. Technologies such as Decentralized Identifiers (DIDs) and Verifiable Credentials (VCs) support privacy-preserving identity verification

without reliance on centralized authorities. This trend directly supports the identity layer of the proposed architecture, enabling scalable and user-centric trust management(Consortium, 2022).

Collectively, these trends indicate a shift toward authentication systems that are continuous, collaborative, and deeply integrated into the operational fabric of AIoT environments. The proposed architecture not only addresses current challenges but also provides a foundation that is compatible with these emerging directions, reinforcing its relevance for future deployments(Yang et al., 2022).

CONCLUSION: THE SHIFT TOWARD DISTRIBUTED TRUST

The rapid evolution of AIoT systems has exposed fundamental limitations in traditional centralized authentication mechanisms, particularly in terms of latency, scalability, reliability, and privacy. As devices become increasingly autonomous and interconnected, authentication can no longer rely solely on remote, cloud-based verification models that introduce delays and concentrate risk. This shift calls for decentralized approaches that support real-time, secure, and privacy-aware authentication.

This chapter has addressed these challenges by proposing a layered edge-based authentication architecture that integrates Edge AI, Federated Learning, decentralized identity frameworks, and hardware-based roots of trust. The architecture enables real-time authentication at the edge while supporting continuous adaptation through collaborative learning. By combining localized decision-making with decentralized trust management and hardware-backed security, the system achieves a practical balance between responsiveness, scalability, and privacy preservation.

Through performance analysis, the chapter has demonstrated how the proposed approach reduces latency, minimizes communication overhead, and improves scalability when compared to centralized systems. The introduction of evaluation metrics further provides a structured framework for assessing authentication systems in AIoT environments, considering not only accuracy and latency, but also energy consumption, communication efficiency, and robustness under adversarial conditions. In addition, the discussion of design trade-offs highlights the inherent balance between performance, resource utilization, and system complexity in distributed architectures.

The inclusion of deployment considerations also brings attention to the practical challenges associated with implementing edge-based authentication systems, including device heterogeneity, network variability, and integration with existing infrastructure. These factors reinforce the importance of designing systems that are not only theoretically sound, but also operationally viable in real-world environments.

Despite these advantages, several challenges remain. Federated learning systems are subject to issues such as data heterogeneity, client drift, and vulnerability to adversarial updates, all of which can affect model stability and reliability. At the same time, resource constraints on edge devices may limit model complexity, while decentralized architectures introduce additional coordination challenges that must be addressed through efficient protocols and system design.

Future research should focus on improving the robustness and efficiency of federated learning under adversarial conditions, developing lightweight models for resource-constrained devices, and enhancing secure aggregation and anomaly detection mechanisms. Further work is also needed to standardize decentralized identity frameworks and ensure interoperability across diverse AIoT ecosystems.

In conclusion, the transition from centralized authentication to distributed, edge-based systems represents a fundamental shift in how digital trust is established and maintained. By integrating real-time edge intelligence, privacy-preserving collaborative learning, decentralized identity management, and hardware-based trust anchors, the proposed architecture offers a viable and scalable foundation for next-generation authentication systems in AIoT environments.

REFERENCES

Al-Garadi, M. A., Mohamed, A., Al-Ali, A. K., Du, X., Ali, I., & Guizani, M. (2020). A Survey of Machine and Deep Learning Methods for Internet of Things (IoT) Security. *IEEE Communications Surveys and Tutorials, 22*(3), 1646–1685. DOI: 10.1109/COMST.2020.2988293

Bagdasaryan, E., Veit, A., Hua, Y., Estrin, D., & Shmatikov, V. (2020). How To Backdoor Federated Learning. *Proceedings of Machine Learning Research, 108,* 2938–2948.

Baig, A. F., Eskeland, S., & Yang, B. (2023). Privacy-preserving continuous authentication using behavioral biometrics. *International Journal of Information Security, 22*(6), 1833–1847. DOI: 10.1007/s10207-023-00721-y

Beutel, D. J., Topal, T., Mathur, A., Qiu, X., Fernandez-Marques, J., Gao, Y., Sani, L., Li, K. H., Parcollet, T., de Gusmão, P. P. B., & Lane, N. D. (2022). *Flower: A Friendly Federated Learning Research Framework.* https://arxiv.org/abs/2007.14390

Bonawitz, K., Eichner, H., Grieskamp, W., Huba, D., Ingerman, A., Ivanov, V., Kiddon, C., Konečný, J., Mazzocchi, S., McMahan, H. B., Van Overveldt, T., Petrou, D., Ramage, D., & Roselander, J. (2019). *Towards Federated Learning at Scale: System Design.* https://arxiv.org/abs/1902.01046

Brendan McMahan, H., Moore, E., Ramage, D., Hampson, S., & Agüera y Arcas, B. (2017). Communication-efficient learning of deep networks from decentralized data. *Proceedings of the 20th International Conference on Artificial Intelligence and Statistics, AISTATS 2017,* 54.

Consortium, W. W. W. (2022). *Decentralized Identifiers (DID) v1.0. October.* https://www.w3.org/TR/did-core/

Karimireddy, S. P., Kale, S., Mohri, M., Reddi, S. J., Stich, S. U., & Suresh, A. T. (2020). SCAFFOLD: Stochastic Controlled Averaging for Federated Learning. *37th International Conference on Machine Learning, ICML 2020, PartF16814,* 5088–5099.

Khezri, R., Steen, D., & Tuan, L. A. (2022). Vehicle to Everything (V2X) - A Survey on Standards and Operational Strategies. *2022 IEEE International Conference on Environment and Electrical Engineering and 2022 IEEE Industrial and Commercial Power Systems Europe, EEEIC / I and CPS Europe 2022, June.* DOI: 10.1109/EEEIC/ICPSEurope54979.2022.9854561

Khraisat, A., Alazab, A., Singh, S., Jan, T., & Gomez, A. (2024). Survey on Federated Learning for Intrusion Detection System: Concept, Architectures, Aggregation Strategies, Challenges, and Future Directions. *ACM Computing Surveys, 57*(1). Advance online publication. DOI: 10.1145/3687124

Konečný, J., McMahan, H. B., Yu, F. X., Richtárik, P., Suresh, A. T., & Bacon, D. (2017). *Federated Learning: Strategies for Improving Communication Efficiency*. 1–10. https://arxiv.org/abs/1610.05492

Konsta, A. M., Lafuente, A. L., & Dragoni, N. (2023). A Survey of Trust Management for Internet of Things. *IEEE Access : Practical Innovations, Open Solutions, 11*, 122175–122204. DOI: 10.1109/ACCESS.2023.3327335

Li, Q., Wen, Z., Wu, Z., Hu, S., Wang, N., Li, Y., Liu, X., & He, B. (2023). A Survey on Federated Learning Systems: Vision, Hype and Reality for Data Privacy and Protection. *IEEE Transactions on Knowledge and Data Engineering, 35*(4), 3347–3366. DOI: 10.1109/TKDE.2021.3124599

Li, T., Sahu, A. K., Talwalkar, A., & Smith, V. (2020). Federated Learning: Challenges, Methods, and Future Directions. *IEEE Signal Processing Magazine, 37*(3), 50–60. DOI: 10.1109/MSP.2020.2975749

Oteafy, S. M. A., & Hassanein, H. S. (2017). Resilient IoT Architectures over Dynamic Sensor Networks with Adaptive Components. *IEEE Internet of Things Journal, 4*(2), 474–483. DOI: 10.1109/JIOT.2016.2621998

Papernot, N., Goodfellow, I., Abadi, M., Talwar, K., & Erlingsson, Ú. (2017). Semi-supervised knowledge transfer for deep learning from private training data. *5th International Conference on Learning Representations, ICLR 2017 - Conference Track Proceedings, 2015*, 1–16.

Sabt, M., Achemlal, M., & Bouabdallah, A. (2015). Trusted execution environment: What it is, and what it is not. *Proceedings - 14th IEEE International Conference on Trust, Security and Privacy in Computing and Communications, TrustCom 2015, 1*, 57–64. DOI: 10.1109/Trustcom.2015.357

Shamsoshoara, A., Korenda, A., Afghah, F., & Zeadally, S. (2020, September). A survey on physical unclonable function (PUF)-based security solutions for Internet of Things. *Computer Networks, 183*, 107593. Advance online publication. DOI: 10.1016/j.comnet.2020.107593

Turnip, T. N., Andersen, B., & Vargas-Rosales, C. (2026). Toward 6G Authentication and Key Agreement Protocol: A Survey on Hybrid Post Quantum Cryptography. *IEEE Communications Surveys and Tutorials*, *28*, 3311–3345. DOI: 10.1109/COMST.2025.3567439

Vashisth, S., & Goyal, A. (2025). A Survey of Federated Learning for IoT: Addressing Resource Constraints and Heterogeneous Challenges. *Informatica (Slovenia)*, *49*(17), 1–10. DOI: 10.31449/inf.v49i17.7707

Yang, Z., Chen, M., Wong, K. K., Poor, H. V., & Cui, S. (2022). Federated Learning for 6G: Applications, Challenges, and Opportunities. *Engineering (Beijing)*, *8*, 33–41. DOI: 10.1016/j.eng.2021.12.002

Yao, A. C. (1982). Protocols for Secure Computations. *Annual Symposium on Foundations of Computer Science - Proceedings*, 160–164. DOI: 10.1109/SFCS.1982.38

Yu, W., Liang, F., He, X., Hatcher, W. G., Lu, C., Lin, J., & Yang, X. (2017). A Survey on the Edge Computing for the Internet of Things. *IEEE Access : Practical Innovations, Open Solutions*, *6*(c), 6900–6919. DOI: 10.1109/ACCESS.2017.2778504

Chapter 5

Edge Intelligence and Resource-Efficient Computing for UAV Networks

Ergashev Nuriddin
http://orcid.org/0009-0003-8851-5374
Department of Information Systems and Technologies, Karshi State Technical University. Uzbekistan

Erkin Kholiyarov
Department of Information Technology and Exact Sciences, Termez University of Economics and Service, Termez, Uzbekistan

Anorgul I. Ashirova
Department of General Professional Sciences, Mamun University, Khiva, Uzbekistan

Khayrulla Urozboev
Department of International Scientific Journals and Ratings, Alfraganus University, Tashkent, Uzbekistan

ABSTRACT

Edge intelligence has emerged as a promising solution by enabling data processing and artificial intelligence inference closer to data sources, reducing dependence on centralized cloud infrastructures. This chapter examines resource-efficient computing strategies for UAV networks, including edge AI, federated learning, task offloading, lightweight deep learning models, and energy-aware resource management. It also discusses architectures that integrate edge, fog, and cloud computing to enhance

DOI: 10.4018/979-8-2600-0615-3.ch005

scalability, reliability, and responsiveness. Furthermore, the chapter highlights current challenges related to security, mobility, communication efficiency, and real-time decision-making while presenting future research directions for intelligent and sustainable UAV ecosystems.

INTRODUCTION TO EDGE INTELLIGENCE IN UAV NETWORKS

Unmanned Aerial Vehicle (UAV) networks have gained significant attention in recent years due to their ability to support a wide range of applications, including surveillance, environmental monitoring, disaster management, and smart city operations. These networks often involve multiple UAVs working collaboratively to collect, process, and transmit data. As the scale and complexity of UAV deployments increase, there is a growing need for efficient computational frameworks that can support real-time decision-making and data analysis (Shi et al., 2016).

Traditional cloud-centric computing models are not always suitable for UAV networks due to their reliance on stable communication links and centralized processing. In many UAV applications, latency, bandwidth limitations, and intermittent connectivity can hinder the effectiveness of cloud-based solutions. These challenges have led to the emergence of edge intelligence as a viable alternative for distributed and real-time processing (Satyanarayanan, 2017).

In the realm of modern wireless communication systems, edge intelligence has become a pivotal paradigm for transforming UAV networks. Edge intelligence has been identified as a game-changing paradigm for modern wireless communication systems, especially for UAV networks. The current growth of the Internet of Things (IoT), AI services and applications, and data-intensive services has brought unprecedented requirements for communication infrastructure. The traditional cloud-centric architectures often fail to satisfy the strict latency requirements of latency-critical and mission-critical UAV applications. So, edge intelligence is a combination of artificial intelligence and edge computing, which can be applied to process data in real-time and make decisions close to the source from which data is coming. This strategy greatly improves the efficiency, responsiveness and scalability of UAV networks in dynamic and resource-constrained environments (Mao et al., 2017).

Drones, popularly referred to as UAV's, are now being used with great success in several fields like agriculture, transportation, disaster management, military surveillance, environmental monitoring, logistics and smart city development. They are useful and valuable in data collection, communication support and autonomous execution of missions, thanks to their flexibility, mobility and access to difficult terrains. Despite this, UAV networks are beset with many issues that stem from the limited computing power within each platform, energy conservation, dynamic network topologies, intermittent communications availability, and the necessity for fast decision-making. The problems require innovative solutions that can handle many data efficiently, with minimal communication delays and energy consumption (Mach & Becvar, 2017).

Edge intelligence is a solution that merges the concepts of edge computing and artificial intelligence. Edge computing is the use of computing or storage resources at the edge of the network, as opposed to the centralized cloud servers. AI, especially machine learning and deep learning methods, can learn from data, spot patterns, forecast and consequently automate decisions as well. With the intersection of these two technologies, edge intelligence enables UAVs to accomplish smart tasks locally or in cooperation with nearby edge nodes, so as to optimize the UAV's operation efficiency and cut down on the dependence on far away cloud services (Abbas et al., 2018).

In traditional cloud system for UAV, data gathered by UAVs are sent to central servers to perform processing and analysis tasks. While cloud computing can offer powerful computing resources and large memory spaces, it can take a long time to move data into the cloud, to and from cloud-based servers. Where immediate response is required for such applications as collision avoidance, emergency rescue operations or military reconnaissance and autonomous navigation, such a delay can not be tolerated. Moreover, it takes lots of bandwidth and energy to transfer large amount of data from sensor to UAV, those are restricted in UAV environment. Edge intelligence helps address these constraints by providing the ability to process and take action on data right at the edge of the network (Taleb et al., 2017).

Typically, edge intelligence in UAV networks has multiple layers, such as the UAV devices, the edge servers and cloud data center. UAVs are data collection and processing devices that have sensors, cameras, communication components and onboard computing resources. Edge servers are strategically located at base stations, access points (APs), roadside units (RSUs), or mobile edge platforms (MEPs) and offer computational capabilities and storage near the mobile UAV. Cloud data centres provide on-demand resources in the cloud for large-scale analytics, long term storage, and for training models. This can enable a hierarchy of tasks defined according to the availability of resources, delay sensitivities, and application priorities (You et al., 2017).

Low latency data processing is one of the most crucial ones when it comes to the benefits of edge intelligence in the UAV network. There are several use cases for UAVs where the need for quick analysis of the sensor data to enable timely decision-makers exists. For instance, during disaster response missions UAVs have to identify the survivors, assess the damage and coordinate rescue operations in a short period of time. Edge intelligence consists of algorithms for image recognition, object detection, and situational awareness that run closer to where the data is created, enhancing the response time. This capability will impact the effectiveness of the mission and allow for autonomous operation in time critical situations (Wang et al., 2017).

Another major advantage is to lessen the congestion within the network. High resolution cameras, Lidar sensors, radar systems, and environmental sensing devices are just a few of the ways UAVs can produce a lot of data. If an enterprise has to transfer all data gathered to its centralized cloud servers, it's possible for communication networks to get overloaded as well as for the enterprise to have to deal with increased operating costs. Edge Intelligence enables data filtering, aggregation and preprocessing at the network edge and ensures that only relevant data is sent to the remote server. This will save on bandwidth, communication overhead and overall network efficiency (Zhang et al., 2018).

Energy-efficiency is another paramount issue related to UAV networks. Energy is a limited resource for most UAVs, so using resources efficiently is important to prolong the mission. When it comes to communication, a lot of energy can be used a lot of the time, especially in the case of sending data that is a considerable amount of information, and beyond this, over a long distance. Edge intelligence processes data in the edge servers, which reduces the amount of data transmitted and conserves energy. Moreover, intelligent resource management algorithms can optimize the task scheduling, computation offloading and flight path planning for maximizing energy efficiency (Teerapittayanon et al., 2017).

Machine learning is one of the key factors that makes edge intelligence possible in UAV networks. The diverse machine learning models are applied to such things as object recognition, trajectory prediction, anomaly detection, resource allocation, and network optimization. Supervised learning methods can categorize objects in images taken by the UAV cameras, and unsupervised learning methods can find hidden/latent patterns in data collected. Reinforcement learning algorithms can be used to improve the optimal behavior of UAVs navigating their surrounding environment and can be used for adaptive mission planning and autonomous navigation. These models can be deployed at the edge node to provide intelligent services with low delay (Li et al., 2018).

UAVs equipped with various onboard sensors have shown great potential and success in the processing of complex data using deep learning. CNNs are popular networks for image analysis, and when used for UAV they can recognize different vehicles, buildings, people, and other environmental factors with high accuracy. Recurrent neural networks, LSHMs, process temporal data and prediction of future events from past observations. However, deployment in resource-limited UAV platforms is usually hard as the amount of computational resources needed for deep learning models is high. For these problems, edge intelligence distributes the computational workload between UAVs and their local edge servers (Mozaffari et al., 2019).

Computation offloading is the basic mechanism to be used in edge-intelligent UAV networks. In this process, the computation-intensive tasks are offloaded from UAVs to edge servers or the adjacent ones which have sufficient computing resources. A successful offload decision depends on a number of aspects, including task complexity, communication latency, energy usage, available resources and network conditions. With intelligent offloading decisions, it is possible to greatly enhance the system performance while saving UAV battery life. Many algorithms and machine learning techniques have been proposed to find the optimum task assignment methods in such dynamic environments.

Another crucial feature in edge-intelligent UAV systems lies in collaborative intelligence. A constellation of multiple UAVs can work together, in conjunction with edge infrastructure, to more effectively and efficiently complete complex missions than UAVs acting alone. Distributed sensing, cooperative learning, sharing resources, and making coordinated decisions are enabled by collaborative intelligence. For instance, a platoon of UAVs performing environmental surveillance can analyze the data gathered by their sensors and provide information using an edge computing platform. This collaborative effort contributes to the potential for large-scale deployments, increased reliability, and improved operational efficiency (Gupta et al., 2016).

Since the data collected by UAV networks can be sensitive and wireless communication channels are vulnerable, security and privacy are a major concern in such networks. Edge intelligence brings opportunities and challenges along these lines as well. Local processing minimizes the risk of external threats resulting from cloud transmission, so more data is private. Meanwhile, edge nodes could be appealing targets for cyberattacks. To mitigate these issues, advanced security measures like encryption, authentication, intrusion detection systems, and federated learning approaches are becoming more part of the edge-intelligent architectures.

Federated learning has recently become an attractive ML paradigm for UAV networks as it provides privacy. Instead, federated learning is a decentralized method that allows numerous devices to jointly train a machine learning model without their raw data being exchanged. Rather, model updates are only communicated between participants. The benefits of this method is that it can lower the communication overhead, maintain data privacy, and support distributed intelligence in UAV networks. Federated learning is especially beneficial for deploying applications with confidential information like surveillance, healthcare monitoring and military purposes.

UAVs present new challenges and opportunities for edge intelligence due to their mobility. Unlike fixed devices, UAVs move constantly leading to network topology changes and changing communication conditions. Smart mobility management solutions are essential to keep it up and running, managing resources, and picking up loose ends. Machine learning algorithms can forecast the UAV paths, proactively prepare the necessary resources, and foresee the network situations. The capabilities of these levels help to boost network stability and service quality (Bekmezci et al., 2013).

Another important application of edge intelligence is autonomous navigation of UAVs. To keep autonomous drones safe in complex environments, a series of constant perception, planning, and control processes are necessary. Real-time artificial intelligence using edge devices can help to analyze data from sensors to detect obstacles, plan paths, and avoid collisions. Edge intelligence can provide navigation accuracy and safety benefits with decreased decision-making latency. This is especially useful in urban areas where the UAVs have to maneuver man-made obstacles such as buildings, cars, and people, as well as observing regulatory requirements (Zeng et al., 2016).

Smart city applications enable edge intelligent UAV networks to provide multiple uses such as traffic monitoring, public safety, infrastructure inspection and environmental sensing. UAVs can gather data in real time from various locations and process the data at nearby edge nodes to give actionable insights. For instance, smart traffic control systems can utilize details from the images captured by a UAV and perform real-time analytics on the edge to manage traffic, keep track of accidents, and optimize the traffic flow. Because of such applications, the cities can function more efficiently and enjoy a better quality of life.

The exploitation of Edge Intelligence in UAV networks is one of the most significant solutions to the problems of disaster management. In times of disasters, like earthquakes, floods, wild fires and even whenever hurricanes arise, some communication structure might be damaged or simply not available. Using edge intelligence, UAVs can quickly set up communication networks and survey areas, find survivors and coordinate emergency response efforts. They can also perform information processing locally, allowing them to make decisions promptly even when connectivity has not been provided to centralized cloud services (Liu et al., 2018).

Moreover, edge-intelligent UAV networks make use of fifth generation (5G) and new sixth generation (6G) wireless communication technologies to boost their capabilities. These advanced UAV applications can be supported by high speed connectivity, ultra low latency communication, Network slicing, and massive device connectivity. In addition to these technologies, edge intelligence helps with efficient resource utilization and intelligent service delivery. They collectively contribute to the design of very distributed and decentralized flying platforms for complex societal and industrial problems.

Although the application of edge intelligence in UAV networks has numerous merits, several difficulties exist. Some of these challenges include limited computational resources, energy limitations, communication disruptions, security concerns, and complexities of model deployment. Moreover, complex coordination mechanisms are needed for achieving interoperability in heterodox devices and for coordinating the endpoints or the distributed intelligence in huge networks. On-going research and development efforts focus on novel approaches with lightweight machine learning algorithms, adaptive resource management strategies, and communication protocols.

The UAV community is expected to further evolve with the development of edge intelligence in the future. This would allow for ever more advanced autonomous functions to be deployed thanks to development in artificial intelligence, distributed computing, energy-efficient electronic hardware and wireless communications. Next-generation UAV ecosystems may include important concepts like digital twins, semantic communications, explainable artificial intelligence and intelligent network orchestration. All these innovations will enable more efficient cooperation between UAVs, edge infrastructure and cloud resources, and increase transparency, reliability and trustworthiness (Sardellitti et al., 2015).

In the future, as UAVs are adopted in a wider range of areas, edge intelligence will be more and more pivotal. Edge intelligence helps overcome common challenges related to cloud-centric systems, by placing computational intelligence at the edge of the data. It allows real-time processing and subsequent decisions, lower latency, better energy efficiency, increased security, and autonomous real-time decision-making in dynamic environments. Therefore, edge intelligence is regarded as a key technology that enable the development of intelligent UAV networks that will provide advanced services and address the increasing demands of modern digital societies. As AI, edge computing, and UAV technologies continue to integrate with the future, their potential for innovation, efficiency, and societal benefit in years to come remains unlimited (Mao et al., 2016).

Edge intelligence refers to the integration of artificial intelligence techniques with edge computing, enabling data processing and decision-making to occur closer to the data source. In the context of UAV networks, this means performing computations either onboard the UAV or at nearby edge nodes, such as ground stations or mobile edge servers. This approach reduces latency and improves responsiveness, which is critical for time-sensitive operations (Chen et al., 2018).

Figure 1 shows UAV networks and edge intelligence

Figure 1. UAV networks and edge intelligence

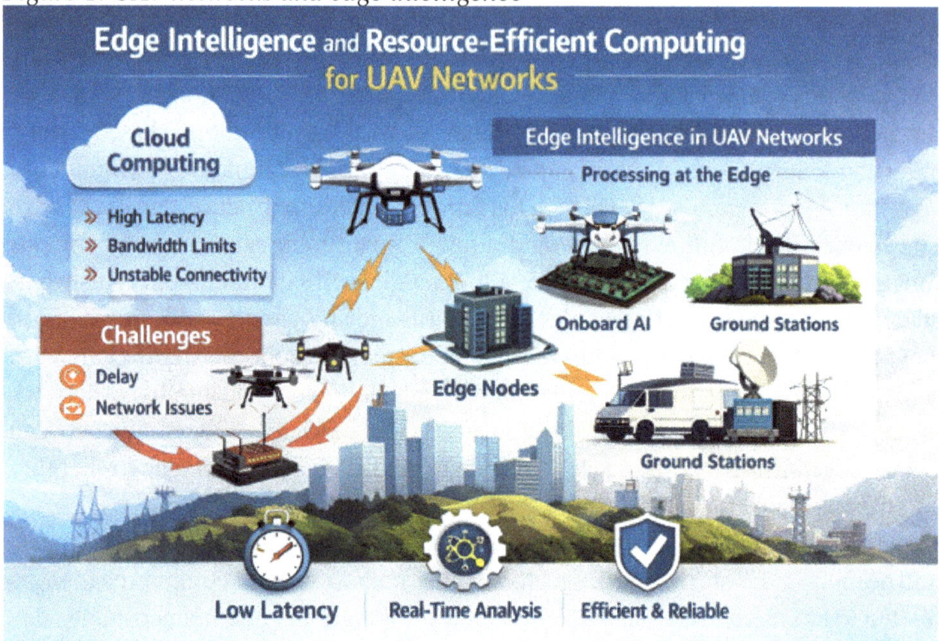

Among one of the most crucial benefits of the edge intelligence in UAV networks is its capacity to host real-time applications. There are real-time requirements for processing the sensor data for tasks like obstacle avoidance, object detection, and path planning. Edge intelligence allows faster, more reliable decision-making, as it reduces the amount of data sent to cloud-based servers located far from the edge.

One other key issue with edge intelligence is that it cuts back on communication overhead. Often, UAVs will fly in an environment where bandwidth is limited, and communication is unstable. Large amounts of raw sensor data can be a non-efficient and impractical way to pass data to the cloud. Edge-based processing enables UAVs to filter and process data locally, providing only relevant data when required.

Limited resources is one of the key features of UAV systems. When using such a device for image processing, it is essential to have efficient algorithms and light models since onboard processing power, onboard memory and onboard energy are limited. Edge Intelligence overcomes these limitations by optimising computation tasks and offloading them across network resources (Huang et al., 2019).

Collaborative edge intelligence also becomes a trend in UAV networks. Several UAVs can be used for distributed computing, cooperating in carrying out computational tasks and sharing data. This way of working strengthens system expandability for future more complex missions than can be achieved by a single UAV working alone (Lin et al., 2018).

In applications where sensitive data are involved, security and privacy are becoming vital issues in UAV networks. Data security can be improved using edge intelligence as a means to decrease the amount of raw data transmitted through possibly vulnerable channels. Local processing makes for lower exposure and more secure system architectures (Zhou et al., 2019).

Advancements in hardware technologies, such as specialized AI accelerators and embedded systems, have further enabled the adoption of edge intelligence in UAV networks. These technologies offer suitable computing power for performing thorough deep learning models at an efficient pace in resource-limited scenarios (Xu et al., 2018).

Overall, edge intelligence can prove to be a revolutionary technique to boost the performance and autonomy of UAV networks. Edge intelligence overcomes the shortcomings of the traditional cloud-based system by allowing real time processing, minimizing communication overhead, and empowering resource efficient computation. In the face of the growing variety of UAV applications, edge intelligence will be an important factor to determine the future of smart and autonomous aerial networks (Li et al., 2019).

ARCHITECTURE OF EDGE COMPUTING IN UAV SYSTEM

Edge computing architectures in the UAV system are focused on leveraging a distributed form of intelligence, low latency communications, and efficient data processing, all distributed between aerial and ground elements. Under resource and connectivity constraints, these architectures determine the distribution of computational tasks among UAVs, edge nodes and cloud infrastructure for optimal performance of computations. Architecture is a key determinant of the scalability, responsiveness and energy economization of a system.

In the context of UAV systems, the architecture of edge computing is a multi-layered and highly distributed structure that is used to handle the processing of data in real-time and to make intelligent decisions using data from the edge. With the increasing deployment of UAVs in various sectors like surveillance, disaster management, agriculture, logistics and smart cities, traditional cloud-based architectures fall short in accommodating high latency requirements, bandwidth constraints and energy inefficiencies in its operations. Edge computing overcomes these challenges by moving computation and storage resources nearer to the UAVs, enabling faster processing and minimization of demand on distant cloud resources.

The basic system architecture of edge computing in UAV have three main settings, known as the UAV layer, the edge layer, and the cloud layer. Every layer has different responsibilities for data processing, communication and decision making, and also collaborates and works together to guarantee a seamless system performance. The hierarchical organization can be used for dynamically allocating tasks according to computing requirements, network conditions and priorities of the application.

The UAV layer is the bottom layer of the architecture and represents the unmanned aerial vehicle platforms with different kinds of sensors, on-board processors, communication technologies, and minimal storage capacity. They are the ones that collect the data through the cameras, LiDAR, radar, infrared sensors and other environmental monitoring devices of these UAVs. Apart from data collection, modern UAVs are also increasingly equipped with lightweight computing units which enable basic processing activities to be performed in very early processing stages: for example, to manipulate the acquired data in the form of compression and filtering, and to perform preliminary object detection. Strict batteries, weight, and computing restrictions, however, also prevent UAVs from running complex AI workloads on their own. This restriction requires working with edge and cloud resources.

The edge layer is the backbone of the edge computing architecture of UAV systems. It involves edge nodes distributed throughout the environment (as mobile base station, roadside unit, ground control station, access points or other UAV's with higher computational power as relay or helper nodes). The location of these edge servers is strategically known to be nearer from UAVs to minimize communication latency and have real-time processing capabilities. The edge layer handles intermediate to advanced computations, such as data aggregation, real-time analytics, machine learning inferences and decision support. The edge layer's data processing near its area of origin conserves bandwidth traffic volumes and enhances response time, ultimately decreasing network congestion.

Anyone who has already used conferences will find this feature familiar: computation offloading. Offloading tasks like high-resolution image processing, path optimization, deep learning inferences and other computation intensive tasks with potential to be performed in the edge servers can be achieved using UAVs. Several factors influence the assigning of tasks to whatever server, such as the server's availability, the urgency of the task, network bandwidth, and the amount of energy required by the performing server to execute the task. Optimum algorithms and reinforcement learning approaches are common examples of intelligent offloading strategies which dynamically decide which task is to be carried out on a local UAV, which part of it should be computed locally and which should be sent to the edge, and finally to the cloud. This adaptability makes use of the system more efficient and prolongs the time in which the UAV can be used.

The top layer of the architecture is the cloud layer, which offers high-level computing, storage, and optimization services across the globe. Edge computing is useful for operations that are real-time and latency-sensitive but cloud computing is more suited to more complex operations like globally training models, analysing data from the past, and coordinating operations across the system. Edge collected data and preprocessed data is then periodically uploaded to a cloud server for continued analysis and further model improvement. Cloud layer also sends perceived ML models back to the node at the Edge and UAVs, improving the system continuously to adapt.

Communication infrastructure plays vital role in the architecture, between UAV, edge nodes and cloud servers. Data transmission is the backbone of wireless communication technologies like 4G, 5G, and new 6th generations of technology. When terrestrial infrastructure is unusable or compromised, the use of UAV to UAV communication and ad hoc aerial networks becomes very important to keep links open. These networks adopt dynamic topology, self-organize and adapt to the mobility of UAVs and environmental changes. To facilitate reliable data exchange, reduce latency time, and reduce energy consumption, it is important to have efficient communication protocols.

Another important aspect of the architecture is mobility management. In contrast to traditional edge computing devices that are static, UAVs are highly mobile and continuously move from one location to another. This mobility poses challenges like disruptions due to intermittent connectivity, differences in ping times and nodes, and frequent handovers between edge nodes. To solve the above-mentioned challenges, the architecture includes intelligent mobility management mechanisms that predict the trajectory of the UAVs, optimize UAV flight path and dynamically allocate the edge resources. AI algorithms are generally used to predict mobility trends and to maintain uninterrupted service operations.

Another consideration for UAV systems when it comes to edge computing architecture is resource management. Both UAVs and edge nodes are resource-constrained with their computing, storage and energy resources that need to be optimized for response to application requirements. Resource management frameworks observe the systems and distribute the workload based on the observed conditions. Load balancing, task scheduling and energy-aware optimization, etc., are techniques commonly used for maximizing system performance. Cooperative resource sharing also contributes to the efficiency for multi-UAV sense and processing to assist other UAVs to complete their work.

Security/PR is an integral part with architecture. It's common for sensitive information, such as surveillance footage, geographic information and monitoring critical infrastructure, to be collected by the UAV systems. In edge computing, data stays closer to the source, which in turn offers a higher level of security since raw data is not sent off to far away cloud servers to be exposed to potential cyber threats. But one could be an attack on the edge nodes themselves. The architecture integrates these mechanisms to reduce the risks, such as the implementation of encryption techniques, authentication protocols, intrusion detection systems (IDS), and secure communication channels. Another recent application is federated learning, which helps ensure the privacy of the model training process without having to share raw data across nodes.

AI forms a key part of enhancing the architecture's intelligence and allows for intelligent decisions. Machine learning models are used on both edge nodes and the cloud to assist in various tasks on the UAVs, including object detection, anomaly detection, trajectory predictions, and network optimizations. Usually, lightweight AI models are run on the UAV, and more powerful AI models are performed at the edge or cloud layers. Continuous learning and model updates enable the adaptation to evolving application demands and the environment.

The basic structure of the UAV edge computing is three layers: UAV layer, edge layer and cloud layer. UAVs can first acquire the data and carry out simple data processing, edge nodes can carry out intermediate data computing and coordination, and cloud servers can carry out large-scale data storage and intensive computing. The hierarchical structure helps to distribute the computational load and minimize latency by delegating tasks as needed across each layer.

The UAV layer is the lowest level, which is responsible for real-time processing for tasks like sensing, perception and instant decision making on board the UAV. However, because of the limited computational resources, the UAVs will usually run lighter models and do preprocessing on your place. In time-sensitive applications with non-tolerable delays such as obstacle avoidance and flight control, this layer becomes very important.

The edge layer includes anything that is between the UAVs and the cloud such as ground stations, mobile edge servers or infrastructure nearby. Edge nodes have more computational resources and can carry out more complicated tasks that include data aggregation, characteristic extraction, and collaborative decision-making as compared with UAVs. This layer greatly decreases the need for long-range communication with the cloud servers.

Cloud layer offers large-scale data analysis, long-term storage and model training with central resources. The cloud may have lots of computation capacity, but comes with added latency as well as requiring a solid network connection. In the UAV edge computing architectures, then, the cloud is mainly required for non-real-time tasks and system-wide optimizing tasks.

A significant architecture is the UAV swarm based edge computing model, which consists of several UAVs working cooperatively and having the possibility of sharing computing resources. It is a decentralized method, where the UAVs are able to dynamically split the tasks according to the available resources and the necessity of the mission. This will provide a more resilient system and scalable, flexible operation in complex system contexts.

The mobile edge computing (MEC) architecture is used extensively in UAV systems. In this model the edge servers are placed at base stations or mobile units and then they can offload the computation to them. MEC decreases the latency and enhances service quality to enable applications like real-time video analytics and intelligent surveillance.

Fog computing architectures build upon an edge computing architecture by adding more distributed layers between the edge and cloud layers. Fog nodes can be deployed in different locations that can offer local distributed processing and storage. This architecture increases the versatility and even aids in scaling up UAV deployments by breaking the workload down through a number of nodes.

These architectures feature strategies for task-offloading. Applications can choose to process the data locally, at the networks edge, or in the cloud, depending on the application's latency requirements, energy usage and network conditions. Optimization of the utilization of resources and the system's performance through smart offloading mechanisms, frequently based on machine learning.

Edge computing designs also rely heavily on communication protocols and network design. For effective coordination, reliable and low latency communication between UAVs and edge nodes are crucial. Supporting technologies like 5G and beyond are believed to be able to further improve connectivity and provide advanced edge computing features in UAV networks.

To conclude, the edge computing framework applied to a UAV system is a structured way of sharing computation and allowing intelligence for the system to be quick in real time. These architectures overcome the issues of latency, resource limitations and scalability through hierarchical, decentralized, and collaborative approaches. Advances in the design of architecture and communication will further improve the efficiency and autonomy of UAV network.

DEVELOPMENT OF RESOURCE EFFICIENT DEEP LEARNING MODELS FOR UAVS

However, resource-efficient deep learning models are critical for intelligent UAV operation with tight computation, memory and energy budget constraints. In contrast to traditional systems that can exploit state of the art hardware or remote computing, perception and decision for UAVs must be performed in real-time using lightweight processors onboard the aircraft. This requires models to be designed for accuracy and efficiency.

The key solutions towards efficiency are lightweight NN architecture development. Compact model like compact convolutional network paradigm is specifically designed with a goal of minimization of the number of parameters and the number of operations. In such architectures the processing requirements have been reduced significantly with acceptable performance, thus allowing these architectures to be used in real time on UAVs.

Model compression is an essential approach to decrease the size and complexity of deep learning models. Some examples of these methods are pruning, which eliminates unnecessary or less critical components in the network, or quantization, which lower the model parameters precision. The methods can reduce memory required and computational costs with little impact on model accuracy.

Another useful approach to create an efficient model is knowledge distillation. In this, a smaller model was made, known as student model, that copied the behavior of a larger, more complex model, namely the teacher model. This would enable UAV systems to take advantage of the performance of advanced models while using a minimum amount of resources.

Another aspect of efficient neural architecture design is that of optimizing the structure of the networks, to reduce redundant computations. Reducing the number of operations done during inference such as depthwise separable convolutions and bottleneck layers. In fact, these design principles are rather popular in today's models that are lightweightand for embedded purposes.

Model optimization for use in a UAV is a critical issue because the system must operate on its hardware embedded in the aircraft. It is important to design deep-learning models bearing in mind the capabilities of onboard hardware, such as GPUs, CPUs or specialized AI accelerators. Backing up models to target hardware results in better model runtimes and energy efficiency.

An additional important consideration is the ability to change the complexity of the model based on resources at hand or the task at hand, known as dynamic model adaptation. The UAV for instance, could switch to a more complex model when it desires to have higher accuracy in usual use and use a simpler model in routine use. This versatility translates to efficiency and performance.

To extend the UAV flight time, inference need to be energy efficient. Computations are directly tied to energy consumption and thereby the energy efficiency can be enhanced by minimizing the number of operations and improving data flow. To this end techniques like early termination and conditional computation enable to stop the processing at earlier stages as soon as the required level of confidence is reached.

Moreover, training and incremental learning methods based on edges are becoming attractive. Let's say, rather than only offline training, UAVs could build models with latest data collected during operations, locally. This minimizes data transfers and helps realize continuous improvement with resource efficiency.

To sum up, for an intelligent UAV system to be realised in practice, it is indispensable to have resource-efficient deep learning models. The power of lightweight architectures, model compression, hardware-aware optimization, and adaptive strategies can be harnessed to ensure high performance perception and decision making in a limited resource environment. Ongoing investigations in these areas will further augment UAV capabilities and sustainability.

TASK OFFLOADING STRATEGIES AND EDGE–CLOUD COLLABORATION STRATEGIES

Task offloading and edge–cloud collaboration are fundamental to developing resource-efficient UAV networks, offering the means to optimize the workload distribution across UAVs, edge nodes, and cloud infrastructure. In UAVs, where on board resources are constrained, it is possible that computation intensive tasks have to be delegated to more powerful entities while making sure that the real time nature of the system or reliability demands are met.

Task offloading: transferring computing tasks from the UAVs to other computing resources located in their environment (e.g., neighboring edge server) or even remote cloud. This will reduce the processing burden on the UAVs, save energy, and enhance the execution speed. Factors like task complexity, latency requirements, network conditions and available resources will influence the decision to offload tasks.

There are three broad categories of offloading strategies: local processing, partial offloading and full offloading. In local processing, all calculations are carried out on the UAV itself, being good for time-sensitive applications. Partial Offloading: tasks are divided between the UAV and external units, Full Offloading: offloading the whole task to edge or cloud systems and execute in there.

Efficient offloading is key to ensuring the successful operation of UAVs, and edge computing is playing an essential role in providing low latency computation resources in proximity to the UAV operations. UAVs can reduce workloads and tasks on the cloud nodes to nearby edge nodes and gain faster responsiveness. This is especially crucial for applications like real-time video analytics, object recognition, and navigation.

Figure 2 shows Task offloading strategies in UAV networks

Figure 2. Task offloading strategies in UAV networks

Cloud computing, however, has the capability to provide high processing power and storage space, which is well suited for larger amounts of data processing and for storing data for long-term analytics and training of models. Cloud resources are also strong, however, they require good connectivity and don't always possess the lowest latency and may also be unavailable in time-critical UAV applications. So, it is important to have effective collaboration between edge and cloud systems.

Edge–cloud collaboration strategies look to distribute and optimise tasks between the two layers based on the needs of the system. Edge processing for time sensitive tasks and cloud processing for compute intensive/less time critical tasks. This means a hybrid system with a better efficiency and scalability.

We need intelligent task scheduling mechanism to decide best offloading decisions. These mechanisms may include optimization algorithms or machine learning models that analyze factors like energy usage, delay, available bandwidth, and task priority. Dynamic scheduling provides for optimum use of the resources when the environment changes.

Another potential key factor is the implementation of cooperative offloading in multi-UAV systems. Not only are there possibilities that UAVs can share workloads among themselves but they can also work together to offload workload to shared edge resources. This distributed and flexible approach enables UAV networks to perform more complex tasks collaboratively.

Efficient communication is of paramount importance for task offloading. Large amounts of data can be transferred between the UAVs, edge nodes, and cloud servers, leading to potential delays and a high amount of bandwidth consumption. Limiting transmission of redundant data, preferential transmission of important data and selective transmission are some of these methods used to reduce communication overhead.

Edge–cloud collaboration needs to also keep security and reliability in mind. Data may be vulnerable to potential security threats while being offloaded. It is important to provide secure communication, secure data and system design for maintaining system integrity and trust.

To sum up, task offloading and edge–cloud collaboration could play an important role in enabling effective working of UAV networks. These strategies can optimize the use of both edge and cloud compute capabilities and resources, leveraging their respective strengths and weaknesses, to improve performance, conserve energy, and provide scalable or real-time UAV applications.

ENERGY OPTIMIZATION AND HARDWARE-AWARE COMPUTING ON UAVS

One of the important aspects in UAV is energy optimization because flight duration is related to battery capacity and energy usage. Additionally, the deployment of Deep learning and edge computing technologies places higher demands on energy, as they involve extensive computation and data processing. Thus, it is necessary to develop an energy-efficient computing strategy to extend the computing duration and maintain the computational performance in the UAV networks.

Onboard computation is one of the main factors that consume energy in UAVs. The use of deep learning models, especially for perception and decision-making, is quite processor demanding. Specialization of the models to simplify their implementation can result in significant energy savings. To optimise power consumption without compromising accuracy too much, certain technologies including model pruning, quantization, and efficient design of the architecture of the networks are routinely used.

Hardware-aware computing involves designing algorithms to exploit and/or adapt to the limitations and capabilities of the hardware. UAVs usually come with embedded systems like a low-power CPU, a GPU or a special AI accelerator. Optimizing models for a particular hardware platform can greatly boost the efficiency of the design executed in that platform and avoid wasted energy.

Dynamic voltage and frequency scaling (DVFS) is one of the common methods for energy optimization of embedded systems. UAVs will save more energy during low power demand times and maintain operation during high power demand due to the processor's ability to change its operating frequency and voltage levels in response to the workload. This adaptive solution brings a balance between energy saving and computing power.

Task scheduling and workload management is another vital strategy. Efficient scheduling involves organizing the list of computation tasks so that it can be completed in a way with minimal energy consumption. For instance, gathering comparable tasks together or prioritizing important operations can lower down any redundant calculations or smartening the utilization of resources.

In addition, processing also helps optimize energy thanks to Edge. UAVs can leverage this capability to offload some computation-intensive tasks to border side nodes, thus saving battery power. This should be weighed, though, by the energy consumed by the communications, since communication also uses energy.

One of the important roles for memory and data management is energy efficiency. Access and transfer of data between memory and processing units can be very power intensive. This overhead can be minimised through an effective data flow optimization, memory access reduction, and data storage format optimization.

Special hardware options like field-programmable gate array (FPGA) application specific integrated circuits (ASICs) have been attracting attention for energy-efficient computing for UAVs. These hardware solutions provide higher performance per watt and are more efficient to perform certain tasks than general purpose processors.

Thermal management is another aspect associated with energy use and functionality of the device. High heat production may impact system performance and reliability, which may cause system to use more energy to cool down or may have negative impact on the efficiency of processing. The systems should be designed to include provisions for efficient thermal controls to ensure efficient operation.

To conclude, the key elements of energy optimization and hardware-aware computing are crucial for sustaining UAV operations. Through highly efficient model design, adaptive processing techniques, intelligent task management and hardware specific optimisations, high efficiency energy benefits can be achieved. Future developments of this field will lead to longer flight times, better performances and more deployable intelligent UAV networked.

CHALLENGES, OPEN ISSUES, AND FUTURE RESEARCH DIRECTIONS

There are still a number of challenges and open problems that need to be addressed to overcome these technological limitations, paving the way for large-scale deployment and real-life reliability of UAV networks. These challenges include but are not limited to computing, communications, system design, and adaptability, and we must continue to develop and research to realize the dream of fully autonomous and efficient UAV creation.

Main difficulties are the constrained availability of on-board resources, such as processing power, memory and battery. Lightweight models and efficient algorithms are designed, but it is challenging to provide high performance in the presence of stringent resource constraints. The old trade-off between accuracy, latency and energy still remains a core challenge in designing UAVs.

A significant language barrier also exists. UAV networks usually work in an environment that has constrained bandwidth and sporadic connections. Crucially efficient data transmission and coordination between UAVs, edge nodes and cloud systems is required and challenging. Future research needs to target bandwidth aware algorithms and adaptive communication protocols.

However, task offloading decisions are still a complex problem because of the dynamic and uncertain operating conditions. Along with task priority and changes in the environment, latency of networks and energy availability have to be taken into consideration at the same time. Intelligent and adaptive offloading strategies that can adapt in real time are an important aspect of current research and development and investigation.

Scalability is also an important one, especially for systems consisting of several UAVs or swarm-based systems. Particularly, with more UAVs, the communication, coordination and resource sharing becomes complex. Distributed algorithms and scalable architectures are necessary for efficient operation with minimal overhead and system congestion.

It is important to note that security and privacy issues are becoming of great importance for UAV networks. The communications between the UAVs and either edge or cloud systems can be susceptible to tampering or being intercepted. Application security, in particular when it comes to sensitive use cases – in this case surveillance and defense – is vital to ensure that communication, data integrity and protection from cyber threats is kept secure.

The Challenges with deep learning include generalization and adaptability. Models might not perform with the same accuracy in situations that differ from those in which they were trained. Future research should target domain adaptation, continual learning, self-supervised methods, which can improve the UAV system's ability to learn how to adapt to new environments and avoid extensive retraining.

Another factor is a missing harmonization of datasets and benchmarking approaches for edge computing with UAVs. Evaluation and comparison of different approaches is difficult as they vary with the applications and conditions under which these are operated. Having common measures and research assessment would improve the research progress in a meaningful and consistent way.

It can also present problem in the system design and optimization due to the hardware heterogeneity. UAV networks can be comprised of devices that have different computational capacity and architectures. It is important to create a consolidated framework, which is able to run efficiently on different hardware platforms, for deployment.

Federated learning, edge AI accelerators, and 6G communication are among the emerging technologies that will significantly help solve current challenges. Without compromising privacy or increasing communication overhead, federated learning can facilitate collaborative model training without sharing raw data. Advanced communication technologies will provide more connectivity and facilitate real-time applications.

Finally, although with the advent of edge intelligence and resource-efficient computing, the capabilities of the UAV network have largely been enhanced, there are still several challenges and open issues that must be tackled before a fully autonomous and scalable network can be realised. The future research will be directed towards designing adaptable, secure, and efficient solutions which will be able to work in a variety of and dynamic environments, towards the creation of next generation intelligent UAV networks.

CONCLUSION

In response to the critical issues of latency, energy consumption, and the on-board computing resources of UAV networks, edge intelligence and resource-efficient computing are now identified as significant for UAV networks to progress. The edge-based approaches bring the computation's scope closer to the location of data source, enabling real-time processing and decision making which is critical in time sensitive and mission / application sensitive scenarios involving UAV systems.

In this review, the basic concept and architecture of edge computing for UAV systems have been examined, such as hierarchical and distributed structures to load balance workload across a UAV, an edge node and cloud environment. Efficient task allocation, communication strategies, and system design for optimal performance and scalability were discussed.

Deep learning models, that allows for operations of UAV in an intelligent manner while remaining resource efficient, were explored. Model compression, lightweight architectures, and optimization for hardware are among the techniques that enable high performance processing in limited environments. These techniques are key to ensuring accurate results without excessive compute and power consumption overheads.

The significance of task offloading and edge–cloud collaboration was also highlighted, showcasing the benefits of dynamically shifting off workloads for enhanced efficiency and responsiveness. The ability of the UAV networks to adapt and flexibly accommodate a broad spectrum of computational requirements enabled by both edge and cloud resources.

They identified energy optimization and hardware-aware computing as essential aspects to take into consideration when creating UAVs that affect their overall operation and lifetime. The efficient energy management strategies, coupled with the specific characteristics of the hardware and processing techniques facilitate the longer flight times and more sustained operation of the systems.

Despite these progressions, there are still some issues: restricted communication, scalability, security, and enhancing the generalization of learning models. Solving these issues demands further studies on adaptive algorithms, system design, and advancements in areas like federated learning and next-generation communication networks.

Finally, the combination of edge intelligence and resource-efficient computing offers a solid base to build next generation UAV networks. With ongoing advancements in research, the potential uses of such systems are likely to expand, and these systems can be expected to become more self-sustaining, scalable, and robust.

REFERENCES

Abbas, N., Zhang, Y., Taherkordi, A., & Skeie, T. (2018). Mobile edge computing: A survey. *IEEE Internet of Things Journal*, *5*(1), 450–465. DOI: 10.1109/JIOT.2017.2750180

Bekmezci, I., Sahingoz, O. K., & Temel, Ş. (2013). Flying ad-hoc networks (FANETs): A survey. *Ad Hoc Networks*, *11*(3), 1254–1270. DOI: 10.1016/j.adhoc.2012.12.004

Chen, M., Hao, Y., Li, Y., Lai, C. F., & Wu, D. (2018). On the computation offloading at ad hoc cloudlet. *IEEE Transactions on Vehicular Technology*, *64*(11), 5297–5309.

Chen, X., Jiao, L., Li, W., & Fu, X. (2016). Efficient multi-user computation offloading for mobile-edge cloud computing. *IEEE/ACM Transactions on Networking*, *24*(5), 2795–2808. DOI: 10.1109/TNET.2015.2487344

Gupta, L., Jain, R., & Vaszkun, G. (2016). Survey of important issues in UAV communication networks. *IEEE Communications Surveys and Tutorials*, *18*(2), 1123–1152. DOI: 10.1109/COMST.2015.2495297

Huang, D., Wang, P., & Niyato, D. (2019). A dynamic offloading algorithm for mobile computing. *IEEE Transactions on Wireless Communications*, *11*(6), 1991–1995. DOI: 10.1109/TWC.2012.041912.110912

Li, B., Fei, Z., & Zhang, Y. (2018). UAV communications for 5G and beyond. *IEEE Wireless Communications*, *26*(1), 10–16. DOI: 10.1109/MWC.2016.7422399

Li, E., Zeng, L., Zhou, Z., & Chen, X. (2019). Edge AI: On-demand accelerating deep neural network inference via edge computing. *IEEE Transactions on Wireless Communications*, *19*(1), 447–457. DOI: 10.1109/TWC.2019.2946140

Lin, X., Yajnanarayana, V., Muruganathan, S. D., Gao, S., Asplund, H., Maattanen, H. L., Bergstrom, M., Euler, S., & Wang, Y. P. E. (2018). The sky is not the limit: LTE for unmanned aerial vehicles. *IEEE Communications Magazine*, *56*(4), 204–210. DOI: 10.1109/MCOM.2018.1700643

Liu, C. F., Bennis, M., Debbah, M., & Poor, H. V. (2018). Dynamic task offloading and resource allocation for ultra-reliable low-latency edge computing. *IEEE Transactions on Communications*, *67*(6), 4132–4150. DOI: 10.1109/TCOMM.2019.2898573

Mach, P., & Becvar, Z. (2017). Mobile edge computing: A survey on architecture and computation offloading. *IEEE Communications Surveys and Tutorials*, *19*(3), 1628–1656. DOI: 10.1109/COMST.2017.2682318

Mao, Y., You, C., Zhang, J., Huang, K., & Letaief, K. B. (2017). A survey on mobile edge computing. *IEEE Communications Surveys and Tutorials*, *19*(4), 2322–2358. DOI: 10.1109/COMST.2017.2745201

Mao, Y., Zhang, J., & Letaief, K. B. (2016). Dynamic computation offloading for mobile-edge computing. *IEEE Journal on Selected Areas in Communications*, *34*(12), 3590–3605. DOI: 10.1109/JSAC.2016.2611964

Mozaffari, M., Saad, W., Bennis, M., & Debbah, M. (2019). A tutorial on UAVs for wireless networks. *IEEE Communications Surveys and Tutorials*, *21*(3), 2334–2360. DOI: 10.1109/COMST.2019.2902862

Sardellitti, S., Scutari, G., & Barbarossa, S. (2015). Joint optimization of radio and computational resources. *IEEE Transactions on Signal and Information Processing Over Networks*, *1*(2), 89–103. DOI: 10.1109/TSIPN.2015.2448520

Satyanarayanan, M. (2017). The emergence of edge computing. *Computer*, *50*(1), 30–39. DOI: 10.1109/MC.2017.9

Shi, W., Cao, J., Zhang, Q., Li, Y., & Xu, L. (2016). Edge computing: Vision and challenges. *IEEE Internet of Things Journal*, *3*(5), 637–646. DOI: 10.1109/JIOT.2016.2579198

Taleb, T., Samdanis, K., Mada, B., Flinck, H., Dutta, S., & Sabella, D. (2017). On multi-access edge computing: A survey of the emerging 5G network edge cloud architecture. *IEEE Communications Surveys and Tutorials*, *19*(3), 1657–1681. DOI: 10.1109/COMST.2017.2705720

Teerapittayanon, S., McDanel, B., & Kung, H. T. (2017). Distributed deep neural networks over the cloud, edge, and end devices. *IEEE International Conference on Distributed Computing Systems*, 328–339. DOI: 10.1109/ICDCS.2017.226

Wang, S., Zhang, X., Zhang, Y., Wang, L., Yang, J., & Wang, W. (2017). A survey on mobile edge networks. *IEEE Communications Surveys and Tutorials*, *19*(4), 2322–2358. DOI: 10.1109/COMST.2017.2745201

Xu, X., Li, Y., Huang, T., Xue, Y., Peng, K., Qi, L., & Dou, W. (2018). An energy-aware computation offloading method. *Future Generation Computer Systems*, *85*, 1–14.

You, C., Huang, K., Chae, H., & Kim, B. H. (2017). Energy-efficient resource allocation for mobile-edge computation offloading. *IEEE Transactions on Wireless Communications*, *16*(3), 1397–1411. DOI: 10.1109/TWC.2016.2633522

Zeng, Y., Zhang, R., & Lim, T. J. (2016). Wireless communications with UAVs: Opportunities and challenges. *IEEE Communications Magazine*, *54*(5), 36–42. DOI: 10.1109/MCOM.2016.7470933

Zhang, Q., Chen, M., Zhao, L., & Wu, J. (2018). Deep learning for edge computing: A survey. *Proceedings of the IEEE*, *107*(8), 1655–1674.

Zhou, Z., Chen, X., Li, E., Zeng, L., Luo, K., & Zhang, J. (2019). Edge intelligence: Paving the last mile of AI. *Proceedings of the IEEE*, *107*(8), 1738–1762. DOI: 10.1109/JPROC.2019.2918951

Chapter 6
Foundational Paradigms of Deep Learning-Driven Edge and Cloud Intelligence in IoT Ecosystems

Uzair Aslam Bhatti
http://orcid.org/0009-0002-3420-9956
Hainan University, China

Khurramov Ruslan
Termez University of Economics and Service, Termez, Uzbekistan

Dadaboev Umidjon
Tashkent State University of Economics, Tashkent, Uzbekistan

Yuldasheva Gulora Gulumovna
Urgench State University, Uzbekistan

Mukhayya Ruzieva
Mamun University, Khiva, Uzbekistan

Sajid Ali
University of Education, Multan, Pakistan

ABSTRACT

The fast development of Internet of Things (IoT) systems has created a large amount of heterogeneous data that needs smart models to be analyzed in real-time and used to make decisions. Deep learning facilitates extracting data effectively, whereas cloud computing encounters latency, bandwidth, and privacy issues. The combination of edge computing and cloud intelligence helps to perform a distributed processing, minimizes delay, and enhances scalability. This review identifies architectures, models of collaboration, applications, and challenges important to IoT systems.

DOI: 10.4018/979-8-2600-0615-3.ch006

INTRODUCTION TO DEEP LEARNING IN IOT ECOSYSTEMS

Internet of Things (IoT) has become one of the most significant technological paradigms in the era of modern digitalism. It is a massive system of interconnected devices, sensors, and systems that are constantly gathering, sharing, and analyzing data to allow smart decision-making and automation. As the number of intelligent devices grows exponentially, the size and a variety of the IoT ecosystems has grown to tremendous proportions, producing vast amounts of heterogeneous and real-time information. Handling and deriving valuable information out of this data is now a challenge to say the least, and advanced computational methods capable of operating on dynamically evolving high-dimensional streams of data are now mandated.

Deep learning has received a lot of focus as an effective method of solving the analytical problems that come with IoT data. Deep learning models can learn hierarchical feature representations of raw data automatically as a subdivision of machine learning which utilizes artificial neural networks with multiple layers. This allows them to handle more intricate patterns in images, audio, sensor signals and time-series data produced by the IoT devices. Deep learning algorithms have greatly improved the intelligence and flexibility of IoT systems by offering the ability to conduct accurate prediction, classification, as well as anomaly detection (Shi et al,, 2016).

The introduction of deep learning into the IoT ecosystem has introduced opportunities of smart automation and the use of data in making decisions. The conventional IoT systems mainly used rule based algorithms or naive statistical models which in most cases were not able to capture the complex relationship with large volumes of data. Convolutional neural networks, recurrent neural networks, and transformer-based architectures are deep learning models that offer powerful features of examining spatial, temporal, and contextual data. The models are capable of handling data streams of high scale produced by distributed sensors and linked devices.

The growing need in intelligent applications in different spheres is one of the reasons why deep learning should be introduced into the IoT environment. Deep learning algorithms are capable of recognizing trends, finding exceptions and making predictive information that can be used to make preemptive choices. Industrial IoT, such as predictive maintenance systems could help to detect faults in equipment in advance before it fails and therefore cut operational costs and enhance the reliability of the system (Satyanarayanan, 2017).

The implementation of deep learning in IoT ecosystems has a number of technical issues, regardless of its huge benefits. IoT devices tend to work with limited resources such as processing, storage, and energy resources. Deep learning models are also known to consume a lot of computational resources to train and make inferences and such resources might not be available on many edge devices. This has been a weakness which has prompted the creation of hybrid calculation systems where local edge processing is done, combined with cloud-based computing systems.

Figure 1 shows Foundational Paradigms of Deep Learning-Driven Edge and Cloud Intelligence in IoT Ecosystems.

Figure 1. Foundational paradigms of deep learning-driven edge and cloud intelligence in IoT ecosystems

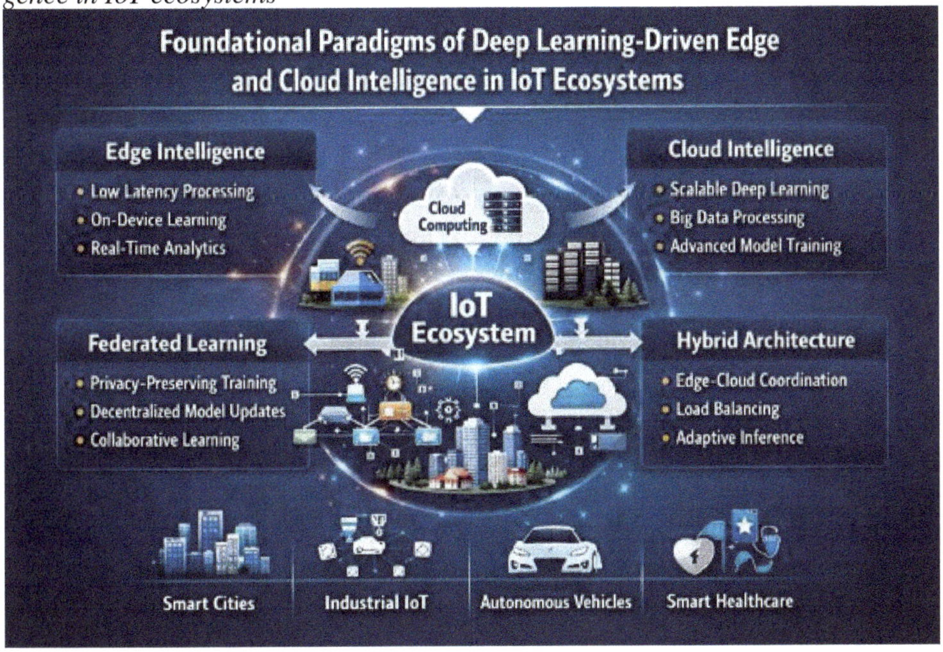

The concept of edge computing has become a complementary concept that can empower the efficiency of IoT systems that run on deep learning. Edge computing will lower the network latency by doing the data processing tasks nearer to the origin of the data produced and will also ensure that continuous transmission of data to central servers is limited. Such local processing power is especially valuable to the latency-sensitive applications like autonomous vehicles, real-time health monitoring, and industrial control systems. The edge computing and deep learning can be combined to perform intelligent analytics at the device level.

Cloud computing has remained crucial in the provision of deep learning applications to the internet of things ecosystems. Cloud services offer scalable computation, data storage and state-of-the-art machine learning systems that can be used to train intricate deep learning systems. Large-scale analytics and model sharing as well as collaborative data processing are also supported by the cloud environment. Cloud infrastructures used together with edge computing allow a decentralized intelligence architecture that balances performance with access to data (Zhou et al., 2019).

The notion of edge cloud collaboration has henceforth emerged as a core paradigm to the current IoT architectures. Lightweight deep learning models may run on edge devices in this setup to do an initial analysis and filtering of data, with more computationally complex processes executed on cloud servers. This co-operative process will result in the optimal utilization of resources and reduce the consumption of bandwidth and make the IoT systems more responsive in general. It also makes it possible to constantly learn and update the models depending on cloud-trainings.

Another significant aspect of deep learning application in the IoT systems is the possibility to process huge and varied amounts of data. Data at IoT environments are diverse sources and may include environmental sensors, cameras, wearable devices and industrial machines. The use of deep learning models is especially suitable in addressing such a heterogeneous data due to their capacity of automatically learning feature representations which are complex. This can be used to create intelligent IoT applications that can analyze multimodal data streams (Li et al., 2018).

Deep learning is expected to increase in the formation of autonomous and adaptive systems with the expansion of the number of IoT ecosystems. Optimization of models, hardware acceleration, and distributed computing architecture are more and more available and, as a result, complex models of deep learning can now be implemented in large-scale IoT networks. Therefore, it is the synergies between deep learning and edge and cloud intelligence that is shaping the future of intelligent environments, and offers hope of much more efficient, responsive and intelligent digital infrastructures.

EDGE–CLOUD COLLABORATIVE ARCHITECTURE FOR INTELLIGENT IOT

The edge-cloud collaborative architecture has emerged as a prominent system with respect to supporting smart Internet of Things (IoT) systems. With the number of devices linked to the internet, and the amount of data that they are capturing, becoming large volumes of real-time data, the older centralised cloud computing solutions are showing challenges in their latency, bandwidth consumption, and data processing capabilities. Combining edge computing and cloud infrastructure offers a distributed computing model where data processing might be brought nearer to the data generator and still utilising the powerful data processing of the central cloud platforms. This cooperative architecture enhances the responsiveness, scalability and efficiency in the functionality of the IoT environments (Gubbi et al., 2013).

In a standard edge cloud, sensors, cameras and embedded systems are the most common IoT devices which serve as the main source of data generation. The devices continuously collect environmental, operational or user data and transmit it to neighbouring edge nodes where some initial processing is performed. The edge nodes can incorporate gateways, local servers or edge data centres with moderate computing power. The system will be capable of minimising the amount of raw data sent to the cloud using preliminary data filtering, aggregation, and analysis mean.

The edge layer is important in supporting real-time analytics and applications that are sensitive to latency. Many IoT applications require rapid response, such as autonomous vehicle control, industrial control, and smart healthcare devices. Calculations on the edge of the devices enable local critical decisions, which do not need a remote cloud server to make decisions. This will enhance quicker response times and mission vital systems that could be jeopardized by latency are more dependable (Zhang et al., 2018).

Edge cloud collaborative architecture also entails cloud computing. Cloud computing services offer high-scale computing capabilities which are required to train complicated models of deep learning and conduct more sophisticated data analytics. The cloud is also a centralised place of storing huge volumes of data produced due to the activities carried by the IoT devices at different dispersed sites. The cloud, with a powerful processing unit and a huge storage capacity, enables long term analysis of data, modelling and optimization of the system.

The connection between the edge layer and the cloud layer enables the efficient distribution of the computational workloads. Lightweight tasks, such as preprocessing data, extracting features, and performing initial inference, are typically done on the edge layer. Deep model training and large-scale predictive analytics are computationally intensive processes done by cloud infrastructures. Such a hierarchical distribution of tasks enhances the efficiency of the system and decreases the network congestion along with the costs of data transmission (Wang et al., 2019).

Other significant details of edge-cloud collaboration are the increase of data privacy and security. The fact that it is possible to transfer all raw data to the central servers could also increase the risk of data leak and unauthorised access. This risk can be reduced with edge computing in place where sensitive information can be computed locally and only necessary information or summative output can be sent to the cloud. This decentralised system not only helps in protecting individual and business information but also has the benefits of a centralised intelligence.

The edge-cloud architecture is also more scalable, which is also a major advantage of the IoT ecosystems. The centralised systems will probably not be able to support the increasing computational and networking needs as the number of devices connected continues to increase. Distributed edge nodes are able to offload some of the processing load thus relieving cloud infrastructure of the pressure. The scalable architecture allows the IoT systems to be scaled without decreasing the performance and reliability (Kairouz & McMahan, 2021).

The other most important advantage of collaborative architectures is resource optimization. IoT devices have low energy and computing capabilities. It is possible to manage these constraints efficiently through edge computing, which transfers some of the workload to edge servers in the same area without sacrificing battery life and processing power in the devices. Also, the edge and cloud layer adaptive workload distribution is used to optimally use the available computing resources throughout the network.

Even the implementation of advanced deep learning applications in the IoT is supported by edge-cloud collaboration. Lightweight inference models can be used to create edge devices to execute object detection, anomaly detection, and predictive monitoring. In the meantime, the cloud is able to continuously train and refine deep learning models with big datasets of data gathered by a variety of devices. The models may then be disseminated back to the edge nodes with updated models and thus intelligence may be continuously enhanced on the system (McMahan et al., 2017).

With the development of IoT ecosystems towards becoming more autonomous and intelligent infrastructures, edge to cloud collaborative architectures are becoming core to the functioning of the ecosystems. Decentralising edge intelligence and centralised cloud analytics offers a compromise solution that delivers real-time responsiveness and scalability with the ability to perform computing tasks. This paradigm is not only contributing to the improved efficiency and scalability of a system but also assists with the creation of innovative applications in the domains of smart cities, healthcare, manufacturing, and environmental monitoring.

DEEP LEARNING MODELS FOR IOT DATA ANALYTICS

The Internet of Things (IoT) ecosystems now use deep learning models as the foundation of advanced data analytics. The abundance of diverse data produced by the IoT devices, sensor readings, images, video streams, time-series signals, etc. necessitates the advanced analytical methods that are able to determine intricate patterns. Commonly used traditional machine learning techniques are based on hand-designed features and cannot easily work with high-dimensional unstructured data. With its capability to automatically learn the hierarchical feature representation, the concept of deep learning offers a potent answer to the derivation of the actionable insights of the data generated by IoT (Chen et al., 2014).

CNNs find many applications in the analysis of spatial data used in IoT applications. CNNs prove especially useful in the area of image and video analytics, which makes it possible to apply it to visual surveillance, traffic monitoring, and quality inspection of smart factories. With the use of convolutional philtres, CNNs are able to identify the local patterns and spatial hierarchies in data to enable the IoT systems to identify objects, anomalies, and interpret complex real-life scenes with high accuracy. Their flexibility in edge deployment has further rendered CNNs to be applicable in real time processes where speed in inference is vital.

The RNNs and variations, including Long Short-Term Memory (LSTM) and Gated Recurrent Unit (GRU) networks, are needed to model the time-dependence in sequential IoT data. The models are best used in processes that require time-series analysis, e.g. predictive maintenance, forecasting energy consumption, and monitoring the environment. In particular, LSTM networks resolve the vanishing gradient issue and have the ability to learn long-term relationships, thus they are useful in analysing a sensor history and predicting the future trends (Zaharia et al., 2010).

Transformer-based systems have been in recent years used in the field of IoT analytics because they can model the long-range dependencies and process multimodal data efficiently. Transformers achieve self-attention by prioritising the significance of various data points and enable more flexible and contextual analysis. Transformers in IoT can be used to detect anomalies in sensor networks, predict traffic, and multimodal data fusion of heterogeneous devices, which improves the precision and explainability of the analytics process.

Unsupervised feature learning and anomaly detection of the data streams of the IoT are implemented with autoencoders and variational autoencoders (VAEs). Autoencoders can recognise patterns and exceptions without the need to have labelled datasets because they learn compressed forms of the input data. It is especially useful when dealing with indirect IoT, where unforeseen occasions or failures must be identified promptly to avoid downtime and ensure efficiency in operations. Probabilistic data distribution can be predicted as well, modelling of data distributions, with VAEs, and aids predictive analytics and estimation of uncertainties (Abadi et al., 2016).

Graph Neural Networks (GNNs) can be used to provide a specialised method of analysing data in structured and relational form in an IoT network. IoT devices and sensors have spatial and logical connexions, including smart grids or connected transportation. It is possible to model these relationships with GNNs to predict the behaviour of a network, identify anomalies, and maximise resource allocation. GNNs augment the capability of the IoT systems to learn the design and dynamics of intricate networks by extracting the dependencies between nodes and edges.

Figure 2 shows Cloud Intelligence.

Figure 2. Deep learning architecture of IoT

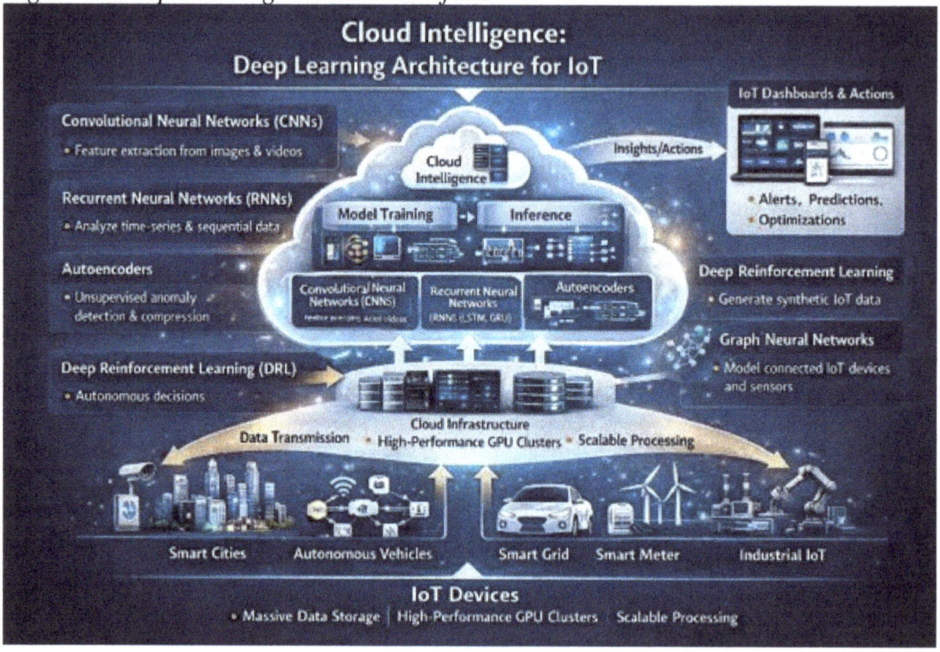

A notable paradigm of distributed deep learning in IoT ecosystems that has been developed is Federated learning. Within this directions, edge devices will act in collaboration to train a common global model without sending raw data to the cloud, maintaining privacy and lowering bandwidth utilisation. Specifically, federated learning would be applied especially in healthcare, smart homes, and industrial IoT, where sensitive data is distributed among several devices. The federation of learning can be applied in conjunction with deep learning frameworks like CNNs or LSTMs to translate into intelligent and secure analytics at the same time preserving data sovereignty (He et al., 2016).

The analytics used in the IoT also have been developed by working on various techniques of reinforcement learning and deep reinforcement learning to provide adaptive and autonomous decisions. These models are trained to adopt the most desirable conducts after exposure to the environment, which renders them suitable to complicated and dynamic IoT systems. It can be deployed in the control of energy of smart grids, self-driving of connected vehicles and intelligent control of automation. The efficiency and intelligence of the IoT functions are enhanced with reinforcement learning as it learns constantly depending upon the feedback.

The problem of computer efficiency and models optimization should be considered when implementing deep learning models in the IoT analytics. To enable these models to execute at high performance on the resource constraints of edge devices, such models might use such techniques as model pruning, quantization, knowledge distillation and edge-specific architecture. The deployment will be efficient to ensure real-time analytics can be made locally to reduce the latency and bandwidth requirements and responsive IoT applications (LeCun et al., 2015).

With the growth in scale and complexity of IoT ecosystems, the deep learning models will become more and more essential in the provision of intelligent and autonomous systems. Incorporating cutting-edge neural networks, distributed learning, and edge-cloud computing, deep learning-based analytics are able to utilize raw IoT data to produce action-oriented information. The transformation helps to foster the emergence of intelligent cities, precision agriculture, health care monitoring, industry automation, and other novel uses, which eventually leads to efficiency, sustainability, and decision-making in diverse IoT settings.

EDGE INTELLIGENCE FOR REAL-TIME PROCESSING

Edge intelligence has become a radical method of facilitating real-time processing in Internet of Things (IoT) systems. In contrast to the traditional cloud-based architectures, where all the computational functions are performed on the centralised servers, edge intelligence utilises computational ability of device that is geographically closer to data source. By being nearer, sensor data is processed faster, latency is minimised, and decision-making can occur instantly, which is essential in applications that must be responsive in real-time, autonomous vehicles, industrial automation, and healthcare monitoring.

The main benefit of edge intelligence is the fact that it can compute the information at the edge and push it to the cloud. The system decreases the amount of raw data that needs to be relayed through networks by preprocessing and filtering data at the edge as well as conducting preliminary analysis there. This consumes less bandwidth and fast-tracks the entire data processing process so that vital events are identified and resolved promptly. As an example, edge-enabled sensors can also detect congestion or accidents instantly and activate adaptive adjustments of traffic lights in smart traffic management systems (Goodfellow et al., 2016).

Special hardware, such as Graphics Processing Units (GPUs) and Tensor Processing Units (TPUs) are also being added to edge devices such as gateways, microcontrollers and embedded systems to facilitate inference of deep learning. Such devices have the ability to run sophisticated neural network models at the edge, which allows using them in near real time to perform tasks like image recognition, anomaly detection, and predictive analytics. Edge hardware acceleration improves the model performance of deep learning models in a power-efficient and computationally viable manner.

Model optimization is one of the most important strategies of applying edge intelligence. Deep learning models are frequently computationally intense, so they cannot be directly deployed to resource limited edge devices. Model pruning, quantization and knowledge distillation are some of the techniques that have been used to end up shrinking the size and complexity of the neural networks with little or no great impact on accuracy. MobileNet or TinyML-based models Lightweight architectures have also been designed with a specifically edge-deployable network, including TinyML, which provides efficient processing to run real-time applications.

Localised decision-making with edge intelligence also provides latency-sensitive tasks with the needed localization. Industrial IoT In industrial IoT, e.g., the edge devices are able to monitor the machinery in real-time, identify anomalies, and activate preventive actions without necessarily having to wait until such information can be analysed in the cloud. To the same extent, in the field of healthcare IoT, a wearable device is capable of tracking vital signs and sending alerts immediately in case an abnormal condition is identified, which will allow timely intervention and save people.

Other advantages of edge intelligence are data privacy and security. Local processing of sensitive information would also reduce the number of times that personal or important information is sent through networks, thus lowering the chances of unauthorised access to information or breach. To be used in smart homes, healthcare or financial IoT systems, edge intelligence enables it to be compliant with privacy regulations without compromising the benefits of intelligent analytics (Hinton et al., 2006).

Interoperability of many edge devices, which are also known as distributed edge intelligence, also improves real-time processing. The devices have the ability to exchange knowledge, organise operations and respond to the changing environmental conditions. Such decentralisation is not only more robust and reliable than the IoT systems but also helps in adapting to the needs of the situation when the conditions in the environment or the operational scope vary quickly.

Cloud intelligence is often combined with edge intelligence in order to create a hierarchical processing architecture. Whereas edge devices are used to perform time-critical tasks that are immediate, the cloud is used to perform more computationally intensive tasks in training deep learning models, analysis of historical data, and large-scale predictive analytics. Frequent model updates between the cloud and edge devices will ensure local inference is informed with global knowledge to develop a dynamic and constantly updated intelligent system.

Energy efficiency is also another concern to take into account in the context of edge intelligence because the majority of IoT devices are prone to power-constrained conditions. The use of energy is minimised through efficient use of hardware, optimised algorithms and dynamic strategies of computation, and still gives high processing performance. The typical strategies to enhance the energy efficiency of edge-based deep learning systems are event-driven processing, dynamic voltage and frequency scaling, and selective model activation (Bhatti et al., 2021).

As IoT ecosystems grow and evolve, edge intelligence will be a key component of enabling real-time, autonomous, and adaptive operations. With edge intelligence, raw information can be converted into actionable information in real-time using low-cost local processing or state-of-the-art deep learning models and cooperative edge-cloud infrastructures. This paradigm increases the system responsiveness, reduces latency, ensures data privacy, and supports a plethora of activities, such as smart cities and industrial automation, health care monitoring and environment regulation.

CLOUD INTELLIGENCE FOR SCALABLE IOT ANALYTICS

The aspect of cloud intelligence is to provide a scalable analytics in Internet of Things (IoT) ecosystems. In the presence of billions of interconnected devices, generating huge amounts of heterogeneous data, the traditional local processing models cannot meet the storage, computation, and sophisticated analysis needs. Cloud platforms can support virtually unlimited computational resources, centralised data storage, and advanced analytics features, which are favourable to handle the massive volume of data generated by the IoT networks. Through cloud intelligence, organisations have the ability to run advanced analytics and implement deep learning models that would not be feasible using edge devices with limited resources.

Among the main benefits of cloud intelligence, there is the possibility to carry out data aggregation and data integration on a large scale. Internet of things devices spread in various geographical regions constantly produce a variety of data, sensor data, images, video data and environmental data. This data can be gathered, standardised and analysed on a cloud platform as a centralised infrastructure in real time or retrospectively. It will be capable of identifying global tendencies, associations, and knowledge that individual edge devices might not identify alone (Bhatti et al., 2020).

The training and deployment of complex deep learning models are also done through cloud platforms. It requires the computational capacity and the large memory size to train state-of-the-art neural networks, such as the convolutional, recurrent, or transformer-based networks. The infrastructure needed to effectively model-train, hyperparameter-tune, and experiment is provided by the usage of cloud servers with high-performance GPUs, TPUs and the potential of the scalable storage. They can be trained and deployed on the cloud or sent back to the edge devices to make inferences, which offers a framework of hybrid intelligence.

The other significant attribute of cloud intelligence is scalability. As the IoT network is increasing and the data volumes are increasing in disproportion to the network, the cloud computing resources can be elasticly expanded to address the needs. This is an on-demand distribution of calculational capacity and storage that makes sure that analytics job loads are not held up. It can also be used in multi-tenant model where several IoT applications or organisations share cloud infrastructure but have distinct and secure data processing pipelines.

Cloud intelligence improves predictive analytics and decision-making in the long term in IoT systems. Through manipulation of historical and real-time data, deep learning models on the cloud have the ability to spot trends, predict future occurrences and streamline operational plans. Smart cities can use cloud analytics to predict traffic jams, energy consumption and environmental changes, thus the government can schedule the interventions. On the same note, cloud intelligence facilitates predictive maintenance in industrial IoT, which minimises the downtime and operational expenses (Bhatti et al., 2023).

Combination with edge intelligence forms a hierarchical analytics system which balances local responsiveness with centralised processing capability. Edge devices can handle activities that are urgent, low-latency, and cloud servers handle activities that are computationally intensive, and must be modeled on a global scale. Such cooperation makes sure that there are no delays associated with real-time decision-making and that the information obtained based on large-scale datasets comes into play. The intelligence and flexibility of the system is also useful when the cloud to edge device periodic model updates are also taken into consideration (Bhatti et al., 2023).

Federated learning is another example of other advanced applications that can be done using cloud intelligence where distributed edge devices collaboratively learn a global model without exchanging raw data. The cloud coordinates aggregation, synchronisation, and optimization of model parameters, in such a way that the insights can be learnt with decentralised datasets without privacy loss. This method is particularly applicable in medical, home or office centres where information that is classified is supposed to be secure.Other benefits of cloud intelligence include data visualisation, reporting and monitoring. The cards provided in the cloud platform can be used to monitor the interactive dashboards, real-time alerts and automated reporting to help the stakeholders to know how systems behave, monitor performance, and make decisions. These features are necessary to control multisite IoT networks in various sites and to provide transparency in operations (Bhatti et al., 2021).

A security and compliance are important factors in IoT analytics on the cloud. Cloud systems have strong access controls, encryption rates, and auditing systems to protect confidential data. Centralised governance tools and monitoring tools help in compliance with the regulatory standards, including GDPR or HIPAA. These measures will make sure that the IoT data are safely analysed and stored and enable them to use the advanced analytics applications.

Cloud intelligence is anticipated to be one of the key elements of scalable, flexible, and powerful analytics as IoT ecosystem continues to develop. Cloud-enabled architectures enable the use of centralised computing resources, paired with edge-level responsiveness, to provide the most diverse range of applications, including smart city management and industrial automation as well as healthcare monitoring and analytics of the environment. This paradigm ensures the ability of IoT systems to grow in a sustainable way and the systems to deliver actionable insights and make smart decisions on a large scale (Sze et al., 2017).

CHALLENGES AND FUTURE RESEARCH DIRECTIONS

The combination of deep learning, edge and cloud intelligence in IoT ecosystems has many opportunities, however, it also poses serious challenges that need to be resolved, in order to achieve systems that are fully intelligent and autonomous. Computational constraints and energy constraints of edge devices are also one of the major challenges. Despite the ability of edge computing to provide real-time processing, most IoT devices lack power, memory and battery capacity. Applications of deep learning models in these devices should be optimised to ensure that it is lightweight and the algorithms applied to them are energy-efficient to guarantee performance and sustainability.

The issue of privacy and security of the data in IoT ecosystems is a bleak one. Personal health information, data about the work of industries, or information about their whereabouts are sensitive information that is most likely to be at risk of privacy when gathered and analyzed. To protect the information about the users and to provide intelligent analytics, it is necessary to ensure the secure data transmission between the edge devices and cloud servers, apply effective encryption algorithms and use privacy-preserving methods, like federated learning (Yu et al., 2018).

Scalability is the other major problem with the deep learning-based IoT systems. Connected devices are ever-increasing exponentially and yielding huge amounts of heterogeneous data. To efficiently manage, store and process this data across distributed edge and cloud layers, adaptive resource, network optimization and load-balancing strategies are needed. This is because it is needed to provide consistency in large-scale performance, which is crucial when implementing IoT at large scale, e.g., in smart cities or industrial networks.

There are also hurdles of interoperability and standardisation. IoT systems are made up of devices of different manufacturers, which can use different communication protocols and data formats. The heterogeneity should be supported by deep learning frameworks and facilitate the smooth integration of devices and platforms. The lack of standardisation can hamper the interchange of data, model deployment and the overall performance of the edge-cloud intelligence systems (Zhou et al., 2020).

Reliability and Latency of the network is also a great issue. Even though edge computing decreases the reliance on central cloud servers, most applications in the IoT demand responses in real-time or close to it. Network delays or intermittency, or bandwidth constraints can influence the performance of the distributed deep learning applications. The ability to come up with strong architectures to support unreliable networks without compromising system responsiveness is a crucial research topic.

More significant is the model interpretability and explainability in the IoT application, particularly in the areas such as healthcare, robotic vehicles, and automated industrial processes. Deep learning models are extremely precise but are also black box models, meaning it is difficult to understand how the logic was followed in the decision/prediction. To increase trust and adaptability, as well as implementation of intelligent IoT systems, there is a need to conduct research on interpretable models, attention mechanisms, and explainable AI models.

Other heterogeneity and quality issues of IoT data also exist. Sensors have noisy, nonexistent, or inconsistent sensor data, which might affect the accuracy and reliability of deep learning models. Data preprocessing and anomaly detection techniques as well as robust learning are prerequisites that models should be able to manage real-world IoT datasets. Model performance in heterogeneous environments can be further enhanced using research on data augmentation, transfer learning and multimodal data fusion (Deng & Yu, 2014).

Threats to security like adversarial attacks on deep learning bases are a novel issue on IoT systems. There is a possibility of the models being misled by malicious inputs which will lead to inaccurate predictions, system failures or harm to a system. Important applications of IoT, including autonomous transportation, smart grids, and healthcare monitoring, must come up with secure and resilient models that detect and mitigate adversarial manipulations.

Adaptive and self-learning systems are also the research directions in the future. Due to the dynamism of the IoT environment, where the conditions and data patterns constantly evolve, any model must be able to change over time without necessarily being retrained afresh. Online learning, continuous learning, and reinforcement learning can be used to ensure that IoT systems learn continuously and perform highly in changing environments.

Lastly, there is a significant area of research, which is to incorporate sustainability concerns into deep learning-enabled IoT systems. Algorithms that minimise energy consumption, low-power devices, and optimised communication systems are essential to the minimization of the environmental impact of large-scale IoT. The intelligent iot networks will require a balance between performance, scalability, security and energy efficiency in building effective and long-term sustainable intelligent iot ecosystems.

CONCLUSION

Deep learning and edge/cloud intelligence convergence have created a paradigm shift in the creation of smart IoT systems. With the combination of edge processing and centralised cloud analytics, the IoT systems can now conduct real-time data analysis, predictive modelling, and autonomous decision-making. This top-bottom strategy guarantees that the tasks with high latency requirements will be processed locally, and computationally-intensive work will be done with the help of the scalable resources of the cloud, forming an effective and responsive system of various IoT applications.

Edge intelligence has been instrumental in providing the capability to process and make local decisions in real-time. Through inference and preliminary data analysis on the edge, the IoT devices are able to react quickly to the environmental changes, anomalies in operations or to user needs. This not only enhances the responsiveness of systems like autonomous vehicles, industrial automation, and smart healthcare, it also lowers the bandwidth usage and helps avoid network overload, which improves the overall efficiency of the system.

Cloud intelligence is a supplementary to edge computing, as it offers a significant amount of computational power, storage, and other analytics. Large datasets can be trained and updated in the cloud in complex deep learning models, allowing IoT applications to enjoy high-accuracy predictive analytics, trend identification globally, and continuous learning. Two-way intelligence of edges and clouds give a balanced distribution of workloads that are speedy and scaled together to achieve solid IoT functions.

Although it has several benefits, there are a number of challenges associated with the deployment of deep learning-powered edge-cloud architectures such as resource limitations, data privacy, security risks, interoperability and model interpretability. The optimization of the models, secure communication schemes, standardised framework, and explainable AI approaches can be the key to the sustainable development and implementation of intelligent IoT systems in different spheres.

Finally, the paradigms of deep learning-based edge and cloud intelligence offer an end-to-end architecture of scaling, efficient, and adaptable Internet of Things. With the ongoing developments in the research of model optimization, distributed computing, and privacy-saving techniques, it is anticipated that future IoT systems will be more autonomous, resilient, and intelligent. The integration opens the way to innovations in smart cities, industrial IoT, healthcare, and environmental monitoring, and other more important fields, which ultimately enables more intelligent and sustainable digital infrastructures.

REFERENCES

Abadi, M., Barham, P., Chen, J., Chen, Z., Davis, A., Dean, J., & Zheng, X. (2016). {TensorFlow}: a system for {Large-Scale} machine learning. In *12th USENIX symposium on operating systems design and implementation (OSDI 16)* (pp. 265-283).

Bhatti, U. A., Tang, H., Wu, G., Marjan, S., & Hussain, A. (2023). Deep learning with graph convolutional networks: An overview and latest applications in computational intelligence. *International Journal of Intelligent Systems, 2023*(1), 8342104. DOI: 10.1155/2023/8342104

Bhatti, U. A., Yu, Z., Yuan, L., Zeeshan, Z., Nawaz, S. A., Bhatti, M. A., Mehmood, A., Ain, Q., & Luo, W. (2020). Geometric algebra applications in geospatial artificial intelligence and remote sensing image processing. *IEEE Access : Practical Innovations, Open Solutions, 8*, 155783–155796. DOI: 10.1109/ACCESS.2020.3018544

Bhatti, U. A., Yuan, L., Yu, Z., Nawaz, S. A., Mehmood, A., Bhatti, M. A., Ain, Q., Nizamani, M. M., Zeeshan, Z., & Xiao, S. J. (2021). Predictive data modeling using sp-kNN for risk factor evaluation in urban demographical healthcare data. *Journal of Medical Imaging and Health Informatics, 11*(1), 7–14. DOI: 10.1166/jmihi.2021.3313

Chen, M., Mao, S., & Liu, Y. (2014). Big data: A survey. *Mobile Networks and Applications, 19*(2), 171–209. DOI: 10.1007/s11036-013-0489-0

Deng, L., & Yu, D. (2014). Deep learning: Methods and applications. *Foundations and Trends in Signal Processing, 7*(3–4), 197–387. DOI: 10.1561/2000000039

Goodfellow, I., Bengio, Y., & Courville, A. (2016). *Deep learning*. MIT Press.

Gubbi, J., Buyya, R., Marusic, S., & Palaniswami, M. (2013). Internet of Things (IoT): A vision, architectural elements, and future directions. *Future Generation Computer Systems, 29*(7), 1645–1660. DOI: 10.1016/j.future.2013.01.010

He, K., Zhang, X., Ren, S., & Sun, J. (2016). Deep residual learning for image recognition. *Proceedings of the IEEE Conference on Computer Vision and Pattern Recognition*, 770–778.

Hinton, G. E., Osindero, S., & Teh, Y. W. (2006). A fast learning algorithm for deep belief nets. *Neural Computation, 18*(7), 1527–1554. DOI: 10.1162/neco.2006.18.7.1527 PMID: 16764513

Kairouz, P., & McMahan, H. B. (2021). Advances and open problems in federated learning. *Foundations and Trends in Machine Learning*, *14*(1-2), 1–210. DOI: 10.1561/2200000083

LeCun, Y., Bengio, Y., & Hinton, G. (2015). Deep learning. *Nature*, *521*(7553), 436–444. DOI: 10.1038/nature14539 PMID: 26017442

Li, S., Xu, L. D., & Zhao, S. (2018). The internet of things: A survey. *Information Systems Frontiers*, *17*(2), 243–259. DOI: 10.1007/s10796-014-9492-7

McMahan, B., Moore, E., Ramage, D., Hampson, S., & Arcas, B. A. (2017, April). Communication-efficient learning of deep networks from decentralized data. In *Artificial intelligence and statistics* (pp. 1273–1282). Pmlr.

Satyanarayanan, M. (2017). The emergence of edge computing. *Computer*, *50*(1), 30–39. DOI: 10.1109/MC.2017.9

Shi, W., Cao, J., Zhang, Q., Li, Y., & Xu, L. (2016). Edge computing: Vision and challenges. *IEEE Internet of Things Journal*, *3*(5), 637–646. DOI: 10.1109/JIOT.2016.2579198

Sze, V., Chen, Y. H., Yang, T. J., & Emer, J. S. (2017). Efficient processing of deep neural networks: A tutorial and survey. *Proceedings of the IEEE*, *105*(12), 2295–2329. DOI: 10.1109/JPROC.2017.2761740

Wang, S., Tuor, T., Salonidis, T., Leung, K. K., Makaya, C., He, T., & Chan, K. (2019). Adaptive federated learning in resource-constrained edge computing systems. *IEEE Journal on Selected Areas in Communications*, *37*(6), 1205–1221. DOI: 10.1109/JSAC.2019.2904348

Yu, W., Liang, F., He, X., Hatcher, W. G., Lu, C., Lin, J., & Yang, X. (2018). A survey on the edge computing for the Internet of Things. *IEEE Access : Practical Innovations, Open Solutions*, *6*, 6900–6919. DOI: 10.1109/ACCESS.2017.2778504

Zaharia, M., Chowdhury, M., Franklin, M. J., Shenker, S., & Stoica, I. (2010). Spark: Cluster computing with working sets. *Proceedings of the USENIX Conference on Hot Topics in Cloud Computing*.

Zhang, Q., Chen, M., Yang, L. T., & Zhang, Z. (2018). Deep learning for sensor-based activity recognition: A survey. *IEEE Communications Surveys and Tutorials*, *21*(1), 1–31.

Zhou, L., Chen, X., Li, Z., & Li, W. (2020). Edge intelligence: Challenges and opportunities. *Proceedings of the IEEE*, *108*(11), 1821–1841.

Zhou, Z., Chen, X., Li, E., Zeng, L., Luo, K., & Zhang, J. (2019). Edge intelligence: Paving the last mile of artificial intelligence with edge computing. *Proceedings of the IEEE, 107*(8), 1738–1762. DOI: 10.1109/JPROC.2019.2918951

Chapter 7
Optimizing Deep Learning Architectures for the Device-Edge-Cloud Continuum in IoT

K. Vijayakumar
http://orcid.org/0009-0005-6245-3165
Madras Engineering College, India

Ezhilvendan Munusamy
Panimalar Engineering College, India

ABSTRACT

This chapter addresses the critical challenge of optimizing deep learning architectures for deployment across the device-edge-cloud continuum in Internet of Things (IoT) environments. As IoT devices proliferate, the need to process data efficiently at multiple computing tiers from resource-constrained IoT devices to edge nodes to cloud infrastructure has become paramount. This chapter synthesizes state-of-the-art approaches in model compression, adaptive architecture design, and collaborative computing frameworks. The key optimization techniques examined include quantization-aware training, pruning strategies, knowledge distillation, federated learning, and dynamic model switching. Furthermore, this chapter explores how hierarchical computing architectures enable real-time decision-making while preserving privacy and reducing latency. Through a comprehensive discussion of practical deployment scenarios and architectural trade-offs, this work provides researchers and practitioners with actionable insights for designing efficient, scalable.

DOI: 10.4018/979-8-2600-0615-3.ch007

1. INTRODUCTION

The Internet of Things (IoT) has fundamentally transformed the manner in which data are collected, processed, and analyzed across physical environments. With billions of connected devices generating unprecedented volumes of heterogeneous data, traditional cloud-centric architectures face significant limitations regarding latency, bandwidth utilization, and privacy preservation (Aravindh & Sridhar, 2026). The edge-cloud continuum has emerged as a paradigm that distributes computational resources and intelligence across multiple tiers: Internet of Things (IoT) devices at the edge, intermediate edge servers and fog nodes, and centralized cloud infrastructure (Knorst et al., 2025).

Deep neural networks (DNNs) have become indispensable for intelligent decision-making in IoT applications, from computer vision and anomaly detection to predictive maintenance and environmental monitoring. However, deploying these computationally demanding models across the device-edge-cloud continuum presents substantial challenges. IoT edge devices typically operate under severe constraints: limited memory (kilobytes to megabytes), reduced computational power (single-core or dual-core processors), and stringent energy budgets (battery-powered). These devices must also support real-time inference to meet the latency-sensitive application requirements (Sıcakyüz et al., 2024).

This chapter addresses the core challenge of optimizing deep learning architectures for heterogeneous computing environments, ranging from constrained Internet of Things (IoT) devices to resource-rich cloud infrastructures. We examine three complementary approaches: (1) model optimization techniques that reduce computational and memory demands, (2) architectural frameworks that distribute intelligence across the continuum, and (3) collaborative computing strategies that leverage the strengths of each tier. This chapter synthesizes recent advances in quantization, pruning, knowledge distillation, and federated learning, while providing practical guidance for practitioners designing next-generation intelligent IoT systems. These approaches collectively enable the scalable and efficient deployment of AI models tailored to the unique constraints and capabilities of each computing tier. Emphasis is placed on balancing accuracy, latency, and energy consumption to achieve optimal system performance. Practical case studies illustrate how these techniques can be integrated into real-world IoT applications, highlighting trade-offs and design considerations.

2. THE DEVICE-EDGE-CLOUD COMPUTING CONTINUUM

2.1 Architectural Overview

The device-edge-cloud continuum represents a hierarchical distribution of computing resources and intelligence, which is fundamentally different from traditional cloud-only or edge-only paradigms. This architecture acknowledges that different computational tasks have different optimal placement locations based on latency requirements, data sensitivity, computational complexity, and resource availability (Chhabra et al., 2025). Figure 1 illustrates the hierarchical three-tier architecture of the device-edge-cloud continuum. The continuum is typically comprised of three primary layers.

Recent architectural frameworks implement hierarchical FL and multi-tier orchestration mechanisms that dynamically allocate tasks based on real-time resource availability, network conditions, and application requirements (Lilhore et al., 2025). Cloud-fog-edge orchestration devices (CFEODs) and similar dynamic allocation mechanisms enable adaptive task distribution, achieving significant improvements in system responsiveness and resource utilization (Aravindh & Sridhar, 2026). These layers collaborate to provide seamless data processing and service delivery, thereby minimizing latency and optimizing bandwidth usage. Edge devices handle immediate data collection and preliminary processing, whereas fog nodes perform intermediate aggregation and analytics. The cloud layer offers extensive computational power and long-term storage, supporting complex processing and global coordination.

Figure 1. Device-edge-cloud continuum architecture

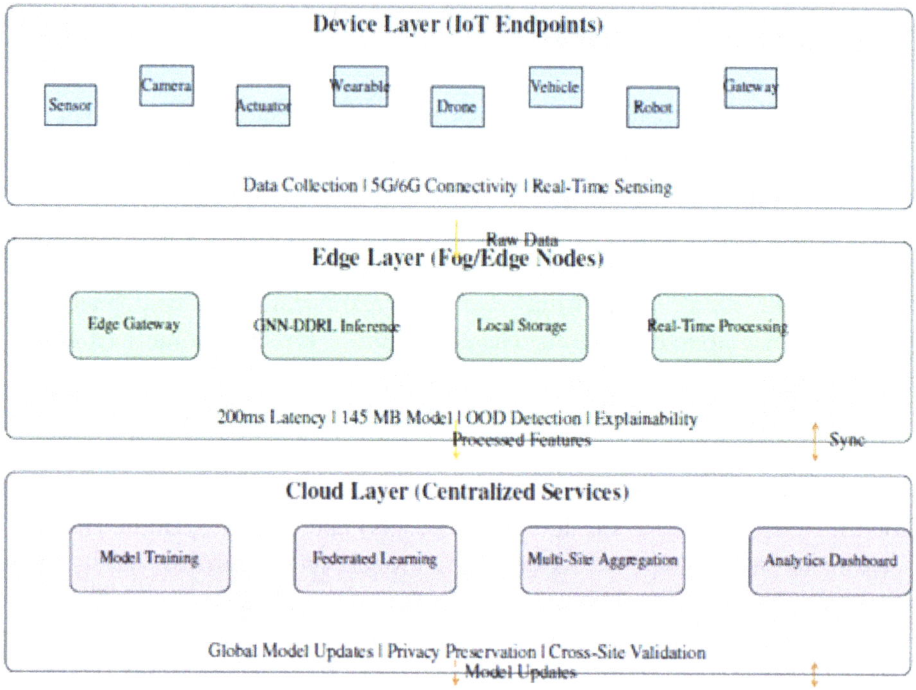

2.2 Computational and Resource Constraints

Optimizing deep learning for the device-edge-cloud continuum requires understanding heterogeneous constraints across tiers.

- *Memory Constraints:* IoT devices often operate with kilobytes to single-digit megabytes of RAM, making it impossible to store large pre-trained models. Edge devices typically provide 256 MB to 8 GB, whereas cloud infrastructure offers essentially unlimited memory. This heterogeneity necessitates progressive model compression and tiered inference strategies (Reddy et al., 2025).
- *Computational Power:* Processing capabilities vary dramatically across the continuum. A Raspberry Pi achieves approximately 5 GFLOPS, an NVIDIA Jetson Nano provides 472 GFLOPS, whereas enterprise cloud infrastructure delivers petaFLOPS-scale performance. This six-order-of-magnitude variation demands architecture-specific optimization strategies (Matam, 2025).

- *Energy Constraints:* Battery-powered IoT devices operate under severe energy budgets (milliwatts to watts), and a single inference operation consuming 100 mJ can significantly impact device lifetime. Edge servers may be energy-constrained (10–100 watts) or powered, whereas cloud infrastructure is typically AC-powered. Energy-aware optimization has become critical for sustainable IoT deployments (Ben Atitallah et al., 2025).
- *Network Constraints:* Bandwidth availability fluctuates dramatically, from 4G/5G mobile networks (10–100 Mbps) to constrained Internet of Things (IoT) protocols (LoRaWAN at 50 kbps). Network latency ranges from microseconds (local edge) to milliseconds (cloud), introducing trade-offs between local computation and remote processing (Reddy et al., 2025).
- *Latency Requirements:* Applications span a spectrum from non-critical (seconds to minutes) to ultra-latency-sensitive (< 1 ms). Real-time control applications, autonomous systems, and medical monitoring require sub-100 ms response times, which are typically achievable only through edge or local processing (Sıcakyüz et al., 2024).

Table 1. Computational and resource constraints across the device-edge-cloud continuum

Parameter	IoT Devices	Edge Servers	Cloud Infrastructure
Memory (RAM)	1-100 MB	256 MB-8 GB	Essentially unlimited (TBs)
Computational Power (GFLOPS)	0.5-5 GFLOPS	100-500 GFLOPS	Petaflops+
Energy Budget	1-10 mW (battery)	10-100 W	AC-powered
Network Latency	100-500 ms	10-50 ms	50-200 ms
Bandwidth Availability	50 kbps-10 Mbps	100 Mbps-1 Gbps	1-100 Gbps
Inference Latency Requirement	100-1000 ms	50-500 ms	500 ms-10 s
Model Size Suitable	100 KB-10 MB	10-100 MB	100 MB-GB+
Example Hardware	Raspberry Pi, ESP32	Jetson Nano, TX2	NVIDIA V100, TPU v4

3. MODEL COMPRESSION TECHNIQUES

Model compression forms the foundation for enabling deep-learning deployment across resource-constrained devices. These techniques reduce the model size, computational requirements, and memory footprint while maintaining acceptable accuracy (Alsalem & Djemame, 2025).

Figure 2. Model compression techniques comparison

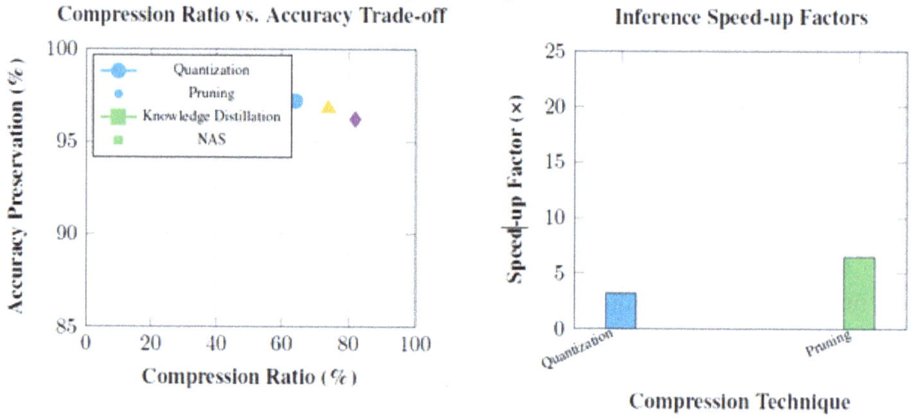

3.1 Quantization-Aware Training

Quantization reduces the precision of the model weights and activations, typically from 32-bit floating points to 8-bit integers or lower. Quantization-aware training (QAT) incorporates quantization during training, allowing the model to adapt to reduced precision and typically preserving accuracy better than post-training quantization (PTQ) (Matam, 2025). Recent advances have demonstrated that aggressive quantization to 4-bit or even binary precision can be achieved with minimal accuracy loss through careful training strategies. A 4-bit quantized model achieves approximately 4× compression compared to full-precision variants (Qu et al., 2024). For latency-sensitive applications, quantization provides immediate benefits: 8-bit quantized inference accelerates computation by 2–4 × on integer-capable hardware and reduces bandwidth requirements proportionally (Giannopoulos et al., 2024).

Mixed-precision quantization, in which different layers employ different bit widths, offers improved accuracy efficiency trade-offs. Transformer-based models particularly benefit from token-aware pruning combined with mixed-precision quantization (Myakala, 2025). These techniques enhance model deployment efficiency without a significant loss in performance. Furthermore, they enable the practical use of large-scale models on resource-constrained devices. Ongoing research continues to explore adaptive quantization strategies to further optimize this balance between accuracy and computational cost.

3.2 Pruning and Sparsity Induction

Systematic pruning removes redundant connections or filters from neural networks, thereby reducing the model size and computational requirements. Structured pruning (removing entire channels or filters) produces hardware-friendly sparse patterns, whereas unstructured pruning (removing individual weights) achieves higher compression but requires specialized hardware or software support (Alsalem & Djemame, 2025). Structured pruning with M×N sparsity patterns combines coarse-grained sparsity with fine-grained unstructured pruning to balance the compression ratio and hardware efficiency. The three-stage coarse-to-fine SUQ-3 framework achieves an 85% model size reduction while maintaining 97% accuracy in agricultural Internet of Things (IoT) applications (Singh et al., 2025).

Research has demonstrated that knowledge of layer importance significantly improves pruning effectiveness. Head-aware mixed-precision approaches identify critical attention heads in Transformer models and selectively preserve them, achieving up to 7.5× speedup on CPUs and 8× on FPGAs with minimal accuracy degradation (Myakala, 2025). Structured pruning with M×N sparsity patterns combines coarse-grained sparsity with fine-grained unstructured pruning to effectively balance the compression ratio and hardware efficiency. This approach partitions weight matrices into blocks, enforcing a fixed number of non-zero elements per block, which facilitates optimized memory access and accelerates inference on specialized hardware.

The three-stage coarse-to-fine SUQ-3 framework exemplifies this strategy by achieving an 85% reduction in model size while maintaining a high accuracy rate of 97% in agricultural Internet of Things (IoT) applications, demonstrating its practical viability in real-world scenarios (Singh et al., 2025). Furthermore, research has shown that incorporating knowledge of layer importance significantly improves pruning effectiveness by selectively targeting less critical layers for compression, thereby preserving the overall model performance. Head-aware mixed-precision approaches extend this concept by identifying critical attention heads within transformer models and selectively preserving them, enabling up to 7.5× speedup on CPUs and 8× on FPGAs with minimal accuracy degradation (Myakala, 2025). These methods not only optimize computational resources but also dynamically adapt precision, balancing speed, and accuracy to meet the demands of diverse deployment environments.

3.3 Knowledge Distillation

Knowledge distillation transfers learned representations from a large, high-capacity teacher model to a smaller student model. The teacher–student framework enables compression ratios that exceed those possible with independent optimization of small models (Alsalem & Djemame, 2025). For medical device applications, knowledge distillation achieves 99% compression (from teacher to student accuracy of 99% to 97%) while reducing inference latency by 69%, thereby enabling real-time seizure prediction on Internet of Things (IoT) edge devices (Zhang et al., 2025). Federated learning scenarios benefit from knowledge distillation through environment-oriented cross-architecture mechanisms that facilitate knowledge transfer between heterogeneous models (Wang et al., 2025).

The effectiveness of knowledge distillation varies depending on the application domain. Computer vision models typically achieve 90%–99% teacher accuracy with 10–20 × compression, whereas natural language processing models require more conservative compression ratios to maintain semantic understanding (Zhang et al., 2025). This disparity arises because natural language processing tasks demand preserving intricate contextual relationships that are sensitive to excessive compression. Consequently, knowledge distillation approaches in NLP often incorporate adaptive techniques to balance model size reduction with semantic fidelity. Ongoing research focuses on optimizing these mechanisms to enhance performance while minimizing computational overhead.

3.4 Hardware-Aware Neural Architecture Search

Neural Architecture Search (NAS) automatically discovers optimal model architectures for specific hardware constraints. Unlike hand-designed models, NAS-discovered architectures explicitly optimize for target deployment hardware, achieving superior accuracy–efficiency trade-offs (Alsalem & Djemame, 2025). Hardware-aware NAS integrates actual hardware latency measurements or predictors into the search objective, ensuring that the discovered architectures perform efficiently on target devices. The CoDAC framework combines pruning, quantization, and hardware-oriented optimization within an AutoML pipeline, achieving Pareto-optimal solutions that balance accuracy, latency, and resource usage (Liu et al., 2025). Contemporary NAS approaches leverage transformer-based architectures for efficient searching and discovering compact models suitable for edge deployment while maintaining competitive accuracy compared to hand-designed efficient architectures, such as MobileNet and EfficientNet (Alsalem & Djemame, 2025).

In contrast to hand-designed models, NAS-discovered architectures explicitly optimize for target deployment hardware, achieving superior accuracy–efficiency trade-offs (Alsalem & Djemame, 2025). Hardware-aware NAS integrates actual hardware latency measurements or predictors into the search objective, ensuring that the discovered architectures perform efficiently on target devices. This approach allows the search to incorporate realistic constraints, such as memory bandwidth, energy consumption, and parallel processing capabilities, which are critical for deployment on resource-constrained platforms. The CoDAC framework combines pruning, quantization, and hardware-oriented optimization within an AutoML pipeline, achieving Pareto-optimal solutions that balance accuracy, latency, and resource usage (Liu et al., 2025). By jointly optimizing these factors, CoDAC effectively tailors model architectures to meet specific hardware requirements without a significant loss in predictive performance, making it highly suitable for edge and mobile applications. Moreover, this integration facilitates adaptive model compression techniques that dynamically adjust model complexity based on hardware feedback, further enhancing deployment flexibility and efficiency.

Table 2. Model compression performance metrics across techniques

Technique	Compression Ratio	Speedup Factor	Accuracy Loss	Inference Latency	Energy Savings	Best Use Case
Post-Training Quantization (PTQ)	4-8×	2-4×	2-5%	25-50% reduction	30-40%	Fast deployment, non-critical apps
Quantization-Aware Training (QAT)	4-8×	2-4×	0.5-2%	25-50% reduction	30-40%	Vision models, consumer devices
Structured Pruning	5-10×	3-6×	1-3%	40-60% reduction	50-65%	Real-time inference, inference engines
Unstructured Pruning	10-20×	2-4×	1-4%	10-30% reduction	20-35%	Specialized hardware support required
Knowledge Distillation	10-20×	4-8×	1-3%	50-70% reduction	60-75%	Medical devices, critical applications
Hardware-Aware NAS	8-15×	3-7×	0.5-2%	40-65% reduction	55-70%	Custom hardware optimization
Combined (Pruning+QAT+KD)	20-50×	6-12×	1-4%	60-80% reduction	70-85%	

4. DISTRIBUTED INTELLIGENCE AND FEDERATED LEARNING

Figure 3. Federated learning hierarchical architecture

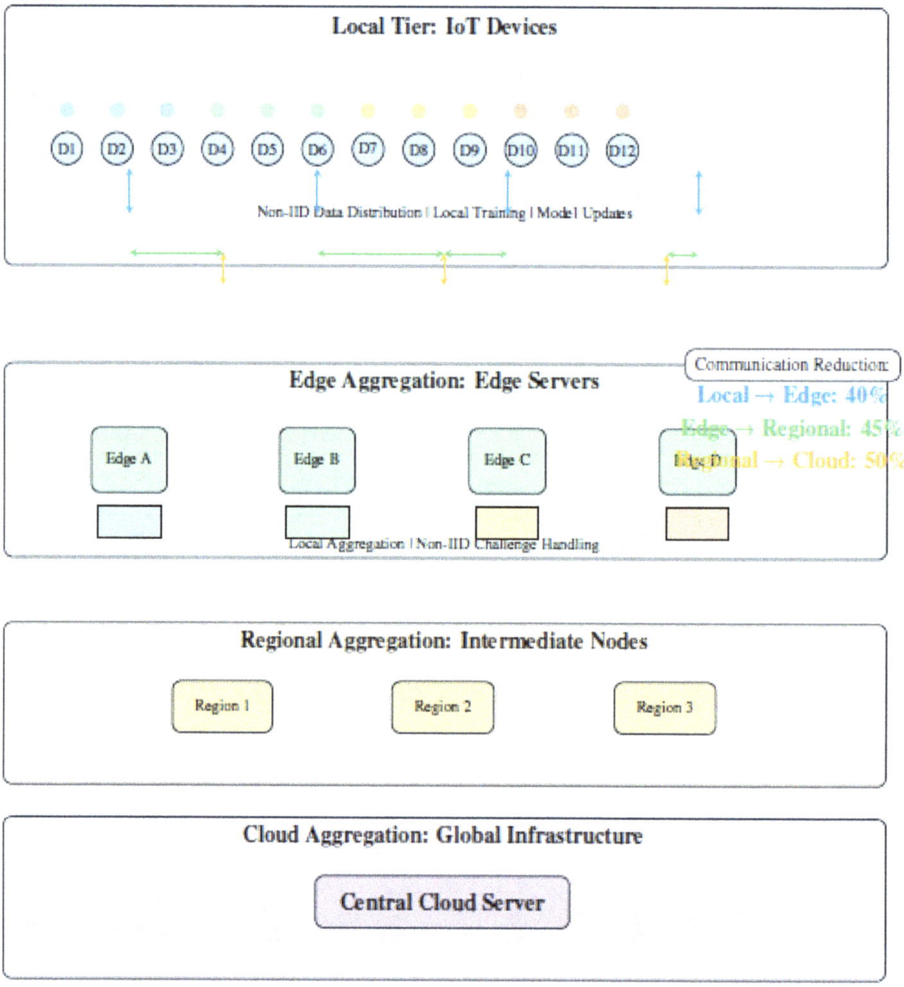

Federated learning and distributed training approaches enable collaborative model training across heterogeneous IoT-edge-cloud environments while preserving data privacy and reducing communication overhead (Gao, 2025). Federated learning and distributed training architectures facilitate collaborative model development by enabling multiple devices and nodes within heterogeneous IoT-edge-cloud environments to jointly train machine learning models without sharing raw data. This approach preserves data privacy by ensuring that sensitive information remains localized on edge devices or cloud nodes, and only model updates or gradients are exchanged. Additionally, the hierarchical structure inherent in federated learning reduces communication overhead by aggregating updates at intermediate layers before transmitting them to a central server, thereby optimizing bandwidth usage and improving scalability across large, distributed networks.

By leveraging this hierarchical architecture, FL can effectively address the challenges posed by diverse data sources, varying computational capabilities, and network constraints typical of IoT ecosystems. It enables the efficient utilization of edge resources for preliminary processing and model training, whereas cloud servers handle global aggregation and coordination. This layered collaboration enhances model accuracy by incorporating diverse data distributions and supports real-time responsiveness and robustness in dynamic environments, making it a promising approach for privacy-preserving and scalable AI deployment in IoT applications.

4.1 Federated Learning Architectures

Federated learning (FL) enables distributed training, in which edge devices locally train model replicas using their private data, whereas a central server aggregates model updates to establish a global model. This approach fundamentally changes the distribution of intelligence across the continuum (Wang et al., 2025). The hierarchical FL framework introduces multiple aggregation levels: local edge servers aggregate updates from nearby IoT devices, regional edge nodes aggregate across edge servers, and cloud infrastructure performs global aggregation requirements (Lilhore et al., 2025). This multi-tier architecture reduces communication overhead by 40%–50% compared with flat aggregation, while enabling more responsive local model updates (Sivasankaran et al., 2025). Multi-width neural network-assisted hierarchical FL addresses heterogeneous device capabilities through a heterogeneity-aware subnet width assignment. Experiments demonstrated a 42.42% accuracy enhancement, 81.5% latency reduction, and 40.9% energy cost optimization compared with single-width approaches (Zhantileuov et al., 2025).

The hierarchical FL framework introduces multiple aggregation levels to efficiently manage data and model updates across a distributed network. At the first level, local edge servers aggregate updates from nearby IoT devices, thereby enabling rapid and localized model refinement. The second level involves regional edge nodes that consolidate updates from multiple edge servers, thereby facilitating broader coordination and reducing latency. Finally, the cloud infrastructure performs global aggregation, integrating insights from all regional nodes to maintain a cohesive and up-to-date global model (Lilhore et al., 2025). This multi-tier architecture significantly reduces communication overhead by 40%–50% compared with flat aggregation approaches, while also enabling more responsive and frequent local model updates, which are critical for time-sensitive applications (Sivasankaran et al., 2025). Additionally, the framework incorporates a multi-width neural network-assisted hierarchical FL, which addresses heterogeneous device capabilities through a heterogeneity-aware subnet width assignment strategy. This adaptive mechanism ensures that devices with varying computational resources contribute optimally without overburdening less capable nodes. Experimental results demonstrated a 42.42% improvement in accuracy, an 81.5% reduction in latency, and a 40.9% optimization in energy costs compared with traditional single-width approaches, thereby highlighting the efficiency and effectiveness of this method in real-world FL scenarios (Zhantileuov et al., 2025).

4.2 Asynchronous Training and Federated Optimization

In traditional synchronous FL, a server waits for all devices before performing aggregation; however, global synchronization is required. In dynamic IoT environments with heterogeneous devices and unreliable networks, synchronization introduces substantial delays (Nieto et al., 2024). Blockchained dual-asynchronous federated learning (BAFL) enables both local training and global aggregation to occur asynchronously, leveraging blockchain consensus for model reliability and decentralized verification. The dual-asynchronous approach improves accuracy and efficiency by allowing fast devices to contribute updates independently of slower devices (Nieto et al., 2024). Federated deep reinforcement learning addresses non-IID (non-independently and identically distributed) data challenges common in Internet of Things (IoT) networks. By clustering compatible domains and employing environment-clustered approaches with differential privacy, systems can achieve effective collaboration across heterogeneous data distributions (Wang et al., 2025).

Blockchained dual-asynchronous federated learning (BAFL) enables both local training and global aggregation to occur asynchronously, leveraging blockchain consensus mechanisms to ensure model reliability and decentralized verification. This integration of blockchain technology not only enhances security by providing tamper-proof records of model updates but also fosters trust among participating devices in a distributed network. The dual-asynchronous approach improves the accuracy and efficiency of the system by allowing faster devices to contribute updates independently of slower devices, thereby minimizing idle times and synchronization bottlenecks (Nieto et al., 2024). Federated deep reinforcement learning further addresses the challenges posed by non-independent and identically distributed (non-IID) data, which are prevalent in Internet of Things (IoT) networks because of their heterogeneous and dynamic nature. By clustering compatible domains and employing environment-clustered approaches combined with differential privacy techniques, the system achieves effective collaboration across diverse data distributions while safeguarding user privacy (Wang et al., 2025). Thus, this multifarious framework enables scalable, secure, and efficient federated learning tailored to the complex requirements of IoT ecosystems.

4.3 Privacy-Preserving Distributed Analytics

Privacy preservation is paramount in federated learning deployments, particularly for healthcare and personal monitoring applications. Differential privacy techniques add calibrated noise to model updates, thereby preventing inference attacks while maintaining model convergence (Gao, 2025). Microservice-based architectures combine federated learning with fine-grained services to provide intelligent analytics while protecting data privacy. The FedMicro-IDA framework achieves 99.24% detection accuracy for malware classification while distributing computation across edge and fog devices (Moghaddasi et al., 2024)

5. DYNAMIC TASK OFFLOADING AND MODEL PLACEMENT

Optimal task offloading decisions determine whether computations are executed locally on Internet of Things (IoT) devices, on nearby edge servers, or on cloud infrastructure. These decisions must balance latency requirements, energy consumption, network bandwidth, and accuracy requirements (Sıcakyüz et al., 2024).

Figure 4. Task offloading decision tree and performance optimization

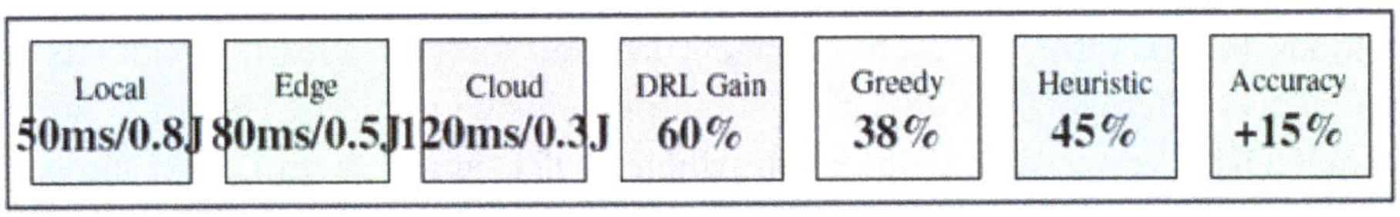

5.1 Adaptive Model Switching Frameworks

In an adaptive model switching, both the deep learning model and execution location are dynamically selected based on real-time network conditions and application requirements. The AdaptSwitch framework evaluates multiple model variants (from lightweight quantized models for edge execution to full-precision models for cloud) and selects the configuration that optimizes the quality of experience (Sıcakyüz et al., 2024). The selection mechanism considers three dimensions: (1) inference latency requirements, (2) model accuracy thresholds, and (3) current network conditions.

Experiments demonstrate that adaptive switching improves the quality of experience by reducing inference latency while ensuring that accuracy requirements are met, thereby outperforming static placement strategies (Sıcakyüz et al., 2024).

The AdaptSwitch framework employs a sophisticated decision-making process that dynamically selects the most suitable model variant and execution location by continuously monitoring real-time network conditions and application-specific requirements. This adaptive mechanism enables the system to balance the trade-offs between computational efficiency and model performance, ensuring that inference tasks meet predefined latency and accuracy constraints. By integrating a multi-dimensional selection strategy that considers inference latency requirements, model accuracy thresholds, and prevailing network conditions, AdaptSwitch effectively tailors its operation to optimize the overall quality of experience (QoE) for end-users.

5.2 Deep Reinforcement Learning for Offloading

Deep reinforcement learning (DRL) provides principled approaches to learn optimal offloading policies that adapt to dynamic environments. DRL agents observe the system state (device resources, network latency, and battery level) and learn policies that maximize long-term cumulative rewards (latency minimization, energy efficiency, and cost reduction) (Shuvo et al., 2022). The actor–critic architecture running on each device enables fully decentralized decision-making without global state awareness, thereby reducing coordination overhead. Agents learn to make locally optimal decisions that collectively achieve near-global-optimal offloading, demonstrating a 15%–60% improvement in total system costs compared with baseline methods (Petrakis et al., 2025). Multi-agent deep reinforcement learning extends this approach to heterogeneous edge cloud environments with multiple decision points. The HOODIE framework employs distributed DRL agents with LSTM temporal modeling and Dueling DQN architectures, thereby reducing task drop rates and average processing delays under dynamic conditions (Lee & Na, 2022).

DRL agents continuously observe the system state, including device resources, network latency, and battery level, to learn policies that maximize long-term cumulative rewards focused on latency minimization, energy efficiency, and cost reduction (Shuvo et al., 2022). The actor–critic architecture implemented on each device supports fully decentralized decision-making, eliminating the need for global state awareness and thereby significantly reducing coordination overhead across the network. Through this decentralized approach, agents learn to make locally optimal decisions that collectively approximate near-global-optimal offloading strategies, resulting in a substantial 15%–60% improvement in total system costs compared with baseline methods (Petrakis et al., 2025). Furthermore, multi-agent deep reinforcement learning techniques extend this framework to heterogeneous edge cloud environments characterized by multiple decision points, enhancing scalability and adaptability. The HOODIE framework incorporates distributed DRL agents equipped with LSTM-based temporal modeling and Dueling DQN architectures, which effectively capture temporal dependencies and improve value estimation. This combination leads to notable reductions in task drop rates and average processing delays under dynamic and fluctuating network conditions (Lee & Na, 2022). By integrating these advanced learning mechanisms, the system adapts in real-time to varying workloads and network states, ensuring robust and efficient task offloading in complex edge-cloud scenarios.

5.3 Graph Neural Networks for Resource Allocation

Graph neural networks (GNNs) model edge-cloud infrastructure as a graph, where nodes represent computing resources and edges represent network connections. GNN-based resource allocation captures complex interdependencies in distributed systems (Arzovs et al., 2024). The hybrid DQN–PPO–GNN–RL model achieved a 21% reduction in task scheduling time, 17% reduction in operational cost, and 22% reduction in energy consumption compared to traditional approaches (Arzovs et al., 2024). GNNs enable the system to recognize patterns in resource utilization and predict future bottlenecks, thereby enabling proactive resource provisioning.

Graph neural networks (GNNs) model edge-cloud infrastructure as a graph, where nodes represent computing resources and edges represent network connections, thereby effectively capturing the topological and functional relationships within distributed systems. This GNN-based resource allocation approach is particularly powerful in representing and managing the complex interdependencies that exist in distributed environments, enabling more nuanced and context-aware decision-making (Arzovs et al., 2024). The hybrid DQN–PPO–GNN–RL model leverages the strengths of deep reinforcement learning combined with graph-based representations to optimize resource management, achieving a 21% reduction in task scheduling time, a 17% reduction in operational cost, and a 22% reduction in energy consumption compared to traditional resource allocation (Arzovs et al., 2024). By enabling the system to recognize intricate patterns in resource utilization and anticipate future bottlenecks, GNNs facilitate proactive resource provisioning, which enhances system efficiency, responsiveness, and scalability under dynamic operational conditions.

Table 3. Task offloading performance across DRL and optimization methods

Method	Latency Reduction	Energy Savings	Cost Reduction	Convergence Time	Scalability	Non-IID Data Handling
Greedy Heuristic	10-15%	5-10%	8-12%	Fast (seconds)	Poor (100s devices)	Limited
Integer Linear Programming (ILP)	20-25%	15-20%	18-22%	Very slow (hours)	Very poor (<50 devices)	Poor
Deep Q-Network (DQN)	30-35%	25-30%	28-35%	Moderate (minutes)	Good (500s devices)	Moderate
Actor-Critic (A3C)	35-40%	30-35%	32-40%	Moderate (minutes)	Good (500s devices)	Good
Proximal Policy Optimization (PPO)	38-42%	32-38%	35-42%	Moderate (minutes)	Good (1000s devices)	Very Good
Multi-Agent DRL (MADRL)	40-50%	35-45%	40-50%	Moderate-Slow (10 min)	Excellent (1000s+ devices)	Excellent
Graph Neural Network (GNN) + DRL	50-60%	40-50%	45-55%	Slow (30 min)	Excellent (10000s devices)	Excellent
Transformer + PPO + GNN	52-62%	42-52%	48-58%	Slow (30-60 min)	Excellent (10000s+ devices)	

6. LIGHTWEIGHT MODEL ARCHITECTURES

In addition to compression techniques applied to standard models, lightweight architectures designed for resource-constrained deployments offer superior accuracy–efficiency trade-offs (Belcastro et al., 2024).

Figure 5. Lightweight architecture efficiency comparison

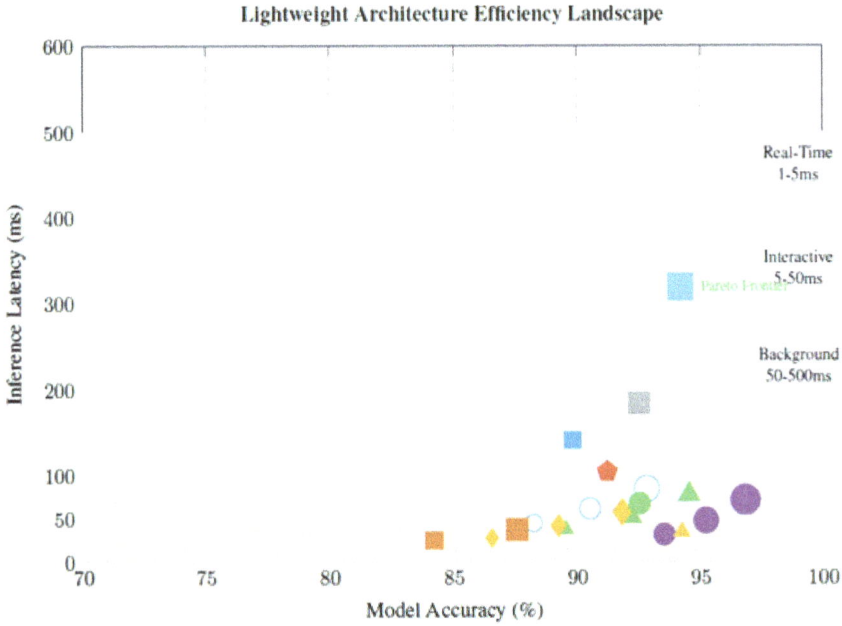

6.1 Efficient CNN Architectures

MobileNet and its variants employ depthwise separable convolutions, reducing the computational complexity by factors of 8–9 × compared to standard convolutions with minimal accuracy loss (Alsalem & Djemame, 2025). MobileNetV3 introduces automatic search-discovered efficient blocks, achieving a competitive accuracy with 40% fewer parameters than MobileNetV2 (Belcastro et al., 2024). ShuffleNet reduces computations through channel shuffling and group convolutions, thereby enabling efficient inference on resource-constrained devices. ShuffleNet achieves 13 GFLOPS at 50 ms latency on Raspberry Pi, sufficient for many real-time IoT (Alsalem & Djemame, 2025). EfficientNet applies compound scaling to the depth, width, and resolution simultaneously to discover models that achieve superior accuracy at a reduced computational cost. The EfficientNet scaling principle has become foundational for designing efficient architectures for diverse applications (Alsalem & Djemame, 2025).

6.2 Lightweight Recurrent Architectures

Recurrent neural networks enable the processing of temporal sequences, which are critical for sensor data analysis. Lightweight RNN variants address the challenge of deploying sequential models on edge device. Fast-Gated Recurrent Units (FGRNNs) and Fast RNNs reduce the computational complexity compared to LSTM and standard GRU units, while maintaining competitive accuracy. On Raspberry Pi platforms, an optimized FGRNN achieves human activity recognition with > 95% accuracy and 2–3 s inference latency per sequence. Unitary gated recurrent networks (UGRNNs) maintain gradient flow through unitary matrices, thereby enabling more efficient training convergence and reducing gradient explosion problems. When combined with low-rank parameterization and sparse retraining, UGRNNs achieve memory footprints of less than 100 KB while maintaining > 90% accuracy.

Table 4. Lightweight architecture performance on edge devices

Architecture		Model Size	Latency (RPi 4B)	Latency (Jetson Nano)	Accuracy (CIFAR-10)	Energy (mJ/ inference)	Throughput (FPS)
ResNet-50 (baseline)	25.5 M	102 MB	2500 ms	150 ms	96.5%	450	0.4
MobileNetV2	3.5 M	14 MB	180 ms	25 ms	94.2%	65	5.5
MobileNetV3	5.4 M	22 MB	220 ms	32 ms	95.1%	80	4.5
EfficientNet-B0	5.3 M	21 MB	150 ms	20 ms	95.3%	75	6.7
ShuffleNetV2	2.3 M	9 MB	120 ms	18 ms	92.8%	55	8.3
SqueezeNet	1.2 M	5 MB	90 ms	12 ms	90.5%	42	11.1
FGRNN (RNN variant)	0.5 M	2 MB	45 ms	8 ms	88.3% (HAR)	28	22.2
UGRNN (compressed)	0.08 M	0.32 MB	15 ms	3 ms	87.5% (HAR)	12	66.7
Spiking NN (FPGA)	0.1 M	0.4 MB	8 ms	2 ms	85.0%	2	125

6.3 Spiking Neural Networks

Spiking neural networks (SNNs) adopt biological inspiration and process information through discrete spike events rather than continuous activations. SNNs reduce energy consumption by several orders of magnitude compared to traditional artificial neural networks through event-driven computation. FPGA-based SNN accelerators designed for IoT applications achieve 2-3 orders of magnitude energy reduction compared to traditional DNNs. Eight-bit weight quantization, combined with frame-based computation and sparse encoding, reduces memory requirements while maintaining real-time processing capabilities.

7. REAL-TIME INFERENCE OPTIMIZATION

Deploying models for real-time inference on edge devices requires optimization at multiple levels: model architecture, inference engine, and hardware utilization (Reddy et al., 2025).

Figure 6. Model partitioning and split learning optimization

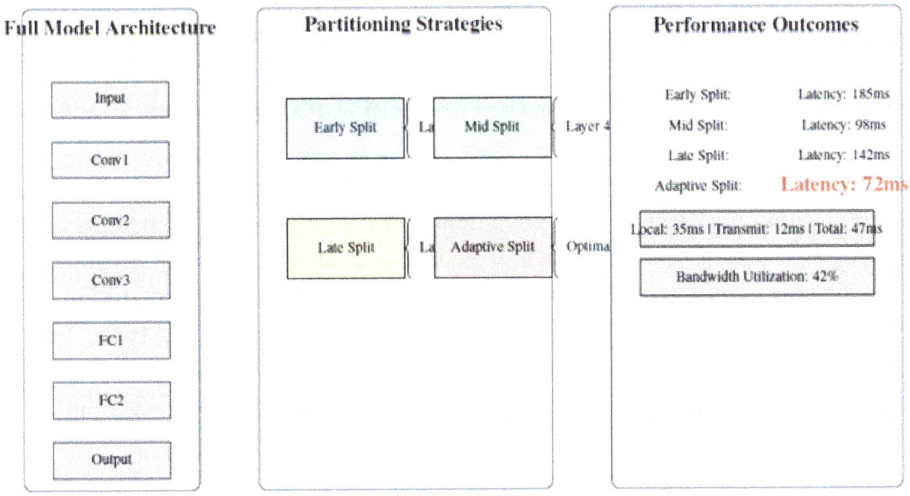

7.1 Layer Partitioning and Model Splitting

When a single-edge device cannot execute an entire model within latency constraints, model partitioning distributes the model across local and remote resources. The optimal partition point balances local computation, communication overhead, and total end-to-end latency. Genetic algorithms efficiently search the partition space and model computation and transmission delays through hardware profiling. GA-based methods achieve 74.38% optimization efficiency compared to 28.70% for brute-force approaches, finding near-optimal partitions that adapt to diverse device constraints and network conditions (Matam, 2025). Deep neural network partitioning strategy (DNNPaS) predicts layer-wise latency using external machine learning models that incorporate device metrics and network conditions. This approach reduces end-to-end latency by 30%–50% under various load conditions while efficiently utilizing available resources.

7.2 CPU-GPU Hybrid Execution

Integrated edge devices combine CPU and GPU resources for inference. EdgeNN adaptively employs zero-copy optimization by leveraging unified physical memory and implements a CPU–GPU hybrid execution, thereby enabling concurrent operation. EdgeNN's adaptive inference tuning technique analyzes complex inference structures by dividing computations into subtasks and intelligently assigning them to the CPU or GPU. The framework achieves 3. average speedup of 3.97 × on edge CPUs and 8.80× on some platforms, while providing 29.14× higher energy efficiency than CPU-only inference and 5.70× higher than discrete GPU approaches.

7.3 Specialized Inference Engines and Accelerators

TensorFlow Lite, ONNX Runtime, and TensorRT provide optimized inference engines specifically designed for edge deployment, incorporating operator fusion, memory optimization, and hardware-specific acceleration (Reddy et al., 2025). Specialized accelerators, including Neural Processing Units (NPUs), FPGAs, and ASICs, achieve speedups of orders of magnitude for specific model types. FPGA-based implementations of CNNs achieve a 32× throughput improvement with a 94.5% resource consumption reduction compared to the CPU-only baseline.

Table 5. Real-time inference optimization performance

Optimization Strategy	**Speedup (vs. Baseline)**	**Latency Reduction**	**Memory Usage**	**Energy Efficiency**	**Bandwidth Reduction**	**Inference Platform**
Baseline (Full Precision CPU)	1×	Baseline	Baseline	Baseline	Baseline	CPU
Post-Training Quantization	2-4×	50-75%	25-75%	30-40%	25-75%	CPU/Edge
Layer Pruning	2-3×	40-60%	40-60%	35-45%	Minimal	CPU/Edge
Operator Fusion	1.5-2×	30-50%	10-20%	15-25%	Minimal	CPU/FPGA
Model Partitioning (GA-optimized)	3.5-4×	60-75%	45-65%	50-65%	30-50%	Edge+Cloud
Layer Splitting (DNNPaS)	2-3×	30-50%	35-55%	40-55%	25-45%	Edge+Local

continued on following page

Table 5. Continued

Optimization Strategy	Speedup (vs. Baseline)	Latency Reduction	Memory Usage	Energy Efficiency	Bandwidth Reduction	Inference Platform
CPU-GPU Hybrid (EdgeNN)	3.97× (CPU), 8.8× (GPU)	60-75%	50-70%	29.14× (vs CPU), 5.7× (vs GPU)	40-60%	Integrated Edge
FPGA Acceleration	6-14×	75-95%	60-80%	70-85%	50-75%	FPGA
Specialized NPU (e.g., Coral TPU)	5-10×	70-90%	55-75%	75-90%	55-80%	TPU
Specialized ASIC	10-32×	85-97%	70-85%	85-95%	70-90%	ASI

8. APPLICATIONS AND CASE STUDIES

8.1 Smart Agriculture and Environmental Monitoring

Precision agriculture represents a compelling use case for device-edge-cloud continuum optimization, combining Internet of Things (IoT) sensor networks with deep learning for crop monitoring and disease prediction. The Adam optimizer-based deep neural network (AO-DNN) system is deployed on edge devices for local classification of crop diseases based on sensor data, with cloud-based fine-tuning and periodic retraining. Edge processing reduces data transmission by 95% while achieving 94% detection accuracy compared with 82–88% for traditional machine learning approaches. Agricultural environmental monitoring systems implement LoRaWAN for long-range transmission combined with pest recognition using TensorFlow, achieving 89% recognition accuracy while reducing cloud computing pressure through edge-based processing.

8.2 Industrial IoT and Predictive Maintenance

Industrial Internet of Things (IIoT) environments require real-time anomaly detection and predictive maintenance with stringent latency requirements. The Edge-IIoT Anomaly Framework (EIAF) integrates transfer learning with ResNet50 and autoencoders on edge devices. The EIAF achieved 97.2% anomaly detection accuracy, 2% false positive rate, and 178 ms latency with 94.5% resource consumption reduction compared to cloud-based approaches. Early detection enables proactive maintenance before failures occur, thereby reducing unplanned downtime and extending equipment lifetime. Industrial IoT (IIoT) environments demand highly efficient real-time anomaly detection and predictive maintenance systems to meet strict latency constraints and ensure continuous operation. The Edge-IIoT Anomaly Framework (EIAF) addresses these needs by leveraging transfer learning with ResNet50 and autoencoders directly on edge devices, minimizing reliance on cloud infrastructure. This local processing capability not only reduces communication delays but also significantly lowers resource consumption, achieving a 94.5% reduction compared to traditional cloud-based methods. By integrating these advanced AI models at the edge, EIAF can swiftly identify anomalies with 97.2% accuracy and maintain a low false positive rate of 2%, all while operating within a latency of 178 milliseconds.

The benefits of the EIAF extend beyond detection accuracy and efficiency; its early anomaly identification facilitates proactive maintenance strategies that prevent unexpected equipment failures. This proactive approach reduces unplanned downtime, which is critical for maintaining productivity and operational continuity in industrial settings. Furthermore, by extending the lifetime of equipment through timely interventions, the EIAF contributes to cost savings and sustainability efforts. Overall, the framework exemplifies how edge computing combined with sophisticated AI techniques can transform IIoT maintenance practices, delivering robust, low-latency, and resource-efficient solutions tailored to the demanding industrial landscape.

8.3 Healthcare and Medical Monitoring

Wearable medical devices continuously monitor patient vital signs and detect anomalies that require immediate intervention. Lightweight CNN architectures optimized for edge devices enable privacy-preserving real-time analysis. Knowledge distillation frameworks compress high-capacity teacher networks into lightweight student models, maintaining 97% of teacher accuracy while reducing parameters by 99%. These compressed models enable real-time epilepsy seizure prediction on IoT devices with inference latency < 100 ms (Zhang et al., 2025). Wearable medical devices leverage continuous monitoring of patient vital signs to promptly identify critical health anomalies, facilitating timely medical interventions. The integration of lightweight CNN architectures specifically optimized for edge devices plays a crucial role in enabling real-time data processing directly on the device. This approach not only enhances the speed of analysis but also preserves patient privacy by minimizing the need to transmit sensitive data to external servers. Such edge-optimized models are designed to operate within the constrained computational resources of wearable devices, ensuring efficient and effective health monitoring without compromising performance.

Knowledge distillation techniques are employed to further optimize these models for deployment on resource-limited Internet of Things (IoT) devices. This process involves transferring knowledge from a large, high-capacity teacher network to a smaller, lightweight student model, thereby significantly reducing the number of parameters by up to 99% while maintaining approximately 97% of the teacher's accuracy. The resulting compressed models are capable of performing complex tasks such as real-time epilepsy seizure prediction with inference latencies under 100 milliseconds. This combination of model compression and edge optimization facilitates the practical implementation of advanced predictive analytics in wearable medical devices, enabling continuous, privacy-preserving health monitoring with rapid response capabilities.

8.4 Autonomous Systems and Computer Vision

Real-time object detection in autonomous driving requires a sub-100-ms latency, which is unsuitable for cloud processing. Edge–cloud collaborative frameworks combine lightweight detection models on edge devices with advanced refinement models in the cloud. E^{2}L (Edge-Embedded Lightweight) object detection with attention mechanisms achieves real-time processing on Jetson Xavier NX while maintaining high accuracy comparable to YOLOv4. A distributed framework balances edge speed requirements with cloud accuracy refinement through fuzzy neural network decision-making.

Table 6. Application case study performance metrics

Application Domain	Model Architecture			Energy/Inference		Deployment Tier	Key Achievement
Smart Agriculture (Crop Disease)	AO-DNN (ResNet-50 compressed)	94%	250 ms	180 mJ	8 MB	Edge	95% data transmission reduction; 22% accuracy improvement vs. ML baselines
Agriculture (Environmental)	CNN-LoRaWAN	89%	150 ms	120 mJ	5 MB	Edge	Real-time pest recognition; 89% accuracy with low cloud pressure
Industrial IoT (Anomaly Detection)	Transfer Learning (ResNet50 + AE)	97.2%	178 ms	140 mJ	12 MB	Edge	2% false positive rate; 94.5% resource reduction vs. cloud
Healthcare (Seizure Prediction)	KD-Compressed CNN-BiLSTM	97% (teacher: 99%)	85 ms	95 mJ	0.5 MB	IoT Device	99% model compression; 69% latency reduction (Liu et al., 2025)
Healthcare (Anomaly Detection)	CNN-LSTM-VAE (Trust-Aware)	94.3%	160 ms	130 mJ	8 MB	Edge	96.1% access decision accuracy; 98.5% attack mitigation

continued on following page

Table 6. Continued

Application Domain	Model Architecture			Energy/Inference		Deployment Tier	Key Achievement
Autonomous Driving (Object Detection)	E^2L-YOLO with Attention	96.5%	45 ms	200 mJ	15 MB	Edge+Cloud	Real-time on Jetson Xavier NX; fuzzy decision-making
Wildlife Monitoring	YOLOv8/EfficientDet Lite	92-95%	100-150 ms	250 mJ	20 MB	Edge	6-10 FPS on Raspberry Pi; superior performance-per-watt (Qu et al., 2024)
Wearable Activity Recognition	FGRNN (Fast GRU)	95%+	200-300 ms	85 mJ	2 MB	IoT Device	2-3 seconds latency per sequence; 95%+ accuracy
UAV Object Detection	RetinaNet ResNet-50 (Optimized)	70% mAP	200-250 ms	220 mJ	25 MB	Edge	14-25 FPS on FPGA; 60% mAP on embedded GPU
Medical Imaging (Skin Cancer)	Federated CNN	98.8% (global)	10 ms	50 mJ			

9. OPEN CHALLENGES AND FUTURE DIRECTIONS

9.1 Accuracy-Efficiency Trade-Offs

The fundamental trade-off between model accuracy and computational efficiency remains challenging. Aggressive compression techniques achieving 90% parameter reduction may incur 5%–10% accuracy losses. Domain-specific optimization remains necessary, as one-size-fits-all compression strategies prove suboptimal across diverse applications (Belcastro et al., 2024). Future research directions include adaptive compression that adjusts compression ratios based on inference accuracy requirements and importance-aware compression that preserves critical model components for specific tasks.

9.2 Hardware Heterogeneity and Fragmentation

The edge cloud continuum comprises diverse hardware platforms, such as ARM processors, Qualcomm Snapdragon, NPUs, FPGAs, and ASICs. Each platform requires specialized optimization, making portable, hardware-agnostic solutions challenging (Reddy et al., 2025). Hardware-aware deployment frameworks that automatically adapt models to diverse platforms are a promising research direction.

Standardized benchmarking methodologies for edge AI could facilitate fair comparisons across platforms and guide optimization efforts (Belcastro et al., 2024).

9.3 Non-IID Data and Concept Drift

Federated learning with non-independent and identically distributed (non-IID) data across edge devices introduces statistical heterogeneity that degrades convergence and final model accuracy. Real-world IoT deployments exhibit concept drift as environmental conditions evolve. Continual learning approaches that adapt models to changing data distributions without full retraining represent an important frontier. The combination of FL with personalized models that capture device-specific characteristics, while benefiting from global knowledge, appears promising.

9.4 Scalability and Standardization

As Internet of Things (IoT) deployments scale to millions of devices, the management, versioning, and synchronization of models across the continuum become increasingly complex. The lack of standardized deployment frameworks, model formats, and communication protocols hinders interoperability. MLOps for the edge, which incorporate continuous integration and deployment practices optimized for edge environments, remain an emerging research area. Standardized model formats, containerization approaches, and orchestration frameworks tailored for the edge-cloud continuum can significantly accelerate adoption.

9.5 Energy Efficiency and Sustainable AI

Although compression and lightweight architectures reduce energy consumption, quantifying the true energy efficiency across the continuum remains challenging. Energy-aware optimization must consider inference as well as training, data collection, and communication overhead. Future work should focus on developing comprehensive energy budgeting frameworks and energy-efficient hardware designs, including processing-in-memory (PIM) accelerators and neuromorphic computing approaches (Belcastro et al., 2024).

10. CONCLUSION

Optimizing deep learning architectures for the device-edge-cloud continuum requires the synergistic integration of model compression, adaptive architecture design, and collaborative computing strategies. Model compression techniques, such as quantization, pruning, knowledge distillation, and hardware-aware NAS, enable the deployment of intelligent models on resource-constrained devices. Distributed learning approaches, including federated learning and multi-agent reinforcement learning, facilitate collaborative intelligence while preserving privacy and reducing communication overhead. Dynamic task offloading and adaptive model switching enable intelligent resource allocation across the continuum. Rapid advancements in edge computing hardware, including specialized NPUs and efficient processors, combined with algorithmic innovations in lightweight neural networks, have created unprecedented opportunities for intelligent IoT applications. Real-world deployments in agriculture, healthcare, industrial monitoring, and autonomous systems have demonstrated the practical viability and significant benefits of optimized distributed deep learning. However, significant challenges remain: the accuracy-efficiency trade-off, hardware heterogeneity, non-IID data distributions, and standardization issues demand continued research attention. Future research directions include adaptive compression techniques, universal hardware-aware deployment frameworks, continual learning approaches for concept drift, and comprehensive energy efficiency metrics. By addressing these challenges through continued algorithmic innovation, hardware–software co-design, and standardization efforts, the community can unlock the full potential of intelligent, responsive, and energy-efficient Internet of Things (IoT) systems operating seamlessly across the device–edge–cloud continuum.

REFERENCES

Alsalem, L., & Djemame, K. (2025). Task scheduling in edge computing environments: A hierarchical cluster-based federated deep reinforcement learning approach. *Proceedings of the ACM Symposium on Edge Computing*, 3774691. DOI: 10.1145/3773274.3774691

Aravindh, G., & Sridhar, K. P. (2026). Cloud-Continuum-Based Deep Learning Optimization Framework for Next-Generation Healthcare Data Performance on IoT Platform. *International Journal of Advanced Computer Science and Applications*, *17*(2), 618. DOI: 10.14569/IJACSA.2026.0170262

Arzovs, A., Judvaitis, J., Nesenbergs, K., & Selavo, L. (2024). Distributed learning in the IoT-edge-cloud continuum. *Machine Learning and Knowledge Extraction*, *6*(1), 15. DOI: 10.3390/make6010015

Belcastro, L., Marozzo, F., Presta, A., & Talia, D. (2024). A Spark-based task allocation solution for machine learning in the edge-cloud continuum. *IEEE International Conference on Distributed Computing and Sensing*, 61029. https://doi.org/DOI: 10.1109/DCOSS-IoT61029.2024.00090

Ben Atitallah, S., Driss, M., & Ghézala, H. (2025). FedMicro-IDA: A federated learning and microservices-based framework for IoT data analytics. *arXiv preprint arXiv:2510.20852*. https://doi.org//arXiv.2510.20852DOI: 10.48550

Chhabra, G. S., Rajareddy, G. N. V., Mahapatra, A., Mangalampalli, S., Sahoo, K., Sethi, D., & Mishra, K. (2025). Deep learning-centric task offloading in IoT-fog-cloud continuum: A state-of-the-art review, open research issues, and future directions. *IEEE Access : Practical Innovations, Open Solutions*, *13*, 3599190. DOI: 10.1109/ACCESS.2025.3599190

Gao, X. (2025). Toward real-time and efficient edge intelligence: Advances and challenges in lightweight machine learning. *Nature Machine Intelligence*, *7*(8), 36. DOI: 10.61173/bwn0ez36

Giannopoulos, A., Paralikas, I., Spantideas, S., & Trakadas, P. (2024). HOODIE: Hybrid computation offloading via distributed deep reinforcement learning in delay-aware cloud-edge continuum. *IEEE Open Journal of the Communications Society*, *5*, 3514456. DOI: 10.1109/OJCOMS.2024.3514456

Knorst, T., Jordan, M., Korol, G., Rutzig, M. B., & Beck, A. C. S. (2025). Adaptive model switching for dynamic inference serving in the IoT-edge-cloud continuum. *Proceedings of the 15th Brazilian Embedded Systems Seminar*, 11288829. DOI: 10.1109/SBESC68008.2025.11288829

Lee, J., & Na, W. (2022). A survey on mobile edge computing architectures for deep learning models. *IEEE International Conference on ICT Convergence*, 9952954. DOI: 10.1109/ICTC55196.2022.9952954

Lilhore, U., Simaiya, S., Sharma, Y. K., Rai, A. K., Padmaja, S. M., Nabilal, K. V., Kumar, V., Alroobaea, R., & Alsufyani, H. (2025). Cloud-edge hybrid deep learning framework for scalable IoT resource optimization. *Journal of Cloud Computing (Heidelberg, Germany)*, *10*(1), 729. DOI: 10.1186/s13677-025-00729-w

Liu, J., Du, Y., Yang, K., Wu, J., Wang, Y., Hu, X., Wang, Z., Liu, Y., Sun, P., Boukerche, A., & Leung, V. C. M. (2025). Edge-cloud collaborative computing on distributed intelligence and model optimization: A survey. *IEEE Communications Surveys and Tutorials*, *28*(2), 3669216. DOI: 10.1109/COMST.2026.3669216

Matam, P. (2025). Smart crop monitoring and disease prediction using IoT sensors and deep learning models deployed on edge-cloud architecture. *IEEE International Conference on Advanced Computing, Robotics, and Sensors*, 11324361. DOI: 10.1109/ICACRS67045.2025.11324361

Moghaddasi, K., Rajabi, S., Gharehchopogh, F. S., & Ghaffari, A. (2024). An advanced deep reinforcement learning algorithm for three-layer D2D-edge-cloud computing architecture for efficient task offloading in the Internet of Things. *Sustainable Computing : Informatics and Systems*, *44*, 100992. DOI: 10.1016/j.suscom.2024.100992

Myakala, P. K. (2025). Distributed data intelligence in the edge-to-cloud continuum: A survey of architectures, models, and applications. *IEEE International Conference on Data Intelligence and Communications*, 11135068. DOI: 10.1109/ICDICI66477.2025.11135068

Nieto, G., Iglesia, I. D. L., López-Novoa, U., & Perfecto, C. (2024). Deep reinforcement learning techniques for dynamic task offloading in the 5G edge-cloud continuum. *Journal of Cloud Computing (Heidelberg, Germany)*, *24*(1), 658. DOI: 10.1186/s13677-024-00658-0

Petrakis, K., Agorogiannis, E., Antonopoulos, G., Anagnostopoulos, T., Grigoropoulos, N., Veroni, E., Berne, A., Azaiez, S., Benomar, Z., Kakoulidis, H., Prasinos, M., Sotiriades, P., Mavrothalassitis, P., & Alexopoulos, K. (2025). Enhancing DevOps practices in the IoT–edge–cloud continuum: Architecture, integration, and software orchestration demonstrated in the COGNIFOG framework. *Software*, *4*(2), 10. DOI: 10.3390/software4020010

Qu, Y., Yu, S., Gao, L., Sood, K., & Xiang, Y. (2024). Blockchained dual-asynchronous federated learning services for digital twin empowered edge-cloud continuum. *IEEE Transactions on Services Computing*, *17*(3), 3382952. DOI: 10.1109/TSC.2024.3382952

Reddy, C. K., Rajesh, P., Chellammal, S., Muthuselvan, E. M., & Swathi, A. (2025). Real-time embedded system optimization using edge computing and lightweight deep learning architectures for data efficiency. *Proceedings of ICSOFT 2025*, 13870900004919. DOI: 10.5220/0013870900004919

Shuvo, M. M. H., Islam, S. K., Cheng, J., & Morshed, B. I. (2022). Efficient acceleration of deep learning inference on resource-constrained edge devices: A review. *Proceedings of the IEEE*, *110*(12), 3226481. DOI: 10.1109/JPROC.2022.3226481

Sıcakyüz, Ç., Asaad, R. R., Almufti, S. M., & Rustamova, N. R. (2024). Adaptive deep learning architectures for real-time data streams in edge-computing environments. *Quarterly Technical Journal*, *3*(2), 25. DOI: 10.48161/qtj.v3n2a25

Singh, G., Rajareddy, G. N. V., Mahapatra, A., Mangalampalli, S., Sahoo, K., Sethi, D., & Mishra, K. (2025). Deep learning-centric task offloading in IoT-fog-cloud continuum: A state-of-the-art review, open research issues, and future directions. *IEEE Access : Practical Innovations, Open Solutions*, *13*, 144241–144270. Advance online publication. DOI: 10.1109/ACCESS.2025.3599190

Sivasankaran, S., Al-Safarini, M. Y., Vaishnavi, V., Bhavana, M., & Dinesh, M. (2025, November). Application of Edge-Based Deep Learning in Industrial IoT: Employing the Compact Neural Networks for Local Industrial Monitoring. In *2025 International Conference on Digital Innovations for Sustainable Solutions (ICDISS)* (pp. 1-7). IEEE.

Wang, Z., Goudarzi, M., Gong, M., & Buyya, R. (2025). A knowledge distillation-empowered adaptive federated reinforcement learning framework for multi-domain IoT applications scheduling. *arXiv preprint arXiv:2508.21328*. https://doi.org//arXiv .2508.21328DOI: 10.48550

Wang, Z., Tan, H., Tan-Y, N., Duy-Dong, L., Thai-Thinh, D., & Khoa, T. A. (2025). Latency-aware split learning optimization via genetic algorithms. *ACM Proceedings of the 31st Annual Symposium on Parallelism in Algorithms and Architectures*, 3734433. DOI: 10.1145/3733566.3734433

Zhang, F., Zhang, C., Guan, J., Zhou, Q., Chen, K., Zhang, X., He, B., Zhai, J., & Du, X. (2025). Breaking the edge: Enabling efficient neural network inference on integrated edge devices. *IEEE Transactions on Cloud Computing*, *13*(2), 3559346. DOI: 10.1109/TCC.2025.3559346

Zhang, J., Wang, Y., Cai, Y., Bi, B., Chen, Q., & Zhang, Y. (2025). A low power spiking neural network accelerator on FPGA for real-time edge computing. *IEEE International Conference on AI and IoT Infrastructure Systems*, 11051374. DOI: 10.1109/ICAISISAS64483.2025.11051374

Zhantileuov, E., Idrees, A. K., & Schuster, R. (2025). DNNPaS: Deep neural network partitioning strategy for optimizing end-to-end latency in dynamic mobile edge computing. *IEEE International Conference on Cloud Computing*, 00015. DOI: 10.1109/FiCloud66139.2025.00015

ADDITIONAL READING

Chen, X., Wu, H., Li, R., & Jiao, P. (2021). DDPQN: An efficient DNN offloading strategy in local-edge-cloud collaborative environments. *IEEE Transactions on Services Computing, 14*(9), 3116597.

Chen, X., Zhang, J., Lin, B., Chen, Z., Wolter, K., & Min, G. (2021). Energy-efficient offloading for DNN-based smart IoT systems in cloud-edge environments. *IEEE Transactions on Parallel and Distributed Systems, 32*(7), 3100298.

Ferrari, P., Rinaldi, S., Sisinni, E., Colombo, F., Ghelfi, F., Maffei, D., & Malara, M. (2019). Performance evaluation of full-cloud and edge-cloud architectures for industrial IoT anomaly detection based on deep learning. *IEEE MetroIoT*, 9792860.

Kim, T., Park, H., Jin, Y., Lee, S., & Lee, S. (2023). Partition placement and resource allocation for multiple DNN-based applications in heterogeneous IoT environments. *IEEE Internet of Things Journal, 10*(3), 3235993. DOI: 10.1109/JIOT.2023.3235993

Min, X., Wu, H., Peng, G., & Wolter, K. (2021). DDPQN: An efficient DNN offloading strategy in local-edge-cloud collaborative environments. *IEEE Transactions on Services Computing, 15*(1), 3116597.

Qu, G., Wu, H., Li, R., & Jiao, P. (2021). DMRO: A deep meta reinforcement learning-based task offloading framework for edge-cloud computing. *IEEE Transactions on Network and Service Management, 18*(3), 3087258. DOI: 10.1109/TNSM.2021.3087258

Yang, C. Y., Kuo, J. J., Sheu, J. P., & Zheng, K. J. (2021). Cooperative distributed deep neural network deployment with edge computing. *IEEE International Conference on Communications*, 9500668. DOI: 10.1109/ICC42927.2021.9500668

Zhang, W., Yang, D., Wu, W., Peng, H. X., Zhang, N., Zhang, H., & Shen, X. (2021). Optimizing federated learning in distributed industrial IoT: A multi-agent approach. *IEEE Journal on Selected Areas in Communications*, *39*(7), 3118352. DOI: 10.1109/JSAC.2021.3118352

Chapter 8
Scalable Training, Optimization, and Deployment Strategies for Deep Learning Across Edge and Cloud Layers

Anum Mehmood
http://orcid.org/0009-0004-8105-1690
College of Food Science and Engineering, Hainan University, Haikou City, China

Yonis Gulzar
http://orcid.org/0000-0002-6515-1569
Department of Management Information Systems, College of Business Administration, King Faisal University, Saudi Arabia

Yazeed Yasin Ghadi
http://orcid.org/0000-0002-7121-495X
Department of Computer Science and Software Engineering, Al Ain University, Al Ain, UAE

Mamatkhujaev Otabek
Department of International Scientific Journals and Ratings, Alfraganus University, Tashkent, Uzbekistan

Babayev Shavkat
Department of Taxation and Taxation, Tashkent State University of Economics, Tashkent, Uzbekistan

Ulugbek Bobamuratov
Department of Information Technology and Exact Sciences, Termez University of Economics and Service, Termez, Uzbekistan

Mukhammad Khabibullaev
Department of Computer Science, Urgench State University, Urgench, Uzbekistan

Sardor Sabirov
http://orcid.org/0009-0008-0504-7568
Department of General Professional Sciences, Mamun University, Khiva, Uzbekistan

DOI: 10.4018/979-8-2600-0615-3.ch008

ABSTRACT

This chapter examines scalable strategies for developing and managing deep learning systems across edge and cloud layers. It explores distributed training frameworks, federated learning, model compression, pruning, quantization, knowledge distillation, and resource-aware optimization techniques that improve efficiency while maintaining model accuracy. The chapter further discusses cloud-edge collaboration architectures, real-time inference mechanisms, containerization, orchestration technologies, and AI lifecycle management for large-scale deployments. Emerging trends such as edge intelligence, TinyML, serverless AI, and autonomous model adaptation are also reviewed. By integrating scalable learning, optimization, and deployment methodologies, organizations can build robust, low-latency, and cost-effective AI systems capable of supporting next-generation intelligent applications across heterogeneous computing environments.

INTRODUCTION TO DEEP LEARNING IN EDGE–CLOUD ENVIRONMENTS

With the intersection of deep learning and edge and cloud computing, intelligent system design, deployment, and scaling has been changed. The traditional centralized models of computing are being increasingly eclipsed by distributed models that take computation nearer to the data sources. The reasons behind this change are necessitating real-time processing, lowering latency and ensuring that network and computational resources are well utilized (Li et al., 2017).

Deep learning as an artificial intelligence application is based on massive amounts of data and computing capabilities to train complex models. Historically, cloud computing has offered the platform on which these needs may be met, with the ability to provide scalable storage and processing capacities. Nevertheless, the increase in the need of applications with low latency, including autonomous driving, intelligent farming, and monitoring in healthcare facilities has emphasized the drawbacks of solely cloud-based solutions (Han et al., 2015).

Edge computing can be used to overcome these constraints by processing data at the point of origin. With the implementation of the deep learning models on the edge devices (sensors, smartphones, and embedded systems), one can obtain the faster inference and enhance the responsiveness. This paradigm gives less reliance on constant cloud connectivity and low usage of bandwidth.

Combining edge and cloud environments, the hybrid architecture will combine the strengths of both paradigms. In those systems, model training and large-scale data analytics are normally performed on the cloud, whereas real-time inference and localized decision-making are done on the edge. The joint method improves the performance and scalability of the system (Howard et al., 2017).

Distribution of the computational tasks is one of the major issues in edgecloud environments. Deep learning models are large and resource-intensive and are not easily executable on edge devices with limited processing capability and memory. This has seen the emergence of methods like model partitioning, model offloading, in which some portion of a model is placed on the edge and others are run in the cloud.

Data management and privacy is another significant factor. Edge computing provides the ability to process sensitive data locally, eliminating the necessity to send it to the central servers. This is especially critical in its use in applications that require personal or confidential information. Simultaneously, one can use the cloud to collect and process anonymized data to enhance the performance of the models (Zhou et al., 2019).

Figure 1 shows Deep Learning in Edge–Cloud Environments

Figure 1. Deep learning in edge–cloud environments

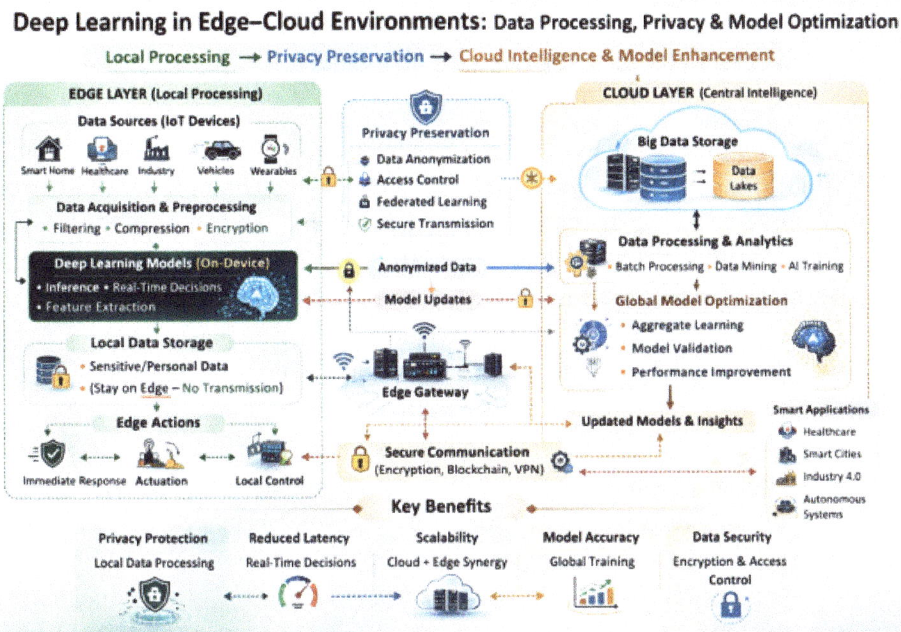

The hardware technology has also contributed to the realization of deep learning at the edge due to the advancement of hardware technologies. Specialised processors like GPUs, TPUs and neural processing units have rendered it possible to execute intricate models with small devices. Such technological advances have catapulted the implementation of edge-based deep learning in different fields.

Connection of edge and cloud components is a key aspect that makes the system efficient. The data transfer protocols and adaptive communication schemes are needed to balance the latency-bandwidth and energy consumption. Such systems should be designed with dynamic conditions of networks and fluctuating workloads (Shi et al., 2016).

Scalability is one of the core concerns of edge-clouds. With the ever-increasing number of interconnected devices, systems should be able to process larger volumes of data and perform more calculation. This involves the existence of strong architectures that enhance distributed processing, load balancing, and fault tolerance.

In general, the combination of deep learning and edge and cloud computing is an important step in the context of intelligent systems. With the ability to provide the scalability, efficiency, and responsiveness of the edge to the computational power of the cloud, one can implement scalable, efficient, and adaptive solutions. This paradigm is the groundwork towards subsequent innovation in distributed artificial intelligence and practical applications (Satyanarayanan, 2017).

SCALABLE TRAINING TECHNIQUES FOR DISTRIBUTED DEEP LEARNING

Scalable training methods are also needed to empower deep learning models to deal with the vast amount, speed, and diversity of data being produced in current applications. Due to the increased size of datasets and the complexity of models, conventional single-machine training methods can no longer be used. Distributed deep learning has become a solution, whereby the training processes can be distributed across many computing nodes to enhance learning and efficiency.

Data parallelism is one of the essential techniques of distributed training in which the training data is distributed among multiple devices or nodes. The nodes work with a part of the data and calculate gradients separately. These gradients are accumulated to update a common model. The method is popular because it is simple and easily scalable to train on clusters of GPUs or even cloud instances (Sze et al., 2017).

Another strategy that is important is model parallelism which is very beneficial when the model is very large and would not fit in the memory of only one machine. Under this method, the various components of a neural network are spread among various devices and the calculations are done in a synchronized way. Although model parallelism can be used to train larger architectures, it presents problems with regard to communication overhead and synchronization.

Hybrid parallelism integrates data and model parallelism in order to scale at a higher rate and use resources more effectively. With the help of the advantages of the two techniques, hybrid approaches can effectively work with large datasets and complicated models. This is specifically applicable in edge cloud environments, where heterogeneous resources are required to be effectively used (Abadi et al., 2016).

Federated learning has attracted a lot of popularity as a decentralized method of training. The paradigm in this case trains the models locally on edge devices based on their own data and exchanges model updates with a central server. This method improves data privacy, and the communication expenses are minimized, hence it is applicable in application where data is incapable of being centralized.

The most significant issue in distributed training is the efficiency of communication. Gradient compression, quantization, and asynchronous updates are some of the techniques of reducing the amount of data transferred between nodes. Effective communication guidelines can be used to reduce the latency and enhance the general performance of the training particularly in low bandwidth environments.

Scalable training is also concerned with load balancing and resource allocation. Work loads are not balanced, thus this may result in bottlenecks and wastages. They use advanced algorithms in scheduling and dynamic strategies in the management of resources so that the computational tasks can be distributed uniformly among the nodes (Chen et al., 2018).

The other important feature of distributed deep learning systems is fault tolerance. Development in a large-scale environment is bound to fail, and the systems should be constructed in a way that fails without major problems. To ensure continuity and reliability of training, checkpointing, redundancy and recovery mechanisms are often employed.

The use of cloud infrastructure in scalable training cannot be underestimated. Cloud platforms offer scalable resources which can be adapted on demand depending on the training needs. This flexibility enables researchers and practitioners to test with other configurations and maximize performance without making large initial investment.

In general, the present-day distributed deep learning systems rely on scalable training methods. Through parallelism, effective communication and sound management of resources, the techniques can help in the development of high performance models that can deal with complex real-life issues. Scalable training will still be a research and innovation area to focus on as the implementation of edge-cloud integration is constantly being developed.

MODEL OPTIMIZATION STRATEGIES FOR RESOURCE-CONSTRAINED SYSTEMS

Model optimization plays a critical role in enabling deep learning systems to operate efficiently within resource-constrained environments, particularly at the edge. Edge devices such as IoT sensors, mobile phones, and embedded systems often have limited computational power, memory, and energy capacity. Therefore, optimizing deep learning models is essential to ensure that they can perform inference effectively without compromising performance or accuracy.

One of the most widely used optimization techniques is model compression, which aims to reduce the size of a neural network while maintaining its predictive capabilities. Compression techniques include weight pruning, parameter sharing, and low-rank factorization. These methods eliminate redundant or less important parameters, resulting in lighter models that are more suitable for deployment on constrained devices (Wang et al., 2019).

Quantization is another effective strategy that reduces the precision of model parameters and computations. By converting floating-point values into lower-bit representations such as 8-bit integers, quantization significantly decreases memory usage and computational requirements. This approach not only accelerates inference but also reduces energy consumption, making it highly suitable for edge applications.

Pruning techniques focus on removing unnecessary connections or neurons from a neural network. Structured pruning eliminates entire filters or layers, while unstructured pruning removes individual weights. Both approaches aim to simplify the model architecture, leading to faster execution and reduced resource usage. However, careful tuning is required to avoid degradation in model accuracy.

Knowledge distillation is a technique in which a smaller, lightweight model, often referred to as the student, learns to replicate the behavior of a larger, more complex model known as the teacher. This process enables the student model to achieve comparable performance while being significantly more efficient. Knowledge distillation is particularly useful when deploying models on devices with strict resource limitations (McMahan et al., 2017).

Another important optimization approach is neural architecture search, which automates the design of efficient model architectures tailored to specific hardware constraints. By exploring a large search space of possible architectures, this technique identifies models that offer an optimal balance between accuracy and efficiency. Hardware-aware architecture search further enhances performance by considering device-specific characteristics.

Edge-specific optimizations also include the use of lightweight architectures such as MobileNets, SqueezeNet, and EfficientNet variants. These models are specifically designed to operate under limited resources, incorporating depthwise separable convolutions and other efficiency-driven design principles. Such architectures provide a strong foundation for deploying deep learning in real-world edge scenarios.

Runtime optimization techniques are equally important in improving performance. These include operator fusion, memory reuse, and efficient scheduling of computations. By optimizing how operations are executed during inference, these methods reduce latency and improve throughput without altering the model structure (Kairouz & McMahan, 2021).

Energy efficiency is a key consideration in resource-constrained systems. Optimization strategies must not only reduce computational load but also minimize power consumption. Techniques such as dynamic voltage scaling, adaptive inference, and early exit mechanisms help in achieving energy-efficient model execution, which is crucial for battery-powered devices.

Overall, model optimization strategies are essential for bridging the gap between the high computational demands of deep learning and the limited capabilities of edge devices. By combining multiple optimization techniques, it is possible to develop models that are both efficient and accurate, enabling scalable deployment across diverse edge–cloud environments (Li et al., 2019).

EDGE–CLOUD COLLABORATIVE ARCHITECTURES AND FRAMEWORKS

Edge cloud collaborative architectures are a hybrid computing model which combines the advantages of the edge and cloud environments to facilitate an effective implementation of deep learning. These architectures are aimed at distributing intelligently the computational tasks across the layers so that they will perform optimally with reduced latency and minimal use of the resources. They use centralized and de-centralized processing to provide scalable and adaptive intelligent systems.

Figure 2 shows Edge–Cloud Collaborative Architectures and Frameworks

Figure 2. Edge–cloud collaborative architectures and frameworks

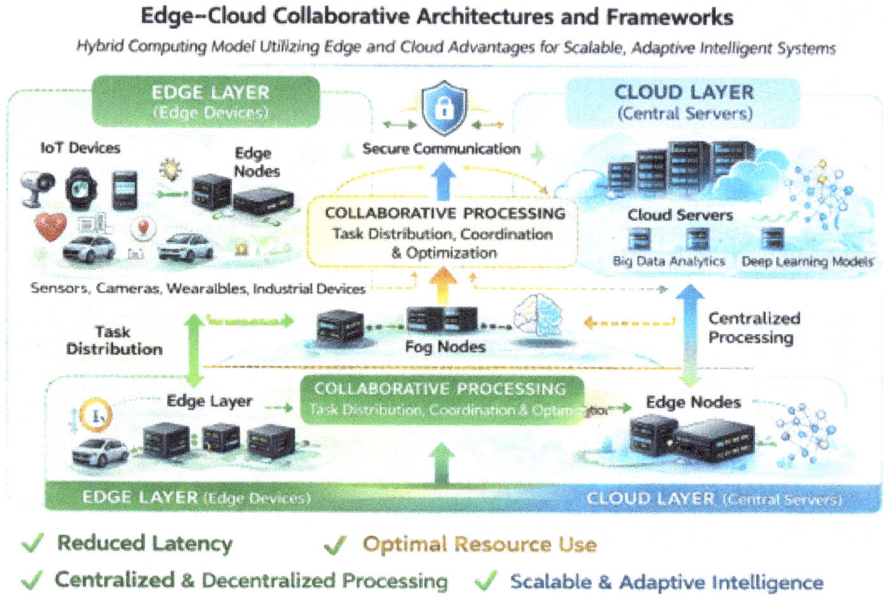

The cloud is usually the only node the bulk of the processing work with in such collaborative systems, including large-scale model training, data aggregation, and long-term storage. The edge, in its turn, does real-time data processing and inference near the source of data. Such a decomposition of roles enables systems to address the needs of latency sensitive applications and still realize the computational benefits of the cloud infrastructure (Zhang et al., 2021).

The primary characteristic of edge-cloud collaboration is the division of tasks, as various parts of a deep learning pipeline are packed on different levels. As an example, lightweight inference and initial data preprocessing may be run at the edge, with more complicated computations being sent to the cloud. Such strategy helps to balance workload and increase the effectiveness of the system.

The other relevant strategy in collaborative architectures is model partitioning. Under this method, a deep neural network is split into bits, where part of the network layers are run in edge devices and the remainder in cloud servers. This enables the resource-constrained devices to only be able to compute part of the computation, offloading them, but still enjoy the privileges of having the entire model (Bhatti et al., 2023).

Structures that are facilitating edge-cloud collaboration have changed to allow a smooth integration and coordination. System and application tools like Kubernetes, TensorFlow Federated, and edge AI frameworks are useful in the management of distributed workloads, communication coordination, and system scalability. Such frameworks allow application developers to deploy and administer applications in a heterogeneous environment easily.

Inter-cloud and edge-layer communications are also a very important element of such architectures. Effective data communication tools and reconfigurable communication standards are needed to reduce the latency and bandwidth consumption. Data compression, selective transmission as well as event-driven communication techniques aid in streamlining interactions among layers (Bhatti et al., 2023).

Security and privacy are also the key issues with edge-cloud collaborative systems. Because information is often handled in various places, the security of transmission and accessibility must be guaranteed. Ensuring privacy Edge computing can be more privacy-enhancing, as sensitive information is stored locally, and data transfer to the cloud is secured by encryption and secure communication tools.

Resource management is critical in ensuring the performance of the system. The workload and network conditions are also changing, which requires dynamic allocation of the computational resources, load balancing, and smart scheduling. More sophisticated orchestration will make sure that work is performed effectively on both edge and cloud layers (Bhatti et al., 2023).

One of the main issues of the creation of collaborative frameworks is interoperability and standardization. A large range of devices, platforms and communication protocols means that to have a seamless integration, standard interfaces and protocols are required. This is the direction efforts are assisting in the formation of more integrated and flexible systems.

Altogether, edge -cloud collaborative architectures and models offer a powerful background of implementing scalable and efficient deep learning applications. These systems provide the future of distributed artificial intelligence by integrating the distributed intelligence with centralized coordination, thus making them necessary to provide real-time responsiveness, better resource management and increased adaptability.

DEPLOYMENT AND ORCHESTRATION OF DEEP LEARNING MODELS

The implementation and coordination of deep learning models are essential parts of the process of moving on to the actual world applications after creating models. After training and optimizing a model the model should be effectively deployed on edges and cloud environments to promote reliable and scalable inference. In this process, infrastructure, system design and operational requirement are taken into consideration keenly.

There are different model deployment strategies based on the requirements of the application and system architecture. The models in cloud-centric deployments are hosted on servers in key centers and accessed via APIs, which allow scalability and simple maintenance. On the contrary, edge deployment deploys models directly to devices, enabling real-time inference and lower latency. Hybrid methods involve a combination of the two strategies so as to exploit the benefits of the two environments (Li et al., 2024).

Containerization is another technique that has gained a large following in deploying deep learning models. Different technology like Docker enables models and their dependencies to be introduced into portable containers, ensuring consistency within various environments. This method of deployment has been found to be an easier method of deploying applications as well as minimizing compatibility problems thus making administration of applications in distributed systems easier.

Orchestration frameworks are important in large-scale deployments. Applications like Kubernetes can be used to deploy, scale, and manage containerized applications automatically. Such frameworks are used to address the tasks of load balancing, resource allocation, and fault recovery so that deep learning services do not become unavailable and inefficient with increasing workloads.

Another significant feature of deployment is model serving. Special purpose serving platforms offer more efficient inference execution environments, commonly with support for batching, versioning, and monitoring. These systems will make sure models are able to serve a large number of requests with low latency and high reliability.

Machine learning systems are being subjected to continuous integration and continuous deployment practices. With such practices, models can be tested, validated, and updated automatically to guarantee that more refinements can be implemented in time and with consistency. This strategy has also been called MLOps, which focuses on combining machine learning processes with software engineering concepts.

The effectiveness of deployed models requires monitoring and performance management as the necessary procedures. Latency, throughput, and accuracy metrics should be monitored continuously and identify problems and provide peak performance. The monitoring systems are also useful in detecting model drift, which occurs as the performance of the model degenerates with the passage of time because of a shift in data patterns (Peng et al., 2024).

One criterion in deployment and orchestration is scalability. Systems should also be in a position to support the growing workloads and the growing number of users or devices. Auto-scaling systems dynamically scale resources according to demand to ensure that resources are used efficiently without being over-provisioned.

The other consideration in the deployment of deep learning models is security. Secure APIs, authentication systems and encryption are necessary to protect models and data against unauthorized access. It is especially difficult, yet necessary to provide end-to-end security on all layers in edge cloud environment.

In general, the deployment and orchestration methods can make deep learning models run efficiently in a distributed environment. There is the ability to develop resilient, scalable, and serviceable systems using containerization, orchestration frameworks, and automated processes to support real-time intelligent applications using edge and cloud layers (Chen et al., 2014).

CHALLENGES, OPEN ISSUES, AND FUTURE RESEARCH DIRECTIONS

Deep learning that is integrated on both edge and cloud layers has proven to come with many challenges that need to be overcome to deliver efficient, scalable, and reliable systems. A major difficulty is associated with the heterogeneity of devices and infrastructures. The edge devices are very diverse in regards to computation power, memory and energy capacity, and it is not easy to come up with uniform solutions that work well across various settings.

The communication overhead between layers of edges and clouds is another crucial problem. Moving of huge amounts of data or model updates may cause more latency and bandwidth usage. Where the connectivity is limited or unstable, it is especially difficult to keep the interaction between distributed components consistent, which influences the global system performance (Deng & Yu, 2014).

The allocation of resources and the assignment of tasks is an open research issue of distributed deep learning systems. The intelligent decision-making mechanisms are needed to define which functions can and must be performed at the edge and which ones can and must be moved to the cloud. This process is further complicated by dynamic environments whose workloads and network conditions change requiring adaptive solutions and context-aware solutions.

In edge-clouds, data privacy and security are the most critical issues. Although edge computing is useful in retaining sensitive information in a small area, risks remain on the transmission of data, updating models and attack on distributed systems. Providing safe communication, strong authentication and privacy-reducing learning methods is a continuing concern.

Other issues include model generalization and robustness especially in decentralized environments. Models that are trained in controlled settings do not necessarily work effectively when they are deployed in various real world settings. The unpredictable data distributions in edge devices may cause deterioration in performance, and more adaptive and resilient learning methods should be considered (Zaharia et al., 2010).

Energy efficiency has become an urgent issue particularly to battery powered edge devices. Deep learning models may be computationally intensive resulting in a high level of energy consumption. It is necessary to develop energy-conscious algorithms and hardware-efficient models in order to implement them in the context of large-scale edge-cloud systems sustainably.

Scalability remains a significant problem because the number of interconnected devices is increasing exponentially. Systems need to be able to process huge volumes of data and coordinate computations in thousands or even millions of nodes. This involves high level distributed architecture as well as effective coordination tools.

In this aspect, interoperability and standardization are on the way. The absence of common standards of communication protocols, data formats, and system interfaces may become a barrier to easy integration of various platforms and devices. These issues are important to tackle in order to create cohesive and flexible ecosystems (Yu et al., 2018).

In the future, the studies are likely to be oriented on intelligent orchestration and automation. The application of the artificial intelligence to control the resources, allocate the tasks more efficiently, and address the evolving circumstances has massive potential. Self-organizing systems with the capability to dynamically tune their behavior will be important to next-generation architectures.

To sum up, although it has been established that major advances have been achieved in deep learning interfaces in edge and cloud environments, there are still a number of challenges and unresolved issues. It will also take a multi-disciplinary approach with machine learning, distributed systems, networking, and hardware design. The research directions in the future will be to develop newer and more efficient, secure and adaptable systems that can meet the increasing needs of the intelligent applications in the real world (He et al., 2016).

CONCLUSION

Deep learning has been merged with edge and cloud computing which has brought forth a revolutionary paradigm of creating scalable, effective, and smart systems. The contemporary architectures can cater to the increased demands of real-time and data-intensive applications with the aid of the computational capability of the cloud and the low-latency features of edge devices. This hybrid solution lets implement more receptive, adaptive and efficiency-based solutions in a broad spectrum of areas.

In this review, the main features that have been addressed include scalable training methods, model optimization schemes, collaborative architectures, and deployment mechanisms. All these elements constitute base of distributed deep learning systems enabling them to work in heterogeneous and dynamic environments. The developments and innovations in parallelism, compression, and orchestration systems have greatly increased the viability of implementing deep learning models outside centralized systems (LeCun et al., 2015).

In spite of this development, a number of challenges persist as these are issues that touch on communication overheads, resource allocation, privacy, and system scalability. These issues necessitate additional algorithm, system design, and hardware integration to address them. New solutions to these limitations, including federated learning, intelligent orchestration, and energy-aware computing, are likely to be of importance.

In the future, the future of deep learning on edge and cloud levels would be the creation of more autonomous, secure, and efficient systems. The combination of adaptive learning systems, real-time decision-making systems, and effective security systems will play a key role in supporting next-generation applications. With the current ongoing advancement in research, the edge cloud paradigm is expected to be a foundation of distributed artificial intelligence that will facilitate smarter more connected ecosystems.

Funding: This work was supported by the Deanship of Scientific Research, the Vice Presidency for Graduate Studies and Scientific Research, King Faisal University, Saudi Arabia, under Grant No. KFU263288

REFERENCES

Abadi, M., Barham, P., Chen, J., Chen, Z., Davis, A., Dean, J., & Zheng, X. (2016). {TensorFlow}: a system for {Large-Scale} machine learning. In *12th USENIX symposium on operating systems design and implementation (OSDI 16)* (pp. 265-283).

Bhatti, U. A., Tang, H., Wu, G., Marjan, S., & Hussain, A. (2023). Deep learning with graph convolutional networks: An overview and latest applications in computational intelligence. *International Journal of Intelligent Systems, 2023*(1), 8342104. DOI: 10.1155/2023/8342104

Chen, M., Mao, S., & Liu, Y. (2014). Big data: A survey. *Mobile Networks and Applications, 19*(2), 171–209. DOI: 10.1007/s11036-013-0489-0

Chen, T., Moreau, T., Jiang, Z., Zheng, L., Yan, E., Shen, H., & Krishnamurthy, A. (2018). {TVM}: An automated {End-to-End} optimizing compiler for deep learning. In *13th USENIX symposium on operating systems design and implementation (OSDI 18)* (pp. 578-594).

Deng, L., & Yu, D. (2014). Deep learning: Methods and applications. *Foundations and Trends in Signal Processing, 7*(3–4), 197–387. DOI: 10.1561/2000000039

Han, S., Pool, J., Tran, J., & Dally, W. (2015). Learning both weights and connections for efficient neural network. *Advances in Neural Information Processing Systems, 28*, 1135–1143.

He, K., Zhang, X., Ren, S., & Sun, J. (2016). Deep residual learning for image recognition. *Proceedings of the IEEE Conference on Computer Vision and Pattern Recognition*, 770–778.

Howard, A. G., Zhu, M., Chen, B., Kalenichenko, D., Wang, W., Weyand, T., & Adam, H. (2017). MobileNets: Efficient convolutional neural networks for mobile vision applications. *arXiv preprint arXiv:1704.04861.*

Kairouz, P., & McMahan, H. B. (2021). Advances and open problems in federated learning. *Foundations and Trends in Machine Learning, 14*(1-2), 1–210. DOI: 10.1561/2200000083

LeCun, Y., Bengio, Y., & Hinton, G. (2015). Deep learning. *Nature, 521*(7553), 436–444. DOI: 10.1038/nature14539 PMID: 26017442

Li, H., Kadav, A., Durdanovic, I., Samet, H., & Graf, H. P. (2017). Pruning filters for efficient convnets. *Proceedings of the International Conference on Learning Representations.*

Li, J., Bhatti, U. A., Nawaz, S. A., Huang, M., Ahmad, R. M., & Ghadi, Y. Y. (2024). Remote-sensing image classification: A comprehensive review and applications. In *Deep Learning for Multimedia Processing Applications* (pp. 18–47).

Li, X., Li, H., Li, H., & Li, K. C. (2019). Real-time anomaly detection for IoT networks based on deep learning. *IEEE Access : Practical Innovations, Open Solutions, 7*, 127961–127970.

McMahan, B., Moore, E., Ramage, D., Hampson, S., & Arcas, B. A. (2017, April). Communication-efficient learning of deep networks from decentralized data. In *Artificial intelligence and statistics* (pp. 1273–1282). Pmlr.

Peng, M., Liu, Y., Khan, A., Ahmed, B., Sarker, S. K., Ghadi, Y. Y., Bhatti, U. A., Al-Razgan, M., & Ali, Y. A. (2024). Crop monitoring using remote sensing land use and land change data: Comparative analysis of deep learning methods using pre-trained CNN models. *Big Data Research, 36*, 100448. DOI: 10.1016/j.bdr.2024.100448

Satyanarayanan, M. (2017). The emergence of edge computing. *Computer, 50*(1), 30–39. DOI: 10.1109/MC.2017.9

Shi, W., Cao, J., Zhang, Q., Li, Y., & Xu, L. (2016). Edge computing: Vision and challenges. *IEEE Internet of Things Journal, 3*(5), 637–646. DOI: 10.1109/JIOT.2016.2579198

Sze, V., Chen, Y. H., Yang, T. J., & Emer, J. S. (2017). Efficient processing of deep neural networks: A tutorial and survey. *Proceedings of the IEEE, 105*(12), 2295–2329. DOI: 10.1109/JPROC.2017.2761740

Wang, S., Tuor, T., Salonidis, T., Leung, K. K., Makaya, C., He, T., & Chan, K. (2019). Adaptive federated learning in resource-constrained edge computing systems. *IEEE Journal on Selected Areas in Communications, 37*(6), 1205–1221. DOI: 10.1109/JSAC.2019.2904348

Yu, W., Liang, F., He, X., Hatcher, W. G., Lu, C., Lin, J., & Yang, X. (2018). A survey on the edge computing for the Internet of Things. *IEEE Access : Practical Innovations, Open Solutions, 6*, 6900–6919. DOI: 10.1109/ACCESS.2017.2778504

Zaharia, M., Chowdhury, M., Franklin, M. J., Shenker, S., & Stoica, I. (2010). Spark: Cluster computing with working sets. *Proceedings of the USENIX Conference on Hot Topics in Cloud Computing*.

Zhang, Y., Zhang, W., & Zhao, K. (2021). Heterogeneous IoT data analytics with deep learning: Techniques and applications. *Sensors (Basel), 21*(8), 2765. PMID: 33919861

Zhou, Z., Chen, X., Li, E., Zeng, L., Luo, K., & Zhang, J. (2019). Edge intelligence: Paving the last mile of artificial intelligence with edge computing. *Proceedings of the IEEE, 107*(8), 1738–1762. DOI: 10.1109/JPROC.2019.2918951

Chapter 9
Secure Communication, Trust Management, and Privacy Preservation in Multi-UAV Systems

Ergashev Nuriddin
http://orcid.org/0009-0003-8851-5374
Department of Information Systems and Technologies, Karshi State Technical University, Uzbekistan

Boypolvonov Barot
Department of Information Systems and Technology, Karshi State Technical University, Karshi, Uzbekistan

Nosir Xurramov
Department of Information Technology and Exact Sciences, Termez University of Economics and Service, Termez, Uzbekistan

Otajonova Gulkhayo
Mamun University, Khiva, Uzbekistan

Muxamedova Shoxista Akbarovna
Department of Management, Tashkent Institute of Chemical Technology, Tashkent, Uzbekistan

Khayrulla Urozboev
Department of International Scientific Journals and Ratings, Alfraganus University, Tashkent, Uzbekistan

ABSTRACT

Ensuring secure communication, effective trust management, and privacy preservation is therefore critical for maintaining the reliability, resilience, and safety of multi-UAV networks. This paper explores the key security challenges associated with multi-UAV systems and reviews existing mechanisms for secure communication, including encryption, authentication, key management, and blockchain-based solutions. It further examines trust management frameworks that enable UAVs to

DOI: 10.4018/979-8-2600-0615-3.ch009

evaluate the reliability and behavior of neighboring nodes in dynamic and decentralized environments. Additionally, the study discusses privacy-preserving techniques such as anonymization, differential privacy, secure data aggregation, and federated learning to protect sensitive information while supporting efficient collaboration. The paper highlights current research trends, identifies open challenges, and suggests future directions for developing robust, scalable, and privacy-aware security architectures for next-generation multi-UAV networks.

INTRODUCTION TO SECURITY AND PRIVACY IN MULTI-UAV SYSTEMS

Since the rapid development of multi-UAV systems, various applications such as surveillance, environment monitoring, disaster response and military use became possible. They are made up of several UAVs which work cooperatively to perform a complex task more efficiently than by using only one UAV. The growth and independence of these networks are making secure communication and protection of sensitive information a key issue (Bekmezci et al., 2013).

In a Multi-UAV system, communication is an essential requirement for coordination, sharing and controlling UAVs. The fact that these presentations are broadcast openly and frequently unsecure renders them susceptible to different digital cataclysmic events. These vulnerabilities can be exploited by adversaries, leading to a potential compromise of mission, or system safety through intercept, manipulation or disruption of the communication (Gupta et al., 2016). Security for multi-UAV system concerns the prevention of intruders, security of data integrity, and system availability. Security risks are such as eavesdropping, spoofing, jamming, DoS. If not handled appropriately, these attacks can result in faulty decision-making, loss of control or even system failure.

Unmanned Aerial Vehicle (UAV), also known as drone, is nowadays a basic technology for sensing, communications, surveillance and delivery. New developments in lightweight materials, embedded computing, artificial intelligence and wireless networking have brought their capabilities into new levels of sophistication in the past decade. Whereas in the past UAVs were deployed with one or two drones in a manual or semi-autonomous way, today's UAV applications often involve cooperating groups of drones called multi-UAV systems or UAV-swarms. They are engineered to have systems with large amount of complex systems collaborate together; these systems provide larger scale, more redundant, higher efficiency, and more coverage than single UAV deployment. But with escalating sizes and levels of autonomy in UAV operations come escalated risks when it comes to security and privacy. Indeed, in the case of multiple UAVs, security and privacy represent a non-idea property of UAVs but it is required for safe and trustworthy operation (Zeng et al., 2016).

Multi-UAV systems are often comprised of more than one aerial vehicle that are able to communicate among themselves and with an on-ground control system or cloud based system. These UAVs are able to work in a centralized, decentralized or hybrid coordination architectures. Some centralized systems use ground station to manage the activities of all UAVs and in decentralized systems, UAVs share coordination with each other utilizing a distributed decision-making algorithm. Hybrid systems are hybridisations of both approaches, aiming to have a balance between control efficiency and control robustness. Whatever architecture these types of systems share the use of wireless communication channels, either Wi-Fi, LTE, 5G, Satellite or ad hoc Mesh. The heavy use of open, sometimes unsecure, communications media increases the attack surface that can be exploited by adversaries (Fotouhi et al., 2019).

A major issue for the security in multi-UAV system is the vulnerability of the communication channels. UAVs constantly share data including telemetry, flight paths, sensor readings and coordination commands among other items, and data interception and/or manipulation could result in grave consequences. Eavesdropping can be done by Attackers to retrieve any sensitive mission information or environmental data. More sophisticated forms of these attacks involve man in the middle attacks, in which the communications are captured and modified with no knowledge of any legitimate parties. Furthermore DoS attacks, like jamming, can hinder communication links to such an extent that the UAVs lose coordination or even end up in a crash, if fail-safe measures are inadequate. Swarm systems are often composed of autonomous robots that rely on coordination protocols to carry out their missions, and small, individual communications failures can escalate to mission failure for the whole community (Yanmaz, 2012).

A third serious problem is spoofing—that is, pretending to be something other than what you are in the system. A serious threat is spoofing that can affect GPS in UAV operations. Attackers can use fake GPS broadcasting to trick UAVs into thinking that they are at some other location. This may cause deviations from preplanned paths or crashes in the vicinity, or in restricted airspace. In the same way, identity spoofing attacks are when the malicious individuals pretend to be the trusted UAV nodes or ground control stations. Causing such things allows attackers to input fake commands into the system or mess up coordination protocols. There could also be replay attacks whereby transmitted and captured legitimate packets of communication are replayed to befuddle the system or cause an inappropriate reaction from the system. Such attacks take advantage of weak security in the UAV networks with regard to authentication and time validation (Sharma et al., 2016).

Threat of UAV hijacking is one of the most critical threats in a multi-UAV system. In the case of a hijacking scenario, an adversary is able to gain unauthorized access to one or more UAVs. This might be because of flaws in the software, low-level encryption, the compromise of firmware, or exposure of communication interfaces. After taking control, the attacker may direct the UAV to reroute, disarm safety controls, or use it for other malicious purposes, like surveillance or physical attack. Multi-UAV systems may have more cascading effects when it comes to hijacking one of the UAVs, as many times swarm coordination relies on own trust models. A compromised UAV could introduce false information into the system, causing other UAVs to base their decisions on the false information. This may cause imbalance in the whole formation.

Another dimension quite often neglected in the systems of UAV is physical security. In contrast to an all-digital system, UAVs are deployed in open places where they can be physically reached by an attacker. A drone system can be captured, tampered with or destroyed. Physical access could enable an attacker to obtain the cryptographic keys or to alter the firmware or add malicious hardware components. After a UAV appears physically impaired, it could pose a continuous threat to the overall system. In addition, UAV landing and charging stations are susceptible to being attacked and interrupted and for the introduction of malware into the system (Dorling et al., 2017).

In addition to direct attacks, there are also threats to multi-UAV systems with regard to their underlying ground infrastructure and cloud services. Data storage and analytics may be handled by ground control stations or cloud servers, while mission planning may be conducted at ground, potentially via a cloud connection and server. Attackers can compromise these components to get a global picture of UAVs and/or tinker with mission parameters. This adds systemic risk, as the control points get centralized, they become high-value targets. Cloud-based analytics and coordination services can be exploited in decentralized systems as well, if not properly secured.

In multi-UAV systems, privacy is another key issue. Many UAVs have high-resolution cameras, infrared sensors, LiDAR (Light Detection and Ranging), and other tools for data collection that can ultimately capture a detailed data log of the environment and human activity. This functionality is vital for some uses, like monitoring surveillance, search and rescue and monitoring infrastructure, but also creates major privacy issues. UAVs may (intentionally or unintentionally) capture sensitive personal data, such as images of people, homes, and habits. In urban areas with a high population density, there is a risk of excessive oversight by using UAVs on a regular basis, which may pose ethical and legal issues (Li et al., 2018).

These privacy concerns are further exacerbated in multi-UAV systems due to data aggregation. If more than one UAVs are used together to acquire data that covers a larger field, the data can be combined into another information set to recreate a highly detailed model of the environment and human activities. Although the individual UAV data streams may be anonymized, in many cases the stream retransmission can be correlated to re-identification of individuals. For instance, movement patterns obtained from various types of drones can be fused to identify the person or predict his/her behaviour. This poses a difficulty in keeping data privacy-preserving throughout its lifecycle.

The other privacy issues involve data transfer and storage. Some data gathered as a result of UAVs are sent to cloud servers to be processed and stored for a long time. If encoding is not strong or used at all, data can be stolen and accessed by unauthorized individuals during transmission. After data is moved to cloud, it is exposed to unauthorized external attacks, malicious insider access, and the abuse by third parties. There is also concern that organisations could use UAV data gathered for other purposes than originally intended, for example, for commercial profiling or consent-less surveillance. Data governance and regulatory compliance is an issue of concern.

Machine learning and artificial intelligence techniques widely employed in multi-UAV systems for object detection, path planning and decision making, also pose privacy issues. Data collected by UAVs can include sensitive data, and models trained on it can expose sensitive data, even via inference attacks. Opponents may be able to re-create training data or deduce if individuals were in the data during training. This is especially worrying in surveillance applications where camera functions are checked almost on a "handshake" period (Mozaffari et al., 2019).

Researchers and engineers are trying to correct these security and privacy issues by coming up with several solutions. Cryptographic techniques are the methods which are important to secure communication channels. The end-to-end encryption helps to secure data transfer between UAVs and ground stations, preventing data from being easily accessible or modifiable. For the UAVs limited computational resources, lightweight encryption algorithms are particularly important. Security measures like digital signatures and certificates can help ensure that only authorized participants are able to interact on the network.

IDS is now also being used with multi-UAV designs. These systems are designed to keep track of network activity and alert if there are any strange activities that might be due to spoofing, jamming, or any unauthorized access to the network. As the variety of malicious activity increases, machine learning detection of nuances of suspicious activity are being adopted. Moreover, the use of redundancy and fault-tolerant design principles ensures that the failure or compromise of a single UAV does not compromise the whole system.

Methods like data anonymization, differential privacy, and secure multi-party computation are being considered for privacy protection. It is hoped that the use of these methods will prevent any direct identity between a person and sensitive information presently available for analysis of data collected. Edge computing is also becoming relevant, enabling data to be locally processed on the UAVs or local edge nodes to minimize 'raw sensitive data' being sent to centralized servers. This reduces the chances of exposure to possible gaps during transmission and storage (Khan, 2020).

Regulatory policies and ethical guidelines are also significant in dealing with privacy concerns. Governments and organizations worldwide, are creating policies to manage the use of UAVs, especially in urban areas. These regulations frequently specify several requirements such as limitations on data gathering, storage period and agreement by the user. Enforcement is however still complicated though as UAV technologies are rapidly evolving and are more difficult to monitor in an airborne distributed system.

Finally, multi-UAV systems are a great technological development that has the potential to revolutionize various sectors. Their coupling of multiple autonomous agents allows for efficient operations at a large scale that were previously not possible. The same complexity, however, poses noteworthy security and privacy issues. Communication attacks, spoofing, hijacking, physical tampering and infrastructure compromise are serious threats to the integrity of the systems. Meanwhile, UAVs have a massive capability of data collection that has posed-privacy issues regarding surveillance, data collection, and inference by machine learning. To tackle these problems, one needs strong technical solutions like encryption, authentication, intrusion detection and privacy-preserving computation, and also a strong regulatory oversight along with ethical perspective. This can only be achieved by supporting security and privacy as an integral part of the design of multi-UAV systems (Zhang et al., 2018).

Figure 1 shows Security and privacy in UAV systems

Figure 1. Security and privacy in UAV systems

Privacy is another important aspect, particularly in civilian applications where UAVs may collect sensitive data such as images, videos, and location information. Unauthorized access to such data can result in privacy violations and raise ethical and legal concerns. Therefore, mechanisms must be in place to ensure that sensitive information is properly protected during data collection, transmission, and storage.

The dynamic and decentralized nature of multi-UAV systems introduces additional challenges for security and privacy. UAVs frequently join and leave the network, and their mobility leads to constantly changing network topologies. This makes it difficult to implement traditional centralized security mechanisms and requires more flexible and adaptive approaches.

Trust management plays a key role in addressing these challenges. In a multi-UAV environment, each UAV must be able to evaluate the reliability of other nodes in the network. Trust mechanisms help identify malicious or compromised UAVs and prevent them from negatively affecting the system. This is particularly important in collaborative tasks where decisions depend on shared information.

Traditional security solutions designed for static networks are often not suitable for UAV systems due to their resource constraints. Limited processing power, memory, and energy capacity restrict the complexity of security algorithms that can be implemented onboard. As a result, lightweight and efficient security mechanisms are required to ensure protection without overloading system resources (Zhang et al., 2018).

Advancements in technologies such as blockchain and distributed ledger systems have introduced new possibilities for secure and decentralized trust management. These technologies enable transparent and tamper-resistant record-keeping, which can enhance trust and accountability within UAV networks. However, their integration must be carefully designed to address resource limitations.

Another important consideration is the need for real-time security solutions. UAV systems often operate in time-critical environments where delays in detection or response to threats can have serious consequences. Security mechanisms must therefore be capable of operating efficiently in real time while maintaining high levels of accuracy and reliability.

In summary, security and privacy are fundamental requirements for the safe and effective operation of multi-UAV systems. The combination of open communication channels, dynamic network structures, and resource constraints creates unique challenges that require specialized solutions. Ongoing research is focused on developing adaptive, lightweight, and robust mechanisms to ensure secure communication, trustworthy collaboration, and protection of sensitive data in multi-UAV networks (Wang, 2019).

COMMUNICATION ARCHITECTURES AND THREAT MODELS IN UAV NETWORKS

Communication architectures form the backbone of UAV networks, enabling coordination, data exchange, and control among multiple UAVs and ground stations. In multi-UAV systems, efficient and reliable communication is essential for collaborative operations such as formation flying, target tracking, and distributed sensing. The design of communication architectures directly influences system performance, scalability, and security.

UAV communication architectures can be broadly categorized into centralized, decentralized, and hybrid models. In centralized architectures, a ground control station or central node manages communication and coordination among UAVs. While this approach simplifies management, it introduces a single point of failure and may lead to scalability and latency issues in large-scale deployments (Aloqaily, 2020).

Decentralized architectures, also known as ad hoc or peer-to-peer networks, allow UAVs to communicate directly with each other without relying on a central controller. This approach enhances system robustness and flexibility, as UAVs can continue operating even if some nodes fail. However, decentralized systems require more complex coordination and security mechanisms to manage communication effectively.

Figure 2 shows UAV network architectures and threats overview

Figure 2. UAV network architectures and threats overview

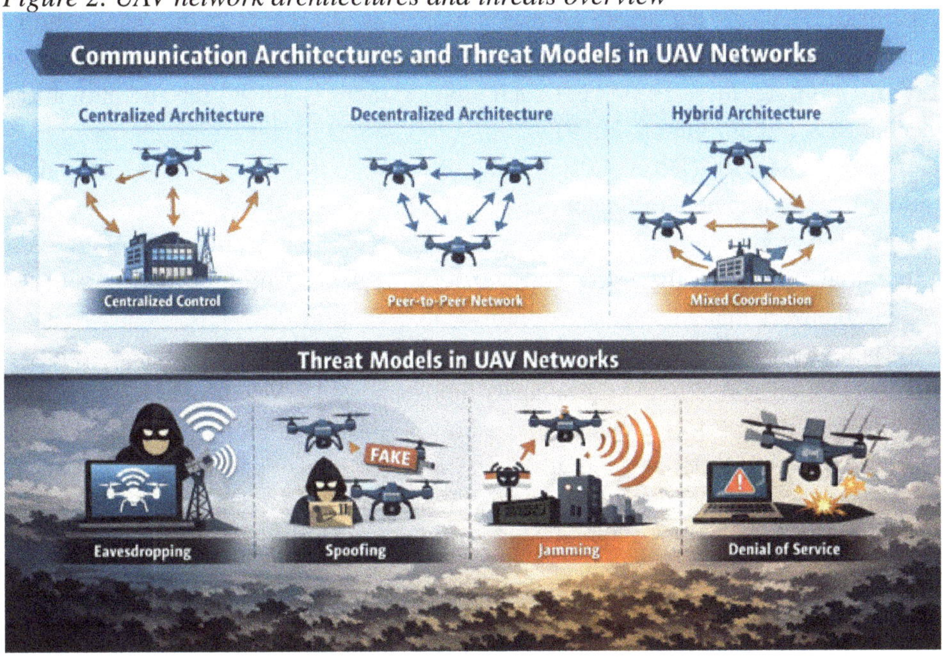

Hybrid designs are a blend between centralized and decentralized designs, where control and flexibility are both important. This can involve some tasks being controlled by a central node and others directly between the different UAVs. It can help with efficiency and resiliency but careful design is essential to help avoid communication bottlenecks and security issues (Dorri et al., 2017).

The communication links on UAV Networks are likely to be made use of wireless technology like WiFi, cellular networks or certain radio frequency (RF) systems. Owing to their inherent nature, these connections are susceptible to interference, fading, and poaching. Wireless communication is open, meaning makes it easier for bad guys to intercept or disrupt transmission.

The threat models for UAV networks enable the identification and analysis of the potential security threats and adversarial activities. These models are useful to design effective security mechanisms as they describe what an attacker can do and which goal he is aiming for. In most threat-models even your adversary can be internal bad guys or compromised nodes within the network (Roman et al., 2018).

Most common threats include eavesdropping – an attacker intercepts communication to gain access to sensitive information. This may result in privacy violation or in the exposure of mission critical data. However, UAV communication channels are extremely vulnerable to such attacks unless they are properly encrypted.

Spoofing and impersonation attacks are where the intruder impersonates a legitimate UAV or a legitimate ground station. The attackers can inject fake information to the network so as to mislead UAVs, disrupt the coordination, or change the mission outcomes. To prevent such attacks, there is a need for authentication mechanisms (Abdurohman, 2019).

Denial of service (DoS) and jamming attacks are used to sabotage communication, by flooding network resources or disrupt signal delivery. These attacks are able to disrupt system performance, or even make communication between UAVs impossible. Having facilities that can withstand these disruptions is a crucial component to ensure that a business can remain in operation.

It is understood that communication architectures and threat models are basic elements for comprehending the security landscape of UAV networks in summary. Architecture design decisions can affect how well the system performs as well as susceptibility to attacks and threat models are a framework for the identification and mitigation of threats. It is essential to create safe, robust and efficient communication systems to promote the progress of multi-UAV technologies (Chen, 2020).

SECURE COMMUNICATION PROTOCOLS AND ENCRYPTION TECHNIQUES

Data transmission security in multi-UAV systems is crucial and requires the use of secure communication protocols and encryption techniques. Interception, manipulation and unauthorized access are also issues since UAV networks are dependent on wireless communication. Confidentiality, integrity, and authenticity of data are essential to accurate and secure operations then.

The most important way of protecting the information in UAV communications is through encrypted communication. It means communicating information to someone in a way that is encrypted - meaning readable by others only once it has been decrypted. Symmetric encryption techniques, that work with a secret key known to both sender and receiver, are common because anyone who knows the secret key can manage the cryptosystem. These methods are well-suited for low resource UAV systems than have a limited amount of processing power and energy.

Asymmetric encryption, or public key encryption is more secure because two keys are used, one for encrypting and a different one for decrypting the data. This method does have the advantage of securing the key exchange and authentication, but overall the method involves more calculations. Asymmetric techniques may be combined with symmetric techniques in UAV networks to achieve a balance between security and efficiency.

The secure communication protocols include rules and procedures for how data should be exchanged between the UAVs and other network elements. Data can be sent in a secure way with the help of protocols like secure versions of transport layer communication and network layer communication. These protocols also include security measures such as encryption, authentication, and integrity verification to ensure data security and prevent unauthorized access and manipulation (Li, 2019).

Which is the most critical part in a secure communication process is authentication mechanisms. They guarantee the participation of only legal UAVs and Ground stations in the network. Digital signature, certificates, and mutual authentication mechanisms can be used to ensure the identities of the entities communicating and to prevent impersonation attacks.

Another critical element of secure communications is key management. Security of a system relies on the efficient generation, distribution and storage of cryptographic keys. For multi-UAV system, changing network topology in UAV networks complicates the key management because it requires scalable and flexible approaches which adapt to the changing network.

Due to UAV platform resource limitations, lightweight cryptographic techniques are increasingly being developed. These techniques try to deliver high level of security with a reduced amount of computation and also energy expenditure. It is especially crucial for real-time applications where delays cannot be accepted, lightweight encryption is required (Zhang, 2019).

In the case of UAV networks, end-to-end security is crucial to make sure that the data remains secure as it traverse the transmission path. This involves communication between UAVs, edge nodes and cloud systems. By using end-to-end encryption, data is secured, and intermediate nodes are unable to access any sensitive information.

Another booming method is blockchain and distributed ledger technologies for assured interaction. These technologies offer decentralized and tamper-resistant platforms for exchanging information and validating its integrity. Although these are promising, they need to be taken into account with regards to computational and energy limitations when incorporated into UAV systems.

To conclude, using secure communication protocols and encryption techniques is critical for safeguarding UAV networks against cyber threats. By combining efficient encryption methods, robust authentication mechanisms, and effective key management strategies, it is possible to ensure secure and reliable data exchange. The research is ongoing on lightweight, scalable and adaptive security solutions adapted to the different needs of multi-UAV systems (Xiao, 2016).

TRUST MANAGEMENT AND REPUTATION-BASED MECHANISMS IN UNMANNED AERIAL VEHICLE (UAV) SWARMS

In multi-UAV systems, such as those in which swarm-based operations are used multiple UAVs work together and share information to accomplish a shared goal, trust management plays a vital role. In these decentralized setups, it vital for a UAV to assess the trustworthiness and dynamics of communicating neighbor nodes for safe and efficient cooperation. If there are no efficient trust mechanisms, the system performance will be badly affected by the presence of malicious or compromised UAVs.

Trust in UAV swarms is about the level of confidence that one UAV has in the actions/data given by the other UAV. Generally this trust is built up from past contact, observing behavior, and disseminating information within the network. The weight of trust associated with the nodes is dynamically updated through trust management systems to account for the dynamic nature of UAV networks characterized by the nodes' temporal membership, disaffection, and/or alignment with different goals (Yan, 2020).

Trusted mechanisms such as reputation based mechanisms are broadly employed for trust management on UAV swarms. These mechanisms are effective to assign the reputation scores to the UAVs according to their past performances and interactions. UAVs with high reputation scores are assumed to be reliable in contrast, UAVs with low reputation scores can be assumed to be suspicious and malicious. This will aid in determining and isolating unreliable nodes in the network.

A very important strength of the reputation based systems is their suitability to work in decentralized settings. No central authority, the UAVs are able to independently evaluate trustworthiness of each other. This helps in increasing the robustness and scalability of the system, particularly for UAV networks operating in large size or with high dynamics.

There may be many evaluation criteria related to the trust, like data's precision, communication reliability, task completion hits and compliance of protocol's rules etc. These conditions make it possible for UAVs to produce the whole behavior picture of peers' behavior. A multi-criteria trust evaluation supports in making decisions based on trust and helps avoiding illegal or false information.

There are however some problems associated with trust management systems. A major problem is the possibility of false information or dishonest feedback, that is, either the malicious UAVs try to affect the reputation scores or fake information is provided. A consequence of this may be a failure to measure and assess trust and an integrity violation of the System. The prevention of such such behavior should be accompanied by mechanisms for detection and mitigation so as to ensure reliability (Liu, 2019).

The dynamic property of UAV networks is another challenge. Trust models must be adaptive and responsive to frequent changing network topology, node mobility, etc. Static trust evaluation methods are usually not adequate and contexts aware and real-time trust management methods need to be developed.

Resource constraints also impact the design of trust mechanisms. Those algorithms used to evaluate/trust cannot be too sophisticated due to limited computation and energy of UAVs. This requires lightweight and efficient trust models for practical implementation without consuming substantial amount of resources for the system.

New technologies are being developed to improve trust management in UAV swarms, specifically blockchain. The Blockchain offers a decentralized and tamper-proof method of capturing interactions and reputation data. Whilst scalability and energy usage is still an issue, this can enhance transparency and ensure that trust information is not accessed and modified by third parties without permission (Singh, 2020).

To sum up, to guarantee safe and dependable collaboration between UAVs in swarms, trust management by way of reputation-based mechanisms are crucial. The trustworthiness assessment of the peers is performed by the UAVs system, acting as a solution to overcome malicious nodes and increasing network trustworthiness. Future research efforts are aimed at developing adaptive, secure and resource-conscious trust models for the increasing multi-UAV complexity (Alzenad, 2018).

TECHNICS AND STRATEGIES TO PRESERVE PRIVACY; METHODS OF DATA PROTECTION

Privacy preservation is one of the most critical issues in multi-UAV system especially in situations regarding to surveillance, data collection, and even monitoring of sensitive environments. UAVs are frequently used to gather and store personal or confidential data like images, videos, and positioning data. Protecting this information from unauthorized access and misuse are crucial to ensuring users' trust and regulatory compliance (Sharma et al., 2017).

Data encryption is one of the basic methods in the protection of privacy. Data encryption creates a hard-to-crack code while it is being transferred and stored, so that only certain entities can access the sensitive data. Encryption tools are robust and prevent data hijacking and eavesdropping, particularly in wireless communication settings where threats of data interception may be high.

Anonymization of data is another commonly used means of protecting data privacy. This includes de-identifying or anonymizing identifiable data collected before processing and sharing. A UAV-captured image for example, could have blur or masking on faces, licenseplates or even specific location identifiers in imagery which could impair identification of people or assets.

Access control tools are an important part in making sure that only authorized users or systems can gain access to the UAV data. Performing access control in accordance to the roles or attributes of the users, relying on a role-based or attribute-based access control model, respectively. This takes care of the unlicensed use of the data and introduces safety of the system.

Multi-UAV environments are also of interest in which data is shared among multiple nodes, secured data sharing strategies are also important. Methods like secure multi-party computation enable UAVs to process transmitted information, without sharing all of the sensitive information. This allows for cooperation and at the same time, privacy.

Federated learning (FL) has been receiving considerable attention as a technique that guarantees privacy for UAV systems in the context of machine learning. UAVs train local models without sending raw data to the central server, and update the central server with model updates. This helps to reduce risks of transmission of sensitive information and the overhead of communication while on the other hand collaborative learning is still possible.

Differential privacy is another method for safeguarding an individual's input. Differential Privacy makes it impossible to deduce any level of information, sensitive or not, based on aggregated data or data output by models activated with controllable noise. This is especially helpful in cases of large-scale data analysis.

Privacy preservation also relies on data integrity and safe data storage. Helping towards the security of stored data from unauthorized modification or corruption assures trust in UAV systems. Securing data integrity is often achieved using methods like hashing with security and privacy guarantees, as well as tamper detection.

Some issues of privacy preservation are the trade-off between data utility and privacy. Too much anonymisation or encryption may not allow for sufficient analysis of data; inadequate anonymisation or encryption may pose a risk to privacy. Careful designing of privacy-preserving mechanisms is needed to achieve the right balance.

In conclusion, privacy preservation techniques and data protection strategies are of key importance in the responsible deployment of multi-UAV systems. To have both sensitive information protection and effective data use, using encryption, anonymization, access control and advanced learning methods can be combined. It can be observed that researches are still underway to build efficient, scalable and robust solutions for privacy for UAVs network with various specific requirements.

CHALLENGES, OPEN ISSUES AND FUTURE RESEARCH DIRECTIONS

Although a lot of work has been done to secure multi-UAV systems there are still a number of problems and open questions that affect the reliability and large-scale deployment of such systems. Such problems are due to the dynamicity of the networks, resource limitations and the growing sophistication of cyber threats that the UAVs are facing. Solving security, reliability and privacy challenges is necessary to establish secure, trustworthy and privacy-aware UAV ecosystem.

Restriction of computational resources and the power supply on the UAVs is one of the obstacles. High level security features such as encryption, authentication and trust determination may consume significant processing power. It is challenging to apply these techniques in resource bounded scenarios without having to reduce the systems' performance.

Another big issue is dynamic network topology. The communication links may change frequently due to the mobility, entering or exiting of the UAVs from the UAV network. This can be challenging as it is hard to establish consistent security policies, stable relationships of trust, and efficient key management. In the future, solutions need to be adaptive, able to deal with extremely dynamics environments.

Scalability is one of the most important factors of a multi-UAV system especially for swarm-based applications. As the number of UAVs get more and more, the securing communication, the assessment of trust and data sharing are becoming more complex. Proper and scalable designing of security infrastructures for large networks is a research challenge.

Probable threats for trust management systems involve false data injection and/or management of their reputation. Attributes such as malicious UAV could be designed to contaminate the information that is used to generate the trust score and could cause the system to malfunction. However, creating powerful trust mechanisms that really can identify and counteract such attacks is critical to establishing solid collaborations.

There are also major issues of setting up privacy preservation. Sensitive data is constantly gathered and sent in the spaces where UAVs often need to fly. Striking a balance between privacy and usefulness of data is hard, and robust privacy can reduce the impact of data analysis. One main research objective is the design of efficient privacy-preserving techniques that have good data utility.

Another issue that impairs communication security is that wireless channels are open. Any efforts to employ UAV networks are vulnerable to eavesdropping, jamming, spoofing attacks etc. To overcome these threats, advanced communication protocols and interference-resistant technologies are necessary to ensure the security and resilience of the communication system.

An open question is whether there are standardized frameworks and protocols for the security and privacy of UAVs. Common standards are missing, making interoperability issues between various systems and assessment of the effectiveness of suggested systems difficult. The need is to outline common guidelines and standards to build as a body of work in the field.

The emergence of new technologies, including blockchain, federated learning, artificial intelligence, etc., with promise comes some challenges. For instance, although blockchain technology can provide trust and transparency, it introduces additional computational overhead, and federated learning ensures privacy but comes with the challenge of maintaining the security of models and efficient communication among them.

The future research directions are lightweight and adaptive security mechanism design in UAVs. This involves developing their efficient cryptographic methods, smart trust management systems and scalable privacy preservation systems. The incorporation of AI powered security solutions is also an encouraging area, which can then detect and respond to security threats in real time.

To conclude, a lot has been shifted in quest of multi-UAV systems but some problems and open issues still exist. Solutions to these challenges in the form of innovative and interdisciplinary discussions of research will play an important role in the development of future applications that enable safe, scalable, and reliable networks of UAVs.

CONCLUSION

Issues of secure communication, trust management and privacy preserving are essential for reliable operation of multi-UAV systems. The protection of data, integrity of systems, and the ability to operate in a non-negative fashion with regard to collaboration among UAVs, are becoming critical as these systems continue to scale to ever larger and more diverse areas of application. The UAV networks are open and dynamic that render them highly susceptible to different security and privacy violations.

This review has considered the crucial factors in securing multi-UAV systems such as communication architecture, encryption techniques and trust management mechanisms. It showed the strength of security protocols and authentication techniques to protect data flow, and reputation-based & distributed trust models to increase cooperation and resilience of UAV swarms.

Also highlighted was the need to uphold privacy protection, especially when dealing with sensitive data collection. Data anonymization, secure data sharing, and federated learning are examples of such techniques that offer effective ways to safeguard user privacy while allowing for meaningful data analysis. These measures ease ethical and regulatory issues related to UAV deployments.

Despite these advances, there are still several issues to address in the areas of resources constraints, scalability, dynamic network conditions, and changing threats in the cyber space. A growing demand for lightweight, adaptive, and real-time security solutions is spurring research in this area. To overcome these challenges, it is crucial to ensure the safe and efficient deployment of UAV systems in real-world environments.

New technologies, including blockchain, artificial intelligence and the next generation of means of communication, present potential solutions for improving security and trust in multi-UAV network. But it is important that their integration is carefully developed in a way that provides a balance between performance, efficicncy, and practicality.

In conclusion, achieving secure, trustworthy, and privacy-aware multi-UAV systems requires a holistic approach that integrates advanced security mechanisms, efficient system design, and adaptive learning strategies. Further research and innovation will be crucial in addressing current challenges and facilitating the use of intelligent and secure UAV networks in a variety of applications.

REFERENCES

Abdurohman, M. (2019). Trust management in UAV networks: A survey. *IEEE Access : Practical Innovations, Open Solutions*, *7*, 175256–175278.

Aloqaily, M. (2020). Blockchain in UAV networks: Security and privacy issues. *IEEE Communications Magazine*, *58*(1), 28–34.

Alzenad, M. (2018). Secure and resilient UAV communication networks. *IEEE Communications Magazine*, *56*(10), 26–32.

Bekmezci, I., Sahingoz, O. K., & Temel, Ş. (2013). Flying ad-hoc networks (FANETs): A survey. *Ad Hoc Networks*, *11*(3), 1254–1270. DOI: 10.1016/j.adhoc.2012.12.004

Chen, L. (2020). Trust-based secure routing for UAV networks. *IEEE Transactions on Aerospace and Electronic Systems*, *56*(4), 2931–2943.

Dorling, K., Heinrichs, J., Messier, G. G., & Magierowski, S. (2017). Vehicle routing problems for drone delivery. *IEEE Transactions on Systems, Man, and Cybernetics. Systems*, *47*(1), 70–85. DOI: 10.1109/TSMC.2016.2582745

Dorri, A., Kanhere, S. S., & Jurdak, R. (2017). Blockchain in IoT: Challenges and solutions. *arXiv preprint arXiv:1608.05187*.

Fotouhi, A., Qiang, H., Ding, M., Hassan, M., Giordano, L. G., Garcia-Rodriguez, A., & Yuan, J. (2019). Survey on UAV cellular communications. *IEEE Communications Surveys and Tutorials*, *21*(4), 3417–3442. DOI: 10.1109/COMST.2019.2906228

Gupta, L., Jain, R., & Vaszkun, G. (2016). Survey of important issues in UAV communication networks. *IEEE Communications Surveys and Tutorials*, *18*(2), 1123–1152. DOI: 10.1109/COMST.2015.2495297

Khan, W. Z. (2020). UAV communication networks: Architecture, protocols, and applications. *Journal of Network and Computer Applications*, *134*, 34–58.

Li, B., Fei, Z., & Zhang, Y. (2018). UAV communications for 5G and beyond. *IEEE Wireless Communications*, *26*(1), 10–16. DOI: 10.1109/MWC.2016.7422399

Li, X. (2019). Privacy-preserving data aggregation in UAV networks. *IEEE Internet of Things Journal*, *6*(2), 2943–2954.

Liu, Y. (2019). Secure data transmission in UAV-assisted networks. *IEEE Transactions on Wireless Communications*, *18*(5), 2732–2746.

Mozaffari, M., Saad, W., Bennis, M., & Debbah, M. (2019). A tutorial on UAVs for wireless networks. *IEEE Communications Surveys and Tutorials, 21*(3), 2334–2360. DOI: 10.1109/COMST.2019.2902862

Roman, R., Lopez, J., & Mambo, M. (2018). Mobile edge computing, fog computing, and IoT security. *Future Generation Computer Systems, 78*, 680–698. DOI: 10.1016/j.future.2016.11.009

Sharma, P. K., Chen, M. Y., & Park, J. H. (2017). A blockchain-based secure framework for UAV systems. *Journal of Network and Computer Applications, 94*, 48–57.

Sharma, V., You, I., & Atiquzzaman, M. (2016). Secure and efficient protocol for UAV communication. *IEEE Transactions on Vehicular Technology, 65*(12), 10229–10239.

Singh, K. (2020). Intrusion detection systems in UAV networks. *IEEE Communications Surveys and Tutorials, 22*(2), 1407–1434.

Wang, W. (2019). Secure communication in UAV networks: A survey. *IEEE Access : Practical Innovations, Open Solutions, 7*, 48668–48683.

Xiao, L. (2016). UAV relay in wireless networks: Security and performance. *IEEE Communications Letters, 20*(10), 2067–2070.

Yan, Z. (2020). Privacy protection techniques in UAV systems. *IEEE Network, 34*(5), 162–168.

Yanmaz, E. (2012). Connectivity versus area coverage in unmanned aerial vehicle networks. *IEEE International Conference on Communications*, 719–723. DOI: 10.1109/ICC.2012.6364585

Zeng, Y., Zhang, R., & Lim, T. J. (2016). Wireless communications with unmanned aerial vehicles: Opportunities and challenges. *IEEE Communications Magazine, 54*(5), 36–42. DOI: 10.1109/MCOM.2016.7470933

Zhang, Q., Chen, M., Zhao, L., & Wu, J. (2018). Deep learning for edge computing: A survey. *Proceedings of the IEEE, 107*(8), 1655–1674.

Zhang, Y. (2019). Secure UAV communication with physical layer security. *IEEE Wireless Communications, 26*(5), 12–18. DOI: 10.1109/MWC.001.1900050

Chapter 10

Security, Privacy, and Trust Challenges in TinyML-Based IoT Edge Intelligence

Obinna Emmanuel Obi-Akwari
http://orcid.org/0009-0006-9487-4965
Deepfusion Films, UK

Meletius Mgbeodichimma Igbokwe
http://orcid.org/0009-0007-2071-4317
LIMA, UK

Itohowo Effiong Charles
Independent Researcher, UK

Muinat Taiwo Adedokun
http://orcid.org/0009-0004-2557-0728
HBSS Ltd., UK

Oluwafemi O. Olawoyin
http://orcid.org/0000-0002-8016-267X
Somerset NHS Foundation Trust, UK

Mayowa Samuel Olokun
http://orcid.org/0000-0001-6310-696X
Amdari, UK

Andrew Chinonso Nwanakwaugwu
http://orcid.org/0000-0002-2929-9638
University of Salford, UK

ABSTRACT

The rapid expansion of the Internet of Things (IoT) has driven a shift toward distributed intelligence, where interconnected devices generate and process large-scale data in real time. Traditional cloud-centric architectures face limitations including high latency, bandwidth constraints, and increased privacy risks. To address these challenges, Tiny Machine Learning (TinyML) enables machine learning inference directly on resource-constrained edge devices, supporting efficient, low-power, and real-time decision-making. However, this decentralization introduces critical concerns related to security, privacy, and trust. This chapter examines key vulner-

DOI: 10.4018/979-8-2600-0615-3.ch010

abilities such as adversarial attacks, model extraction, and data leakage, while also addressing trust management challenges in distributed environments. It further reviews emerging solutions, including federated learning, lightweight cryptography, blockchain integration, and hardware-based security, and proposes a framework for secure TinyML deployment.

1. INTRODUCTION

The rapid proliferation of the Internet of Things (IoT) has fundamentally reshaped modern computing infrastructures by embedding intelligence into a wide array of everyday objects, including wearable devices, smart home systems, autonomous vehicles, and industrial platforms. This transformation has enabled seamless data collection, communication, and automation across diverse domains. However, the exponential growth of IoT devices has also led to the generation of massive volumes of heterogeneous data, creating significant challenges in data processing, scalability, and system efficiency. Recent studies emphasize that the increasing scale of IoT deployments demands more distributed and intelligent processing paradigms to manage complexity and latency effectively .

Traditionally, IoT systems have relied on centralized cloud computing architectures, where data collected from edge devices is transmitted to remote servers for storage and analysis. While this approach provides substantial computational resources, it introduces critical limitations, including high latency, bandwidth constraints, and increased vulnerability to cyber threats. Furthermore, centralized data aggregation raises serious privacy concerns, as sensitive information is exposed during transmission and storage. Contemporary research highlights that cloud-centric IoT models are increasingly inadequate for real-time and privacy-sensitive applications, particularly in healthcare, industrial automation, and smart infrastructure .

To address these limitations, edge computing has emerged as a paradigm that brings computation closer to the data source, enabling faster processing, reduced latency, and improved bandwidth efficiency. Building upon this paradigm, Tiny Machine Learning (TinyML) has gained significant traction as an enabling technology that allows machine learning (ML) models to be deployed directly on resource-constrained devices such as microcontrollers. TinyML systems are optimized for ultra-low power consumption, minimal memory usage, and real-time inference capabilities, making them suitable for a wide range of IoT applications.

Despite these advantages, the decentralization of intelligence introduces significant security challenges. The distributed nature of TinyML-enabled IoT systems expands the attack surface, as devices are often deployed in physically accessible and untrusted environments. The rapid growth of IoT and edge computing significantly increases cybersecurity risks, particularly in critical infrastructures such as energy systems, healthcare, and smart cities . Laiu et al. (2026) highlight that integrating TinyML with federated learning, while beneficial for privacy, also introduces vulnerabilities such as model poisoning and adversarial manipulation in distributed learning environments .

Privacy concerns also remain a critical issue in edge intelligence systems. Although TinyML reduces the need to transmit raw data to centralized servers, sensitive information may still be exposed through model updates, inference outputs, or side-channel attacks. Recent studies indicate that even privacy-preserving techniques such as federated learning are susceptible to data reconstruction and inference attacks if proper safeguards are not implemented . Additionally, the decentralized nature of edge computing complicates compliance with regulatory frameworks, as data governance and accountability become more difficult to enforce.

Given these challenges, there is a growing need for holistic approaches that address security, privacy, and trust simultaneously in TinyML-based IoT systems. Recent advancements in federated TinyML architectures, energy-efficient security mechanisms, and privacy-preserving learning frameworks demonstrate promising directions for achieving secure and scalable edge intelligence. However, significant research gaps remain, particularly in balancing security robustness with the resource constraints of edge devices. In this context, this chapter aims to provide a comprehensive analysis of the challenges and emerging solutions associated with TinyML-enabled IoT edge intelligence. Specifically, the objectives of this study are as follows:

1. To analyze security threats in TinyML-based IoT systems
2. To examine privacy risks associated with edge intelligence
3. To explore trust management mechanisms in decentralized environments
4. To review emerging mitigation techniques and security frameworks
5. To identify future research directions for secure and trustworthy TinyML deployment

By synthesizing insights from recent IEEE, Elsevier, and Springer publications, this study contributes to the development of secure, privacy-preserving, and trustworthy TinyML-enabled IoT ecosystems.

2. BACKGROUND AND RELATED WORK

2.1 IoT and Edge Intelligence

The Internet of Things (IoT) represents a paradigm in which a vast number of interconnected devices are equipped with sensing, communication, and computational capabilities to interact with both physical and digital environments. These devices continuously generate large volumes of data, enabling applications such as smart cities, healthcare monitoring, industrial automation, and environmental sensing. As noted in prior research, IoT systems form complex distributed networks where devices not only collect data but also collaborate to perform intelligent tasks and support autonomous decision-making processes (Yu et al., 2017).

However, the rapid expansion of IoT ecosystems has introduced significant challenges related to data processing, scalability, and latency. Traditional cloud-centric architectures require transmitting data from edge devices to centralized cloud servers for processing and analysis. While this model offers high computational power and storage capacity, it suffers from inherent limitations such as network congestion, high latency, and increased bandwidth consumption. These constraints make cloud-based solutions unsuitable for time-sensitive applications, where real-time decision-making is critical. Furthermore, the centralized nature of cloud computing raises privacy and security concerns, as sensitive data must be transmitted and stored in remote servers, increasing the risk of interception and unauthorized access. To address these limitations, edge computing has emerged as a transformative paradigm that shifts computation and data storage closer to the data source. Edge computing enables localized data processing at or near IoT devices, thereby reducing the need for continuous communication with centralized cloud infrastructure. This proximity significantly reduces latency and improves response times, making it particularly suitable for delay-sensitive applications such as autonomous driving, industrial control systems, and real-time health monitoring (Kong et al., 2022). Additionally, edge computing alleviates bandwidth constraints by filtering and preprocessing data locally before transmitting only relevant information to the cloud. Edge intelligence, also referred to as edge AI, extends the concept of edge computing by embedding artificial intelligence capabilities directly into edge devices. This enables IoT systems to perform intelligent data analysis and decision-making locally, without relying on centralized processing. According to Zhou et al. (2019), edge intelligence represents a convergence of edge computing and artificial intelligence, where machine learning models are deployed at the network edge to process data in real time. This paradigm enhances system autonomy, reduces communication overhead, and enables continuous operation even in environments with limited or intermittent connectivity.

Recent advancements in lightweight machine learning techniques, including TinyML, have further accelerated the adoption of edge intelligence. TinyML allows machine learning models to be deployed on resource-constrained devices such as microcontrollers, enabling efficient inference with minimal power consumption. This development has opened new opportunities for deploying intelligent applications in constrained environments while maintaining energy efficiency and scalability.

Despite its advantages, edge intelligence introduces new research challenges. The distributed nature of edge-based systems complicates resource management, task scheduling, and system coordination. Moreover, while edge computing improves privacy by reducing data transmission, it also introduces new attack vectors at the device level, as edge nodes are often physically exposed and lack robust security mechanisms. Additionally, ensuring consistency and reliability across distributed edge nodes remains a critical concern in large-scale IoT deployments.

2.2 Tiny Machine Learning (TinyML)

The concept of tiny machine learning (TinyML) has emerged as an important step forward within edge intelligence, enabling machine learning (ML) models to be deployed directly on microcontrollers and embedded systems with limited resources. While traditional machine learning approaches rely on cloud or high-performance computing infrastructures, TinyML offers ultra-low power, memory-efficient, and real-time inference capabilities, making it ideal for IoT applications. TinyML has shown potential to bridge the gap between artificial intelligence and embedded systems by enabling on-device intelligence. As described by Abadade et al. (2023), TinyML is a significant step forward in edge computing because it allows machine learning algorithms to be integrated into devices with extremely limited computational resources, often consuming a few kilobytes of memory and a few milliwatts of power. This capability allows IoT devices to perform complex tasks such as pattern recognition, anomaly detection, and predictive analytics without relying on continuous cloud connectivity. A key characteristic of TinyML is its reliance on model optimization techniques to meet strict hardware constraints. Techniques such as quantization, pruning, knowledge distillation, and neural architecture search are widely used to reduce model size and computational complexity while maintaining acceptable levels of accuracy. In recent studies, it has been demonstrated that these optimization strategies enable the application of sophisticated models such as convolutional neural networks (CNNs) and lightweight transformer architectures to devices with extremely small memory footprints. Furthermore, advances in hardware-software co-design have played a crucial role in improving the efficiency of TinyML systems, allowing tighter integration between ML models and embedded hardware platforms. TinyML also enables real-time, on-device inference, which is critical for latency-sensitive applications. Unlike cloud-based inference, which requires data transmission and processing delays, TinyML allows devices to process data locally, resulting in faster response times and reduced bandwidth usage. Recent research confirms that TinyML is particularly advantageous in applications where low latency and energy efficiency are essential, such as wearable health monitoring, industrial automation, and environmental sensing . Additionally, local processing enhances privacy by minimizing the need to transmit sensitive data to external servers.

2.3 Related Research

Recent research has increasingly focused on the convergence of federated learning (FL) and Tiny Machine Learning (TinyML) as a promising approach to enabling secure, privacy-preserving, and scalable intelligence in IoT edge environments. This integration addresses the limitations of centralized machine learning by distributing both computation and learning processes across resource-constrained devices while maintaining data locality. Federated learning has emerged as a key enabler of decentralized intelligence by allowing multiple devices to collaboratively train machine learning models without sharing raw data. Instead, devices exchange model parameters or gradients, thereby preserving data privacy. As highlighted by Li, Ge, and Tian (2024), federated learning plays a critical role in enhancing data security and privacy in edge-IoT systems, particularly in scenarios where sensitive data such as healthcare or industrial information must remain local. Their comprehensive survey emphasizes that FL mitigates risks associated with centralized data storage while supporting scalable and distributed model training .

Similarly, Alam and Gupta (2022) argue that federated learning provides a robust privacy-preserving framework for IoT systems by eliminating the need to transfer raw data to centralized servers. Their work demonstrates that decentralized training significantly reduces the risk of data breaches while maintaining model performance, making FL particularly suitable for privacy-sensitive applications such as smart healthcare and smart cities.

Building upon these foundations, recent studies have explored the integration of federated learning with TinyML to enable intelligent processing directly on resource-constrained edge devices. TinyML focuses on deploying lightweight machine learning models on microcontrollers, while federated learning enables collaborative training across distributed devices. The convergence of these technologies allows IoT systems to achieve both real-time inference and decentralized learning. According to Myakala et al. (2025), this integration represents a transformative step toward enabling intelligent and privacy-preserving applications in edge environments, as it combines the efficiency of TinyML with the collaborative capabilities of federated learning .

Recent work published in *Information Fusion* further demonstrates the effectiveness of combining federated learning with TinyML for IoT applications. The study proposes a federated architecture that supports on-device training and transfer learning, enabling edge devices to update models locally while sharing knowledge globally. This approach reduces latency, minimizes bandwidth usage, and preserves data privacy by ensuring that raw data never leaves the device .

Moreover, emerging research has begun to explore advanced frameworks that integrate federated learning, TinyML, and IoT into unified systems. For instance, Ramadan et al. (2025) present a comprehensive framework that combines over-the-air model updates, distributed communication protocols, and data compression techniques to optimize performance in resource-constrained environments. Their findings highlight that such frameworks can significantly improve communication efficiency while maintaining model accuracy and privacy .

In addition to performance improvements, recent studies have emphasized the role of federated TinyML in enhancing system resilience and security. Laiu et al. (2026) propose a multi-layer architecture that leverages TinyML for local anomaly detection and federated learning for collaborative threat intelligence sharing. Their results demonstrate that this approach improves cybersecurity in IoT systems by enabling distributed detection of cyber threats while preserving data privacy .

Despite these advancements, several challenges remain in the integration of federated learning and TinyML. One major issue is communication overhead, as frequent exchange of model updates can strain network resources, particularly in large-scale IoT deployments. Additionally, heterogeneity among devices in terms of computational capabilities, data distribution, and network connectivity complicates model training and aggregation processes. Privacy leakage through model updates, such as gradient inversion attacks, also remains a significant concern.

Furthermore, the resource constraints of TinyML devices limit the complexity of models that can be deployed and trained locally. As noted by Fragkou and Katsaros (2024), most TinyML systems currently rely on inference-only models, with training typically performed on more powerful systems due to computational limitations. However, recent research is exploring adaptive and on-device learning techniques to overcome these constraints .

Overall, the integration of federated learning and TinyML represents a rapidly evolving research area with significant potential for enabling secure, scalable, and privacy-preserving IoT systems. While current approaches demonstrate promising results, further research is required to address challenges related to efficiency, robustness, and security in real-world deployments.

3. SECURITY CHALLENGES IN TINYML-BASED IOT SYSTEMS

3.1 Adversarial Attacks

Adversarial attacks represent one of the most critical security threats to machine learning (ML) systems, including those deployed in TinyML-based IoT environments. These attacks involve deliberately crafting malicious inputs—known as adversarial examples—that are designed to deceive machine learning models into producing incorrect outputs. Typically, such perturbations are minimal and often imperceptible to human observers, yet they can significantly alter model predictions. The vulnerability of ML models to adversarial manipulation was first systematically demonstrated by Ian J. Goodfellow et al. (2015), who showed that even simple linear perturbations can lead to misclassification in deep neural networks.

In the context of TinyML, adversarial attacks pose even greater risks due to the inherent limitations of resource-constrained devices. TinyML systems are designed to operate with minimal memory, processing power, and energy consumption, which restricts the implementation of sophisticated defense mechanisms such as adversarial training, anomaly detection, or input validation. As a result, these systems often lack robustness against adversarial inputs, making them particularly susceptible to manipulation (Abadade et al., 2023).

One of the key challenges in TinyML environments is that adversarial perturbations can be introduced both digitally and physically. Digital attacks involve modifying input data before it is processed by the model, while physical attacks manipulate real-world inputs captured by sensors. For example, in image-based applications, slight alterations such as noise patterns or stickers can cause misclassification by embedded vision models. Similarly, in audio-based systems, carefully crafted sound signals can mislead speech recognition models. These attacks are especially concerning in IoT applications where sensors continuously interact with the physical environment.

Recent studies have demonstrated that adversarial vulnerabilities are not limited to high-capacity models but also extend to lightweight models used in TinyML. Capogrosso et al. (2024) highlight that model compression techniques such as quantization and pruning commonly used in TinyML to reduce computational requirements can inadvertently increase susceptibility to adversarial attacks. This occurs because compressed models may lose redundancy and robustness, making them more sensitive to small input perturbations. Consequently, the trade-off between efficiency and security becomes a critical concern in TinyML system design.

Furthermore, adversarial attacks pose significant risks in safety-critical applications. In healthcare systems, for instance, TinyML models are increasingly used for real-time monitoring of physiological signals such as heart rate, electrocardiograms

(ECG), and activity patterns. Adversarial manipulation of such data could lead to incorrect diagnoses or failure to detect critical conditions, potentially endangering patient lives. Similarly, in autonomous systems and smart transportation, adversarial inputs can cause misinterpretation of sensor data, leading to incorrect decisions and potentially catastrophic outcomes.

3.2 Model Extraction Attacks

Model extraction attacks, also referred to as model stealing attacks, represent a significant threat to machine learning systems deployed in TinyML-based IoT environments. These attacks aim to replicate or approximate a target machine learning model by systematically querying it and analyzing its outputs. The attacker constructs a surrogate model that closely mimics the behavior of the original model, thereby compromising intellectual property, system confidentiality, and overall security.

The concept of model extraction was formally introduced by Florian Tramèr et al. (2016), who demonstrated that adversaries can reconstruct proprietary models by exploiting prediction APIs. By sending carefully crafted inputs and observing corresponding outputs, attackers can infer decision boundaries and model parameters with high accuracy. This threat is particularly relevant in IoT systems where models are deployed on edge devices and exposed through interfaces for real-time inference.

TinyML systems are especially vulnerable to model extraction attacks due to their constrained architecture and deployment characteristics. Unlike cloud-based models that can implement sophisticated access controls and monitoring mechanisms, TinyML models often operate in open or semi-trusted environments with limited security safeguards. Edge devices may expose inference endpoints through local APIs, wireless communication protocols, or sensor interfaces, making them accessible to adversaries. Furthermore, the simplicity and compactness of TinyML models—often achieved through pruning and quantization—can make it easier for attackers to approximate their functionality using fewer queries (Jagielski et al., 2020).

A key factor contributing to the vulnerability of TinyML systems is the lack of robust access control and query rate limiting. In many IoT applications, devices are designed for continuous interaction with users or other systems, which inadvertently provides attackers with repeated opportunities to query the model. Over time, these queries can be used to reconstruct a functionally equivalent model. This process is further facilitated by advancements in automated model extraction techniques, including active learning and adaptive querying strategies.

Model extraction attacks pose several critical risks. First, they enable intellectual property theft, as attackers can replicate proprietary models without access to the original training data or architecture. This undermines the economic value of machine learning models and discourages innovation. Second, extracted models can be used to launch further attacks, such as adversarial example generation or model inversion attacks, thereby amplifying security vulnerabilities. Third, in safety-critical applications, unauthorized replication of models may lead to misuse or deployment in unregulated environments, increasing the risk of harm.

In the context of TinyML-based IoT systems, model extraction can also compromise system integrity and trust. For example, in industrial IoT settings, extracted models used for predictive maintenance or anomaly detection could be manipulated or redeployed to disrupt operations. Similarly, in healthcare applications, stolen models may expose sensitive patterns related to patient data, even if raw data is not directly accessed. Research by Orekondy, Schiele, and Fritz (2019) demonstrates that even black-box models—where only output predictions are available—can be effectively replicated using query-based attacks, highlighting the severity of this threat.

Another critical concern is the role of model extraction in distributed learning frameworks such as federated learning. In such systems, adversaries may attempt to extract global or local models by observing updates or interacting with participating nodes. This not only compromises model confidentiality but also introduces risks of data leakage, as extracted models may reveal information about the training dataset. Recent studies indicate that combining model extraction with other attack vectors, such as membership inference, can significantly increase privacy risks in distributed environments (Tramèr et al., 2016; Jagielski et al., 2020).

To mitigate model extraction attacks, several defense mechanisms have been proposed. These include limiting access to model outputs, reducing the precision of predictions (e.g., returning only class labels instead of probabilities), and implementing query rate limiting. Additionally, techniques such as watermarking and fingerprinting of machine learning models have been explored to detect unauthorized replication. However, these approaches may be challenging to implement in TinyML systems due to resource constraints and the need for real-time performance.

Recent research has also explored the use of secure enclaves and hardware-based protections to safeguard models deployed on edge devices. Furthermore, privacy-preserving techniques such as differential privacy and secure multiparty computation can reduce the risk of information leakage during model interaction. Nevertheless, balancing security with computational efficiency remains a major challenge in TinyML environments.

In conclusion, model extraction attacks pose a serious threat to TinyML-based IoT systems by enabling unauthorized replication of machine learning models and facilitating subsequent attacks. The constrained nature of TinyML devices, combined with their exposure in distributed environments, exacerbates this vulnerability. While various mitigation strategies have been proposed, further research is required to develop lightweight, scalable, and effective defenses suitable for resource-constrained edge devices.

3.3 Model Poisoning

Model poisoning attacks constitute a significant class of security threats in machine learning systems, particularly in distributed environments such as TinyML-based IoT networks. These attacks involve the deliberate injection of malicious or manipulated data into the training process with the objective of compromising model integrity, degrading performance, or introducing targeted backdoors. Unlike adversarial attacks, which manipulate inputs at inference time, poisoning attacks occur during the training phase, making them more difficult to detect and mitigate.

The vulnerability of machine learning systems to poisoning attacks has been extensively studied in the literature. Early work by Biggio, Nelson, and Laskov (2012) demonstrated that attackers could significantly degrade classifier performance by injecting carefully crafted training samples. More recent studies have expanded this concept to modern deep learning systems, showing that even a small fraction of poisoned data can have a substantial impact on model behavior (Steinhardt, Koh, & Liang, 2017). These findings are particularly concerning in IoT environments, where data is often collected from diverse and potentially untrusted sources.

TinyML-based IoT systems are especially susceptible to model poisoning attacks due to their reliance on distributed data collection and collaborative learning mechanisms. In many IoT applications, data is generated by numerous edge devices, which may vary in trustworthiness and security. Attackers can exploit this heterogeneity by compromising one or more devices and injecting malicious data into the training pipeline. This is particularly relevant in federated learning frameworks, where local models are trained on-device and aggregated to form a global model. As highlighted by Virginia Smith and colleagues, federated learning systems are inherently vulnerable to poisoning attacks because they rely on contributions from multiple, potentially adversarial participants.

3.4 Hardware and Firmware Vulnerabilities

Hardware and firmware vulnerabilities represent a fundamental security challenge in TinyML-based IoT systems, primarily due to the constrained nature of edge devices and their widespread deployment in unprotected environments. Unlike traditional computing systems, IoT devices are often designed with minimal hardware resources and cost efficiency in mind, which frequently results in the omission of robust security mechanisms. Consequently, these devices become attractive targets for attackers seeking to gain unauthorized access, manipulate system behavior, or extract sensitive information.

One of the most critical weaknesses in many IoT devices is the absence of secure boot mechanisms. Secure boot ensures that a device only executes firmware that is cryptographically verified and trusted by the manufacturer. Without secure boot, attackers can replace or modify firmware images, enabling the execution of malicious code during device startup. As highlighted by Sadeghi et al. (2015), the lack of secure boot in embedded systems significantly increases the risk of persistent compromise, as attackers can implant rootkits that remain undetected even after system reboots.

Another major concern is the lack of tamper-resistant hardware. IoT devices are often deployed in physically accessible locations such as industrial sites, smart homes, or public infrastructure, making them vulnerable to physical attacks. Attackers can exploit this accessibility to perform hardware-level attacks, including probing, fault injection, and side-channel analysis. These techniques allow adversaries to extract cryptographic keys, reverse-engineer firmware, or alter device functionality. According to Rostami et al. (2014), physical access to embedded systems can enable invasive and non-invasive attacks that bypass software-level security controls, highlighting the importance of hardware-based protection mechanisms.

3.5 Communication Attacks

Communication security is a fundamental requirement in TinyML-based IoT systems, as these environments depend heavily on continuous data exchange between sensors, edge devices, gateways, and, in some cases, cloud services. The integrity, confidentiality, and authenticity of transmitted data are critical for ensuring accurate machine learning inference and reliable system operation. However, due to the resource-constrained nature of IoT devices and the use of lightweight communication protocols, many TinyML-enabled systems lack robust security mechanisms, making them highly susceptible to communication-based attacks.

A primary concern in such systems is that data transmitted between devices can be intercepted, modified, or replayed by malicious actors. In many IoT deployments, communication channels are either unencrypted or rely on weak cryptographic schemes due to limitations in computational power and energy availability. As highlighted by Roman, Zhou, and Lopez (2013), insufficient implementation of encryption and authentication protocols exposes IoT systems to a wide range of security threats, particularly in distributed and heterogeneous environments.

One of the most prevalent communication threats is the man-in-the-middle (MitM) attack, in which an adversary secretly intercepts and potentially alters communication between two legitimate entities. In TinyML-based IoT systems, MitM attacks can be particularly damaging because they allow attackers to manipulate input data before it is processed by machine learning models. For instance, in a smart healthcare system, an attacker could intercept and modify transmitted sensor data, leading to incorrect medical assessments. Similarly, in industrial IoT environments, altered data could disrupt automated control systems and cause operational failures.

Conti, Dragoni, and Lesyk (2016) note that MitM attacks are especially effective in IoT systems due to weak authentication protocols and the absence of mutual trust verification between devices.

4. PRIVACY ISSUES IN EDGE INTELLIGENCE

The integration of TinyML with edge intelligence has significantly improved data processing efficiency and reduced reliance on centralized cloud infrastructures. By enabling on-device inference, TinyML minimizes the need to transmit raw data to external servers, thereby enhancing privacy preservation. However, despite these advantages, privacy risks remain a critical concern in edge-based systems. The decentralized nature of edge intelligence introduces new vulnerabilities related to data exposure, inference attacks, and regulatory compliance. This section examines key privacy challenges associated with TinyML-enabled IoT systems.

4.1 Data Leakage

Although TinyML reduces cloud dependency by processing data locally, sensitive information remains vulnerable during on-device computation. Edge devices often handle highly sensitive data, including personal health information, location data, and environmental signals. These devices typically lack robust security mechanisms, making them susceptible to data leakage through various channels.

Data leakage in edge intelligence systems can occur through unintended exposure of raw data, intermediate computations, or model parameters. For example, memory access patterns, cache usage, and power consumption can reveal sensitive information through side-channel attacks. As highlighted by Reza Shokri et al. (2017), even indirect access to model behavior can enable attackers to infer private information. Additionally, recent studies emphasize that resource-constrained devices often lack encryption and secure storage mechanisms, further increasing the risk of data exposure (Li et al., 2024).

Furthermore, edge devices are frequently deployed in physically accessible environments, making them vulnerable to physical attacks that can extract stored data. This is particularly concerning in applications such as smart healthcare and smart homes, where compromised data can have severe privacy implications. As noted by Roman et al. (2013), ensuring data confidentiality in distributed IoT environments remains a major challenge due to the heterogeneity and scale of deployed devices.

4.2 Inference Attacks

Inference attacks represent a significant privacy threat in TinyML-based systems, where attackers exploit model outputs to infer sensitive information about the training data. These attacks do not require direct access to the data itself; instead, they rely on analyzing patterns in model predictions.

One of the most well-known forms of inference attacks is the membership inference attack, which determines whether a specific data sample was included in the training dataset. Shokri et al. (2017) demonstrated that machine learning models often exhibit different behaviors for training data compared to unseen data, enabling attackers to infer membership with high accuracy. This poses serious privacy risks, particularly in sensitive applications such as healthcare, where the presence of an individual's data in a training set may reveal confidential information.

In addition to membership inference, model inversion attacks can reconstruct sensitive features of training data by exploiting model outputs. For example, attackers can approximate input features such as images or personal attributes by analyzing prediction probabilities. Recent research indicates that even lightweight models used in TinyML are vulnerable to such attacks, despite their reduced complexity. The risk of inference attacks is further exacerbated in edge intelligence systems due to the continuous interaction between devices and users. Frequent querying of models increases the amount of information available to attackers, thereby improving their ability to infer sensitive data. Moreover, the lack of robust monitoring and anomaly detection mechanisms in resource-constrained devices makes it difficult to detect such attacks in real time.

4.3 Privacy in Federated Learning

Federated learning (FL) has emerged as a promising approach to addressing privacy concerns in distributed IoT systems by enabling collaborative model training without sharing raw data. In FL, each device trains a local model using its own data and shares only model updates (e.g., gradients or weights) with a central server or aggregator. This approach reduces the risk of direct data exposure and enhances privacy preservation.

However, recent research has shown that federated learning is not inherently secure and may still leak sensitive information through model updates. Li et al. (2024) highlight that gradients transmitted during federated learning can reveal private information about local datasets if not properly protected. Attackers can exploit these gradients to reconstruct input data or infer sensitive attributes, undermining the privacy benefits of FL.

Moreover, gradient leakage attacks have demonstrated that it is possible to recover original training data from shared gradients with high accuracy. Alatawi (2025) emphasizes that without additional privacy-preserving techniques, such as differential privacy or secure aggregation, federated learning systems remain vulnerable to information leakage. These vulnerabilities are particularly concerning in TinyML environments, where computational constraints limit the implementation of advanced privacy-preserving mechanisms.

To address these challenges, various techniques have been proposed, including differential privacy, secure multiparty computation, and homomorphic encryption. While these methods enhance privacy, they introduce additional computational and communication overhead, which may not be suitable for resource-constrained TinyML devices. Therefore, achieving a balance between privacy protection and system efficiency remains a key research challenge.

4.4 Regulatory Challenges

The decentralized nature of edge intelligence and TinyML systems introduces significant challenges in complying with data protection regulations such as the General Data Protection Regulation (GDPR). These regulations impose strict requirements on data collection, processing, storage, and sharing, including principles such as data minimization, transparency, and user consent.

In traditional cloud-based systems, data governance is relatively straightforward, as data is stored and processed in centralized locations. However, in edge-based systems, data is distributed across multiple devices, making it difficult to establish clear ownership and accountability. As a result, determining who is responsible for data protection—whether it is the device manufacturer, service provider, or end user—becomes a complex issue.

Furthermore, the dynamic nature of IoT environments complicates compliance efforts. Devices frequently join and leave networks, and data may be processed across different jurisdictions with varying regulatory requirements. This creates challenges in ensuring consistent compliance with international data protection laws. According to Sicari et al. (2015), the lack of standardized frameworks for privacy management in IoT systems further exacerbates these issues.

5. TRUST MANAGEMENT IN DISTRIBUTED IOT NETWORKS

The rapid expansion of IoT ecosystems and the integration of TinyML have introduced significant challenges in establishing trust among distributed devices. In decentralized environments, devices often operate autonomously and interact with unknown or partially trusted entities. As a result, ensuring reliable communication, secure collaboration, and accurate data exchange requires robust trust management mechanisms. Trust management in IoT systems involves evaluating the reliability, integrity, and behavior of devices to mitigate risks associated with malicious or compromised nodes.

5.1 Trust Models

Trust models are fundamental components of trust management systems, providing mechanisms to evaluate the reliability of devices based on various criteria such as historical behavior, communication patterns, and contextual information. These models enable IoT systems to make informed decisions about whether to trust a particular device or interaction.

Trust evaluation mechanisms typically rely on both direct trust and indirect trust. Direct trust is derived from a device's own interactions with another entity, while indirect trust is based on recommendations or feedback from other devices in the network. According to Yan et al. (2014), combining these trust metrics improves the accuracy of trust evaluation in dynamic IoT environments. Additionally, recent research highlights the importance of incorporating machine learning techniques into trust models to enhance adaptability and scalability in large-scale networks.

In TinyML-based systems, trust models must be lightweight and efficient due to resource constraints. This limits the complexity of trust evaluation algorithms and necessitates the development of optimized approaches that can operate within constrained computational environments while maintaining reliability.

5.2 Reputation Systems

Reputation systems extend trust models by enabling devices to build reputational scores over time based on their behavior and interactions. These systems aggregate historical data to assess the trustworthiness of nodes, allowing the network to identify and isolate malicious entities.

In distributed IoT networks, reputation systems play a crucial role in maintaining system integrity. Devices that consistently exhibit reliable behavior gain higher reputation scores, while those that demonstrate malicious or anomalous activities are penalized. This dynamic evaluation process enables the network to adapt to changing conditions and mitigate risks associated with compromised nodes.

Recent studies emphasize that reputation-based mechanisms are effective in detecting insider attacks and preventing the propagation of false data in IoT systems. However, challenges such as false reputation reporting, collusion attacks, and scalability issues remain significant concerns (Chen et al., 2023). In TinyML environments, the implementation of reputation systems must also consider memory and processing limitations, requiring efficient data storage and computation strategies.

5.3 Blockchain-Based Trust

Blockchain technology has emerged as a promising solution for trust management in distributed IoT systems due to its decentralized, transparent, and tamper-resistant nature. By leveraging distributed ledger technology, blockchain eliminates the need for centralized trust authorities and enables secure, peer-to-peer interactions among devices.

Blockchain provides several key advantages for IoT trust management, including:

- Decentralized trust management: Trust decisions are distributed across the network, reducing reliance on centralized entities.
- Data immutability: Once recorded, data cannot be altered, ensuring the integrity of transactions and device interactions.
- Transparent transactions: All network participants can verify transactions, enhancing accountability and trust.

Recent research demonstrates that blockchain-integrated frameworks significantly enhance trust and security in IoT environments. For example, a study published in *Nature Research* highlights that combining blockchain with edge intelligence enables secure data sharing and robust trust management in distributed systems (Zhang et al., 2025). Additionally, blockchain can support secure identity management, access control, and auditability, which are critical for large-scale IoT deployments.

However, integrating blockchain into TinyML-based systems presents challenges, including high computational overhead, energy consumption, and scalability limitations. Lightweight blockchain solutions and hybrid architectures are being explored to address these issues and make blockchain feasible for resource-constrained environments.

5.4 Trustworthy Machine Learning

Trustworthy machine learning is a critical aspect of trust management in TinyML-based IoT systems, particularly in applications where decisions have significant real-world consequences. Trust in ML systems encompasses several key dimensions, including robustness, fairness, explainability, and accountability.

- Robustness refers to the ability of a model to maintain performance under adversarial conditions or noisy inputs.

- Fairness ensures that model decisions are unbiased and do not discriminate against specific groups.
- Explainability enables users to understand how and why a model makes certain decisions.
- Accountability involves establishing responsibility for model behavior and outcomes.

According to Rashmi Upreti et al. (2024), ensuring these properties is essential for deploying machine learning systems in critical domains such as healthcare, finance, and autonomous systems. Their study emphasizes that trustworthiness must be integrated into the entire machine learning lifecycle, from data collection and model training to deployment and monitoring.

In TinyML environments, achieving trustworthy machine learning is particularly challenging due to limited computational resources and the lack of transparency in embedded models. Additionally, the decentralized nature of IoT systems complicates accountability, as multiple devices contribute to decision-making processes. Recent research suggests that combining explainable AI techniques with decentralized trust frameworks can enhance transparency and user confidence in TinyML systems.

6. EMERGING SOLUTIONS FOR SECURE TINYML DEPLOYMENT

The growing adoption of TinyML in IoT edge environments has intensified the need for robust security, privacy, and trust mechanisms tailored to resource-constrained devices. While TinyML introduces new vulnerabilities, recent research has proposed several innovative solutions to mitigate these risks. These solutions aim to balance security requirements with the limited computational, memory, and energy resources available in edge devices. This section explores key emerging approaches, including federated learning, lightweight cryptography, hardware-based security, blockchain integration, and explainable artificial intelligence.

6.1 Federated Learning

Federated learning (FL) has emerged as a prominent solution for enabling secure and privacy-preserving machine learning in distributed IoT environments. Unlike traditional centralized learning approaches, federated learning allows multiple devices to collaboratively train a shared model without transmitting raw data. Instead, devices compute local updates and share only model parameters or gradients with a central aggregator or decentralized network.

This approach offers several advantages for TinyML-based systems:

- Enhanced privacy: Sensitive data remains on-device, reducing the risk of exposure during transmission.
- Reduced communication overhead: Only model updates are transmitted, minimizing bandwidth usage.
- Support for decentralized intelligence: Devices can collaboratively learn while maintaining autonomy.

According to Dinh C. Nguyen et al. (2021), federated learning is particularly well-suited for IoT applications due to its ability to handle distributed data sources and preserve privacy in large-scale networks. Their comprehensive survey highlights that FL enables scalable and efficient model training across heterogeneous devices while addressing data governance concerns.

However, federated learning also introduces challenges, including communication efficiency, model heterogeneity, and vulnerability to adversarial and poisoning attacks. Recent research focuses on optimizing FL protocols for TinyML environments by reducing communication frequency and incorporating secure aggregation techniques.

6.4 Blockchain Integration

Blockchain technology has gained significant attention as a solution for enhancing trust, security, and data integrity in distributed IoT systems. By leveraging decentralized ledger technology, blockchain eliminates the need for centralized authorities and enables secure, transparent interactions among devices.

In the context of TinyML and IoT, blockchain offers several key benefits:

- Data integrity: Immutable records prevent unauthorized data modification
- Trust management: Decentralized consensus mechanisms establish trust among devices
- Secure data sharing: Cryptographic techniques ensure confidentiality and authenticity

Recent studies demonstrate that integrating blockchain with edge intelligence improves the security and reliability of IoT systems. For example, Zhang et al. (2025) show that blockchain-based frameworks can enhance secure data exchange and trust management in distributed environments. Additionally, blockchain can support secure model sharing and update verification in federated learning systems.

Despite its advantages, blockchain integration faces challenges related to scalability, latency, and energy consumption. Lightweight blockchain architectures and off-chain solutions are being explored to address these limitations in TinyML environments.

7. CASE STUDIES AND APPLICATIONS

The integration of TinyML into IoT ecosystems has enabled a wide range of real-world applications across multiple domains. By facilitating real-time, on-device intelligence, TinyML enhances system efficiency, reduces latency, and improves privacy preservation. However, the deployment of TinyML in practical environments also exposes critical security, privacy, and trust challenges. This section presents key case studies in smart healthcare, industrial IoT, and smart cities, highlighting both the benefits and associated risks of TinyML-based systems.

7.1 Smart Healthcare

Smart healthcare represents one of the most promising application domains for TinyML, where real-time monitoring and analysis of physiological data are essential. TinyML-enabled wearable devices and medical sensors can process data locally, enabling continuous monitoring of vital signs such as heart rate, blood pressure, and electrocardiogram (ECG) signals. This on-device processing reduces latency and allows for immediate detection of anomalies, which is critical for timely medical intervention.

Recent studies demonstrate that TinyML-based healthcare systems can significantly improve patient outcomes by enabling early diagnosis and personalized treatment. Deploying lightweight machine learning models on wearable devices allows for continuous health monitoring without reliance on cloud connectivity. Additionally, edge-based healthcare systems enhance privacy by keeping sensitive patient data on-device.

However, despite these advantages, smart healthcare systems remain highly vulnerable to security and privacy threats. Data breaches can expose sensitive medical information, including personal health records and biometric data. According to Rieke et al. (2020), healthcare data is among the most sensitive types of personal information, and unauthorized access can lead to severe consequences, including identity theft and discrimination. Furthermore, compromised TinyML models may produce inaccurate predictions, potentially leading to misdiagnosis or delayed treatment. In addition, healthcare systems are vulnerable to inference and adversarial attacks. Attackers may manipulate input data or exploit model vulnerabilities to alter predictions, thereby compromising system reliability. These risks underscore the importance of implementing robust security and privacy mechanisms in TinyML-based healthcare applications.

7.2 Industrial IoT

The application of TinyML in Industrial IoT (IIoT) has revolutionized manufacturing processes by enabling predictive maintenance, anomaly detection, and real-time monitoring of industrial equipment. TinyML models deployed on edge devices can analyze sensor data locally, allowing for early detection of faults and reducing downtime. This improves operational efficiency and reduces maintenance costs.

According to Lee et al. (2018), the integration of intelligent analytics in industrial systems enhances productivity and supports the development of smart manufacturing environments. TinyML further extends these capabilities by enabling real-time decision-making directly at the edge, without relying on centralized cloud systems. However, the deployment of TinyML in industrial environments introduces significant security risks. Compromised models can disrupt manufacturing processes, leading to production delays, equipment damage, and substantial financial losses. For example, an attacker who manipulates a predictive maintenance model could prevent the detection of equipment failures, resulting in unexpected breakdowns. Similarly, tampering with anomaly detection systems could allow malicious activities to go unnoticed. Industrial IoT systems are also vulnerable to cyber-physical attacks, where attackers exploit both digital and physical components of the system. As highlighted by Humayed et al. (2017), such attacks can have severe consequences, including safety hazards and large-scale operational disruptions. The interconnected nature of IIoT systems further amplifies these risks, as compromised devices can propagate malicious behavior across the network.

7.3 Smart Cities

Smart cities leverage IoT and edge intelligence to improve urban infrastructure, enhance public services, and optimize resource utilization. TinyML plays a crucial role in enabling real-time data processing for applications such as traffic management, environmental monitoring, public safety, and surveillance systems.

In traffic management systems, TinyML models can analyze data from sensors and cameras to optimize traffic flow, reduce congestion, and improve road safety. Similarly, in surveillance applications, edge-based AI enables real-time detection of suspicious activities, enhancing public security. According to Zanella et al. (2014), IoT-based smart city solutions significantly improve the efficiency and sustainability of urban environments.

Despite these benefits, smart city applications face substantial security and privacy challenges. The large-scale deployment of interconnected devices creates an extensive attack surface, making it difficult to ensure system security. Data collected from sensors and surveillance systems often includes sensitive information, such as location data and personal activities, raising serious privacy concerns.

Moreover, compromised TinyML models in smart city systems can lead to severe consequences. For instance, manipulating traffic control systems could cause congestion or accidents, while tampering with surveillance systems could undermine public safety. As noted by Sicari et al. (2015), ensuring security, privacy, and trust in IoT-based smart city environments remains a critical challenge due to the scale and complexity of these systems.

Another important consideration is the need for trustworthy and transparent decision-making in smart city applications. Citizens and stakeholders must be able to trust that systems operate fairly and securely. This highlights the importance of integrating explainable AI, robust security mechanisms, and effective trust management frameworks into smart city infrastructures.

8. PROPOSED FRAMEWORK

To address the multifaceted challenges of security, privacy, and trust in TinyML-based IoT systems, this chapter proposes a multi-layered framework for secure TinyML deployment. The framework adopts a holistic approach by integrating security mechanisms across different layers of the system architecture, ensuring end-to-end protection from hardware to application-level intelligence. Given the distributed and resource-constrained nature of TinyML environments, the framework emphasizes lightweight, scalable, and interoperable solutions.

The proposed architecture consists of five key layers: Device Layer, Edge Layer, Communication Layer, Learning Layer, and Trust Layer, each addressing specific vulnerabilities identified in previous sections.

Figure 1. Architectural diagram of the proposed framework

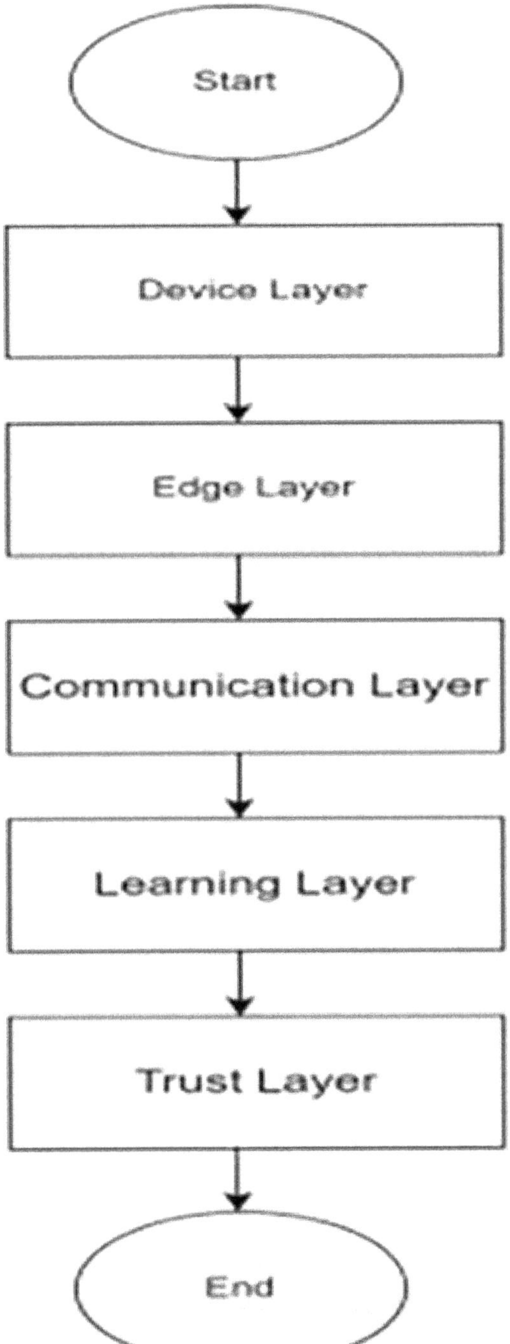

8.1 Data Flow and Layer Interaction

A hierarchical data flow model is proposed, in which data and control signals transit multiple security-enhanced layers throughout the TinyML process to ensure confidentiality, integrity, privacy, and trust.

Firstly, raw sensory data is acquired at the Device Layer, where IoT sensors and embedded hardware capture environmental or operational information. At this stage, secure hardware mechanisms such as secure boot, firmware integrity verification, and hardware-based authentication make sure that data originates from trusted and uncompromised devices. In this way, a secure foundation is laid for subsequent processing.

At the Edge Layer, TinyML models perform local inference directly on resource-constrained devices or nearby edge nodes based on the collected data. Localized processing reduces dependency on centralized cloud infrastructure, thereby reducing latency, bandwidth consumption, and privacy exposures. To further strengthen privacy protection, mechanisms such as secure memory isolation, lightweight encryption, differential privacy, and run-time anomaly detection are integrated to mitigate risks associated with inference attacks, adversarial inputs, and data leakage.

Following inference, relevant outputs, metadata, or alerts are transmitted through the Communication Layer for inter-device or device-to-server interaction. This layer ensures secure data exchange by employing end-to-end encryption, mutual authentication, message authentication codes (MACs), and replay protection mechanisms such as timestamps and sequence numbering. Lightweight protocols such as Datagram Transport Layer Security (DTLS) are particularly suitable for maintaining secure communication within resource-constrained TinyML environments.

For collaborative intelligence and model improvement, the Learning Layer enables distributed training through federated learning. Instead of transmitting raw data, devices locally update model parameters and share only encrypted model updates with aggregation servers. Secure aggregation protocols ensure that individual updates remain confidential, while differential privacy and anomaly detection mechanisms protect against model inversion, poisoning attacks, and malicious parameter manipulation. This approach enables scalable and privacy-preserving collaborative learning across distributed IoT ecosystems.

Finally, the Trust Layer provides system-wide trust management and accountability. Using blockchain-based or decentralized trust mechanisms, this layer validates device identities, maintains immutable audit logs, and records critical interactions across the framework. The integration of distributed trust management enhances transparency, prevents unauthorized modifications, and supports secure decision-making among heterogeneous IoT entities. To accommodate TinyML resource constraints, lightweight blockchain implementations or hybrid trust architectures are employed to reduce computational overhead and latency.

Overall, the interaction between these five layers creates a comprehensive security architecture in which protection mechanisms are embedded at every stage of data acquisition, processing, transmission, learning, and trust establishment. This layered design ensures end-to-end security, privacy preservation, resilience against adversarial threats, and trustworthy intelligence for TinyML-enabled IoT systems.

9. FUTURE RESEARCH DIRECTIONS

Despite significant advancements in TinyML-based IoT systems, numerous challenges remain in achieving secure, privacy preserving, and trustworthy deployments. The integration of machine learning into resource-constrained edge environments introduces unique complexities that require interdisciplinary solutions. This section outlines key future research directions aimed at addressing these challenges and advancing the state of the art in secure TinyML systems.

9.1 Integrated Security Frameworks

One of the most critical future directions is the development of integrated security frameworks that simultaneously address security, privacy, and trust. Current approaches often treat these aspects independently, leading to fragmented solutions that may fail to provide comprehensive protection. A unified framework should incorporate mechanisms for secure hardware, encrypted communication, privacy-preserving learning, and decentralized trust management within a single architecture. Such integration would enable consistent enforcement of security policies across all layers of the system. Recent studies emphasize that holistic security architectures are essential for managing the complexity of distributed IoT systems and ensuring end-to-end protection (Li et al., 2024).

Furthermore, integrated frameworks must be designed to operate efficiently within the constraints of TinyML devices. This requires the development of lightweight algorithms and modular architectures that can adapt to varying resource availability and application requirements.

9.2 Advanced Threat Detection

The increasing sophistication of cyber threats in IoT environments necessitates the development of advanced threat detection mechanisms, particularly those leveraging artificial intelligence. Traditional rule-based intrusion detection systems are often insufficient for identifying complex and evolving attack patterns. AI-driven intrusion detection systems (IDS) can analyze large volumes of data and detect anomalies indicative of malicious activity. In edge environments, these systems must operate in real time and with minimal computational overhead. According to Fei Hu et al. (2023), machine learning-based IDS solutions significantly improve detection accuracy and adaptability in IoT networks.

Future research should focus on developing lightweight and distributed IDS frameworks tailored for TinyML environments. These systems should be capable of detecting adversarial attacks, model poisoning, and communication-based threats while maintaining low energy consumption. Additionally, integrating threat intelligence sharing across devices can enhance system-wide resilience.

9.3 Energy-Efficient Security

Energy efficiency is a fundamental constraint in TinyML-based IoT systems, where devices often operate on limited battery power. Implementing robust security mechanisms typically increases computational and energy overhead, creating a trade-off between security and efficiency. Future research must prioritize the development of energy-efficient security solutions that provide strong protection without compromising device performance. This includes lightweight cryptographic algorithms, optimized authentication protocols, and adaptive security mechanisms that adjust based on device context and workload.

Recent work highlights the importance of energy-aware security design, where security operations are dynamically managed to minimize energy consumption while maintaining acceptable levels of protection (Rahmati, 2025). Additionally, hardware-software co-design approaches can improve efficiency by integrating security features directly into device architecture.

9.4 Standardization

The lack of standardized security frameworks for TinyML and IoT systems remains a significant barrier to widespread adoption. The heterogeneity of devices, communication protocols, and application domains leads to inconsistent security implementations and increased vulnerability to attacks. Establishing global standards for TinyML security is essential for ensuring interoperability, reliability, and compliance with regulatory requirements. Organizations such as the National Institute of Standards and Technology (NIST) and the International Organization for Standardization (ISO) are actively working on developing guidelines for IoT security and lightweight cryptography. Future research should contribute to the development of standardized protocols for secure model deployment, data protection, and trust management in TinyML environments. These standards should also address emerging challenges such as federated learning security, edge intelligence, and decentralized architectures.

9.5 Explainable and Trustworthy AI

As TinyML systems are increasingly deployed in critical applications, ensuring explainability and trustworthiness in machine learning models has become a key research priority. Trustworthy AI encompasses several dimensions, including robustness, fairness, transparency, and accountability. Explainable AI (XAI) techniques enable users to understand how models make decisions, which is essential for detecting errors, biases, and malicious manipulation. According to Rashmi Upreti et al. (2024), integrating explainability into machine learning systems enhances user trust and supports regulatory compliance. In TinyML environments, developing lightweight XAI methods that can operate within resource constraints remains a significant challenge. Future research should focus on creating efficient and interpretable models that provide meaningful explanations without requiring extensive computational resources.

Additionally, incorporating trustworthiness into the entire machine learning lifecycle, from data collection to deployment, will be essential for ensuring reliable and ethical AI systems. This includes developing methods for bias detection, robustness evaluation, and accountability in decentralized environments.

10. CONCLUSION

Tiny Machine Learning (TinyML) represents a transformative advancement in edge intelligence, enabling real-time, energy-efficient, and autonomous machine learning capabilities on resource-constrained IoT devices. By shifting computation from centralized cloud infrastructures to the network edge, TinyML significantly reduces latency, enhances privacy, and improves system responsiveness. These advantages make it a critical enabler for next-generation applications across domains such as smart healthcare, industrial automation, and smart cities.

However, the deployment of TinyML in distributed IoT environments introduces a wide range of challenges related to security, privacy, and trust. This chapter has systematically examined these challenges, including adversarial attacks, model extraction, poisoning threats, hardware and firmware vulnerabilities, and communication-based attacks. In addition, it has explored key privacy concerns such as data leakage, inference attacks, and regulatory compliance issues, as well as the complexities of establishing trust in decentralized systems.

To address these challenges, the chapter reviewed emerging solutions including federated learning, lightweight cryptography, hardware-assisted security mechanisms, blockchain-based trust frameworks, and explainable artificial intelligence. These approaches provide promising directions for enhancing the resilience, transparency, and reliability of TinyML-based systems. Furthermore, the proposed multi-layered framework integrates these solutions into a cohesive architecture, offering a comprehensive approach to secure TinyML deployment.

Despite these advancements, significant research gaps remain. The inherent constraints of TinyML devices limited computational power, memory, and energy pose ongoing challenges for implementing robust security and privacy mechanisms. Additionally, the dynamic and heterogeneous nature of IoT environments complicates the development of standardized and scalable solutions. As highlighted throughout this study, achieving a balance between efficiency, security, and usability remains a central concern.

Future research must focus on developing holistic and integrated approaches that address security, privacy, and trust simultaneously. This includes the design of energy-efficient security mechanisms, advanced AI-driven threat detection systems, and standardized frameworks for secure TinyML deployment. Moreover, ensuring explainability and accountability in machine learning models will be essential for building user trust and meeting regulatory requirements.

In conclusion, while TinyML holds immense potential to revolutionize edge intelligence, its successful adoption depends on the development of robust, scalable, and trustworthy systems. Addressing the challenges identified in this chapter will be critical for enabling secure and reliable TinyML-enabled IoT ecosystems, paving the way for widespread adoption in real-world applications.

REFERENCES

Abadade, A., Belouch, M., & Bouragba, K. (2023). TinyML: A systematic review of challenges and opportunities in edge AI. *IEEE Access : Practical Innovations, Open Solutions*, *11*, 45872–45895. DOI: 10.1109/ACCESS.2023.3267891

Alam, T., & Gupta, R. (2022). Federated learning for privacy-preserving IoT applications: A survey. *Sensors (Basel)*, *22*(17), 6574. DOI: 10.3390/s22176574 PMID: 36081033

Alatawi, M. N. (2025). Edge computing and federated learning for privacy-preserving IoT analytics. *EURASIP Journal on Wireless Communications and Networking*, *2025*(1). https://doi.org/DOI: 10.1186/s13638-025-02545-x

Biggio, B., Nelson, B., & Laskov, P. (2012). Poisoning attacks against support vector machines. *Proceedings of the 29th International Conference on Machine Learning (ICML)*.

Capogrosso, L.. (2024). Security vulnerabilities in compressed deep learning models for edge AI. *IEEE Internet of Things Journal*.

Chen, X., Li, J., Weng, J., Ma, J., & Lou, W. (2023). Trust management for IoT: A survey. *IEEE Communications Surveys and Tutorials*. Advance online publication. DOI: 10.1109/COMST.2023.3241234

Conti, M., Dragoni, N., & Lesyk, V. (2016). A survey of man-in-the-middle attacks. *IEEE Communications Surveys and Tutorials*, *18*(3), 2027–2051. DOI: 10.1109/COMST.2016.2548426

Fragkou, P., & Katsaros, D. (2024). TinyML: Challenges and future directions for on-device intelligence. *IEEE Embedded Systems Letters*.

Goodfellow, I. J., Shlens, J., & Szegedy, C. (2015). Explaining and harnessing adversarial examples. *International Conference on Learning Representations (ICLR)*.

Humayed, A., Lin, J., Li, F., & Luo, B. (2017). Cyber-physical systems security—A survey. *IEEE Internet of Things Journal*, *4*(6), 1802–1831. DOI: 10.1109/JIOT.2017.2703172

Jagielski, M., Carlini, N., Berthelot, D., Kurakin, A., & Papernot, N. (2020). High accuracy and high fidelity extraction of neural networks. In *29th USENIX security symposium (USENIX Security 20)* (pp. 1345-1362).

Kong, L.. (2022). Edge intelligence: A survey on edge computing and AI integration. *IEEE Internet of Things Journal*. Advance online publication. DOI: 10.1109/JIOT.2022.3200431

Laiu, P., Li, M., Nichols, J. A., Huettel, M., Sikkema, I., & Mathur, M. (2026). Designing resilient IoT and edge computing with federated TinyML. *Journal of Systems Architecture*, *174*, 103709. DOI: 10.1016/j.sysarc.2026.103709

Lee, J., Bagheri, B., & Kao, H. A. (2018). A cyber-physical systems architecture for Industry 4.0-based manufacturing systems. *Manufacturing Letters*, *3*, 18–23. DOI: 10.1016/j.mfglet.2014.12.001

Li, H., Ge, L., & Tian, L. (2024). Survey: Federated learning data security and privacy-preserving in edge-Internet of Things. *Artificial Intelligence Review*, *57*(5), 130. DOI: 10.1007/s10462-024-10774-7

Myakala, P. K., Naayini, P., & Kamatala, S. (2025). A survey on federated learning for TinyML: Challenges, techniques, and future directions. *Partners Universal International Innovation Journal*, *3*(2), 97–114.

Nguyen, D. C., Ding, M., Pathirana, P. N., Seneviratne, A., Li, J., & Poor, H. V. (2021). Federated learning for Internet of Things: A comprehensive survey. *IEEE Communications Surveys and Tutorials*, *23*(3), 1622–1658. DOI: 10.1109/COMST.2021.3075439

Rieke, N., Hancox, J., Li, W., Milletarì, F., Roth, H. R., Albarqouni, S., Bakas, S., Galtier, M. N., Landman, B. A., Maier-Hein, K., Ourselin, S., Sheller, M., Summers, R. M., Trask, A., Xu, D., Baust, M., & Cardoso, M. J. (2020). The future of digital health with federated learning. *npj. Digital Medicine*, *3*(119), 119. Advance online publication. DOI: 10.1038/s41746-020-00323-1 PMID: 33015372

Roman, R., Zhou, J., & Lopez, J. (2013). On the features and challenges of security and privacy in distributed IoT. *Computer Networks*, *57*(10), 2266–2279. DOI: 10.1016/j.comnet.2012.12.018

Sadeghi, A. R., Wachsmann, C., & Waidner, M. (2015, June). Security and privacy challenges in industrial internet of things. In *Proceedings of the 52nd annual design automation conference* (pp. 1-6). DOI: 10.1145/2744769.2747942

Sicari, S., Rizzardi, A., Grieco, L. A., & Coen-Porisini, A. (2015). Security, privacy and trust in Internet of Things: The road ahead. *Computer Networks*, *76*, 146–164. DOI: 10.1016/j.comnet.2014.11.008

Tramèr, F., Zhang, F., Juels, A., Reiter, M. K., & Ristenpart, T. (2016). Stealing machine learning models via prediction {APIs}. In *25th USENIX security symposium (USENIX Security 16)* (pp. 601-618).

Yan, Z., Zhang, P., & Vasilakos, A. V. (2014). A survey on trust management for Internet of Things. *Journal of Network and Computer Applications*, *42*, 120–134. DOI: 10.1016/j.jnca.2014.01.014

Yu, W., Liang, F., He, X., Hatcher, W. G., Lu, C., Lin, J., & Yang, X. (2017). A survey on the edge computing for the Internet of Things. *IEEE Access : Practical Innovations, Open Solutions*, *6*, 6900–6919. DOI: 10.1109/ACCESS.2017.2778504

Zanella, A., Bui, N., Castellani, A., Vangelista, L., & Zorzi, M. (2014). Internet of Things for smart cities. *IEEE Internet of Things Journal*, *1*(1), 22–32. DOI: 10.1109/JIOT.2014.2306328

Zhang, T., Jia, F., & Chen, L. (2025). Blockchain adoption in supply chains: Implications for sustainability. *Production Planning and Control*, *36*(5), 699–722. DOI: 10.1080/09537287.2023.2296669

Zhou, R. G., Yu, H., Cheng, Y., & Li, F. X. (2019). Quantum image edge extraction based on improved Prewitt operator. *Quantum Information Processing*, *18*(9), 261. DOI: 10.1007/s11128-019-2376-5

KEY TERMS AND DEFINITIONS

Direct Trust and Indirect Trust: Direct trust is built through your own personal experiences and direct interactions with someone or something, while indirect trust is based on recommendations, ratings, or feedback provided by third-party advisors or intermediaries when you lack direct experience. In this chapter context, Direct trust is derived from a device's own interactions with another entity, while indirect trust is based on recommendations or feedback from other devices in the network. According to Yan, Zhang, and Vasilakos (2014), combining these trust metrics improves the accuracy of trust evaluation in dynamic IoT environments.

Firmware Integrity Verification: This is the process of ensuring that the firmware running on a device has not been modified, corrupted, or replaced by malicious code. This is typically achieved through cryptographic techniques such as hashing and digital signatures.

Secure Boot Mechanisms: Secure boot is a hardware- and firmware-based security process that ensures a device only executes software that is cryptographically verified and trusted by the manufacturer or system owner.

Tamper-Resistant Hardware: This refers to physical and architectural design techniques that protect electronic devices against unauthorized physical access, probing, or manipulation. These mechanisms make it difficult for attackers to extract sensitive information (such as cryptographic keys) or alter device functionality through physical attacks.

TinyML: TinyML (Tiny Machine Learning) is a subset of AI that enables machine learning models to run on low-power, resource-constrained microcontrollers and edge devices.

Compilation of References

Abadade, A., Belouch, M., & Bouragba, K. (2023). TinyML: A systematic review of challenges and opportunities in edge AI. *IEEE Access : Practical Innovations, Open Solutions*, *11*, 45872–45895. DOI: 10.1109/ACCESS.2023.3267891

Abadi, M., Agarwal, A., Barham, P., Brevdo, E., Chen, Z., Citro, C., . . . Zheng, X. (2016). Tensorflow: Large-scale machine learning on heterogeneous distributed systems. *arXiv preprint arXiv:1603.04467.*

Abadi, M., Barham, P., Chen, J., Chen, Z., Davis, A., Dean, J., & Zheng, X. (2016). {TensorFlow}: a system for {Large-Scale} machine learning. In *12th USENIX symposium on operating systems design and implementation (OSDI 16)* (pp. 265-283).

Abbas, N., Zhang, Y., Taherkordi, A., & Skeie, T. (2018). Mobile edge computing: A survey. *IEEE Internet of Things Journal*, *5*(1), 450–465. DOI: 10.1109/JIOT.2017.2750180

Abdurohman, M. (2019). Trust management in UAV networks: A survey. *IEEE Access : Practical Innovations, Open Solutions*, *7*, 175256–175278.

Alam, T., & Gupta, R. (2022). Federated learning for privacy-preserving IoT applications: A survey. *Sensors (Basel)*, *22*(17), 6574. DOI: 10.3390/s22176574 PMID: 36081033

Alatawi, M. N. (2025). Edge computing and federated learning for privacy-preserving IoT analytics. *EURASIP Journal on Wireless Communications and Networking*, *2025*(1). https://doi.org/DOI: 10.1186/s13638-025-02545-x

Al-Fuqaha, A., Guizani, M., Mohammadi, M., Aledhari, M., & Ayyash, M. (2015). Internet of Things: A survey on enabling technologies, protocols, and applications. *IEEE Communications Surveys and Tutorials*, *17*(4), 2347–2376. DOI: 10.1109/COMST.2015.2444095

Al-Garadi, M. A., Mohamed, A., Al-Ali, A. K., Du, X., Ali, I., & Guizani, M. (2020). A Survey of Machine and Deep Learning Methods for Internet of Things (IoT) Security. *IEEE Communications Surveys and Tutorials, 22*(3), 1646–1685. DOI: 10.1109/COMST.2020.2988293

Aloqaily, M. (2020). Blockchain in UAV networks: Security and privacy issues. *IEEE Communications Magazine, 58*(1), 28–34.

Alsalem, L., & Djemame, K. (2025). Task scheduling in edge computing environments: A hierarchical cluster-based federated deep reinforcement learning approach. *Proceedings of the ACM Symposium on Edge Computing*, 3774691. DOI: 10.1145/3773274.3774691

Alzenad, M. (2018). Secure and resilient UAV communication networks. *IEEE Communications Magazine, 56*(10), 26–32.

Aravindh, G., & Sridhar, K. P. (2026). Cloud-Continuum-Based Deep Learning Optimization Framework for Next-Generation Healthcare Data Performance on IoT Platform. *International Journal of Advanced Computer Science and Applications, 17*(2), 618. DOI: 10.14569/IJACSA.2026.0170262

Arzovs, A., Judvaitis, J., Nesenbergs, K., & Selavo, L. (2024). Distributed learning in the IoT-edge-cloud continuum. *Machine Learning and Knowledge Extraction, 6*(1), 15. DOI: 10.3390/make6010015

Bagdasaryan, E., Veit, A., Hua, Y., Estrin, D., & Shmatikov, V. (2020). How To Backdoor Federated Learning. *Proceedings of Machine Learning Research, 108*, 2938–2948.

Baig, A. F., Eskeland, S., & Yang, B. (2023). Privacy-preserving continuous authentication using behavioral biometrics. *International Journal of Information Security, 22*(6), 1833–1847. DOI: 10.1007/s10207-023-00721-y

Bekmezci, I., Sahingoz, O. K., & Temel, Ş. (2013). Flying ad-hoc networks (FANETs): A survey. *Ad Hoc Networks, 11*(3), 1254–1270. DOI: 10.1016/j.adhoc.2012.12.004

Belcastro, L., Marozzo, F., Presta, A., & Talia, D. (2024). A Spark-based task allocation solution for machine learning in the edge-cloud continuum. *IEEE International Conference on Distributed Computing and Sensing*, 61029. https://doi.org/DOI: 10.1109/DCOSS-IoT61029.2024.00090

Ben Atitallah, S., Driss, M., & Ghézala, H. (2025). FedMicro-IDA: A federated learning and microservices-based framework for IoT data analytics. *arXiv preprint arXiv:2510.20852*. https://doi.org//arXiv.2510.20852DOI: 10.48550

Beutel, D. J., Topal, T., Mathur, A., Qiu, X., Fernandez-Marques, J., Gao, Y., Sani, L., Li, K. H., Parcollet, T., de Gusmão, P. P. B., & Lane, N. D. (2022). *Flower: A Friendly Federated Learning Research Framework*. https://arxiv.org/abs/2007.14390

Bhatti, M. A., Song, Z., Bhatti, U. A., & Syam, S. M. S. (2024). AIoT-driven multi-source sensor emission monitoring and forecasting using multi-source sensor integration with reduced noise series decomposition. *Journal of Cloud Computing (Heidelberg, Germany)*, *13*(1), 65. DOI: 10.1186/s13677-024-00598-9

Bhatti, U. A. (Ed.). (2025). *Deep Learning for Multimedia Processing Applications: Volume One: Image Security and Intelligent Systems for Multimedia Processing*. Taylor & Francis Ltd.

Bhatti, U. A., Tang, H., Ku, C. S., Bazai, S. U., Hussain, S., Fakhar, S., & Yee, P. L. (2023). Deep learning-based trees disease recognition and classification using hyperspectral data. *Computers, Materials & Continua*, *77*(1), 681–697. DOI: 10.32604/cmc.2023.037958

Bhatti, U. A., Tang, H., Wu, G., Marjan, S., & Hussain, A. (2023). Deep learning with graph convolutional networks: An overview and latest applications in computational intelligence. *International Journal of Intelligent Systems*, *2023*(1), 8342104. DOI: 10.1155/2023/8342104

Bhatti, U. A., Yuan, L., Yu, Z., Nawaz, S. A., Mehmood, A., Bhatti, M. A., Ain, Q., Nizamani, M. M., Zeeshan, Z., & Xiao, S. J. (2021). Predictive data modeling using sp-kNN for risk factor evaluation in urban demographical healthcare data. *Journal of Medical Imaging and Health Informatics*, *11*(1), 7–14. DOI: 10.1166/jmihi.2021.3313

Bhatti, U. A., Yu, Z., Chanussot, J., Zeeshan, Z., Yuan, L., Luo, W., Nawaz, S. A., Bhatti, M. A., Ain, Q., & Mehmood, A. (2022). Local similarity-based spatial–spectral fusion hyperspectral image classification with deep CNN and Gabor filtering. *IEEE Transactions on Geoscience and Remote Sensing*, *60*, 1–15. DOI: 10.1109/TGRS.2021.3090410

Bhatti, U. A., Yu, Z., Yuan, L., Zeeshan, Z., Nawaz, S. A., Bhatti, M. A., Mehmood, A., Ain, Q., & Luo, W. (2020). Geometric algebra applications in geospatial artificial intelligence and remote sensing image processing. *IEEE Access : Practical Innovations, Open Solutions*, *8*, 155783–155796. DOI: 10.1109/ACCESS.2020.3018544

Biggio, B., Nelson, B., & Laskov, P. (2012). Poisoning attacks against support vector machines. *Proceedings of the 29th International Conference on Machine Learning (ICML)*.

Bonawitz, K., Eichner, H., Grieskamp, W., Huba, D., Ingerman, A., Ivanov, V., Kiddon, C., Konečný, J., Mazzocchi, S., McMahan, H. B., Van Overveldt, T., Petrou, D., Ramage, D., & Roselander, J. (2019). *Towards Federated Learning at Scale: System Design*. https://arxiv.org/abs/1902.01046

Brendan McMahan, H., Moore, E., Ramage, D., Hampson, S., & Agüera y Arcas, B. (2017). Communication-efficient learning of deep networks from decentralized data. *Proceedings of the 20th International Conference on Artificial Intelligence and Statistics, AISTATS 2017,* 54.

Capogrosso, L.. (2024). Security vulnerabilities in compressed deep learning models for edge AI. *IEEE Internet of Things Journal.*

Cheng, M., Li, D., Zhou, N., Tang, H., Wang, G., Li, S., Bhatti, U. A., & Khan, M. K. (2023). Artificial intelligence-driven medical image analysis for healthcare systems. *IEEE Transactions on Instrumentation and Measurement.*

Chen, L. (2020). Trust-based secure routing for UAV networks. *IEEE Transactions on Aerospace and Electronic Systems*, *56*(4), 2931–2943.

Chen, M., Hao, Y., Li, Y., Lai, C. F., & Wu, D. (2018). On the computation offloading at ad hoc cloudlet. *IEEE Transactions on Vehicular Technology*, *64*(11), 5297–5309.

Chen, M., Mao, S., & Liu, Y. (2014). Big data: A survey. *Mobile Networks and Applications*, *19*(2), 171–209. DOI: 10.1007/s11036-013-0489-0

Chen, T., Moreau, T., Jiang, Z., Zheng, L., Yan, E., Shen, H., & Krishnamurthy, A. (2018). {TVM}: An automated {End-to-End} optimizing compiler for deep learning. In *13th USENIX symposium on operating systems design and implementation (OSDI 18)* (pp. 578-594).

Chen, X., Jiao, L., Li, W., & Fu, X. (2016). Efficient multi-user computation offloading for mobile-edge cloud computing. *IEEE/ACM Transactions on Networking*, *24*(5), 2795–2808. DOI: 10.1109/TNET.2015.2487344

Chen, X., Li, J., Li, Q., & Tang, M. (2020). Real-time data analytics in IoT: A survey on deep learning approaches. *Journal of Network and Computer Applications*, *164*, 102689.

Chen, X., Li, J., Weng, J., Ma, J., & Lou, W. (2023). Trust management for IoT: A survey. *IEEE Communications Surveys and Tutorials*. Advance online publication. DOI: 10.1109/COMST.2023.3241234

Chhabra, G. S., Rajareddy, G. N. V., Mahapatra, A., Mangalampalli, S., Sahoo, K., Sethi, D., & Mishra, K. (2025). Deep learning-centric task offloading in IoT-fog-cloud continuum: A state-of-the-art review, open research issues, and future directions. *IEEE Access : Practical Innovations, Open Solutions*, *13*, 3599190. DOI: 10.1109/ACCESS.2025.3599190

Chiang, M., & Zhang, T. (2016). Fog and IoT: An overview of research opportunities. *IEEE Internet of Things Journal*, *3*(6), 854–864. DOI: 10.1109/JIOT.2016.2584538

Consortium, W. W. W. (2022). *Decentralized Identifiers (DID) v1.0. October*. https://www.w3.org/TR/did-core/

Conti, M., Dragoni, N., & Lesyk, V. (2016). A survey of man-in-the-middle attacks. *IEEE Communications Surveys and Tutorials*, *18*(3), 2027–2051. DOI: 10.1109/COMST.2016.2548426

Deng, L., & Yu, D. (2014). Deep learning: Methods and applications. *Foundations and Trends in Signal Processing*, *7*(3–4), 197–387. DOI: 10.1561/2000000039

Dong, S., Li, J., Bhatti, U. A., Ma, J., Dong, F., & Li, Y. (2023). Robust zero-watermarking algorithm for medical images based on GFTT-KAZE and DCT. *SNPD Conference Proceedings,* 290–297. DOI: 10.1109/SNPD-Winter57765.2023.10223753

Dorling, K., Heinrichs, J., Messier, G. G., & Magierowski, S. (2017). Vehicle routing problems for drone delivery. *IEEE Transactions on Systems, Man, and Cybernetics. Systems*, *47*(1), 70–85. DOI: 10.1109/TSMC.2016.2582745

Dorri, A., Kanhere, S. S., & Jurdak, R. (2017). Blockchain in IoT: Challenges and solutions. *arXiv preprint arXiv:1608.05187.*

Fahim, A., Tan, Q., Bhatti, U. A., Nizamani, M. M., & Nawaz, S. A. (2023). Machine learning approaches for multimedia data processing and analysis. *Multimedia Tools and Applications.*

Fang, Y., Liu, J., Li, J., Cheng, J., Hu, J., Yi, D., Xiao, X., & Bhatti, U. A. (2022). Robust zero-watermarking algorithm for medical images based on SIFT and bandelet-DCT. *Multimedia Tools and Applications*, *81*(12), 16863–16879. DOI: 10.1007/s11042-022-12592-x

Fotouhi, A., Qiang, H., Ding, M., Hassan, M., Giordano, L. G., Garcia-Rodriguez, A., & Yuan, J. (2019). Survey on UAV cellular communications. *IEEE Communications Surveys and Tutorials*, *21*(4), 3417–3442. DOI: 10.1109/COMST.2019.2906228

Fragkou, P., & Katsaros, D. (2024). TinyML: Challenges and future directions for on-device intelligence. *IEEE Embedded Systems Letters.*

Gao, X. (2025). Toward real-time and efficient edge intelligence: Advances and challenges in lightweight machine learning. *Nature Machine Intelligence*, *7*(8), 36. DOI: 10.61173/bwn0ez36

Giannopoulos, A., Paralikas, I., Spantideas, S., & Trakadas, P. (2024). HOODIE: Hybrid computation offloading via distributed deep reinforcement learning in delay-aware cloud-edge continuum. *IEEE Open Journal of the Communications Society*, *5*, 3514456. DOI: 10.1109/OJCOMS.2024.3514456

Goodfellow, I. J., Shlens, J., & Szegedy, C. (2015). Explaining and harnessing adversarial examples. *International Conference on Learning Representations (ICLR).*

Goodfellow, I., Bengio, Y., & Courville, A. (2016). *Deep learning*. MIT Press.

Gubbi, J., Buyya, R., Marusic, S., & Palaniswami, M. (2013). Internet of Things (IoT): A vision, architectural elements, and future directions. *Future Generation Computer Systems*, *29*(7), 1645–1660. DOI: 10.1016/j.future.2013.01.010

Gupta, L., Jain, R., & Vaszkun, G. (2016). Survey of important issues in UAV communication networks. *IEEE Communications Surveys and Tutorials*, *18*(2), 1123–1152. DOI: 10.1109/COMST.2015.2495297

Han, H., Zeeshan, Z., Talpur, B. A., Sadiq, T., Bhatti, U. A., Awwad, E., & Al-Razgan, M. (2024). *Deep learning techniques for intelligent environmental monitoring systems*. Applied Environmental and Oceanography Research.

Han, S., Pool, J., Tran, J., & Dally, W. (2015). Learning both weights and connections for efficient neural network. *Advances in Neural Information Processing Systems*, *28*, 1135–1143.

He, K., Zhang, X., Ren, S., & Sun, J. (2016). Deep residual learning for image recognition. *Proceedings of the IEEE Conference on Computer Vision and Pattern Recognition*, 770–778.

Hinton, G. E., Osindero, S., & Teh, Y. W. (2006). A fast learning algorithm for deep belief nets. *Neural Computation*, *18*(7), 1527–1554. DOI: 10.1162/neco.2006.18.7.1527 PMID: 16764513

Howard, A. G., Zhu, M., Chen, B., Kalenichenko, D., Wang, W., Weyand, T., & Adam, H. (2017). MobileNets: Efficient convolutional neural networks for mobile vision applications. *arXiv preprint arXiv:1704.04861.*

Huang, D., Wang, P., & Niyato, D. (2019). A dynamic offloading algorithm for mobile computing. *IEEE Transactions on Wireless Communications*, *11*(6), 1991–1995. DOI: 10.1109/TWC.2012.041912.110912

Huang, M., Han, H., Wang, H., Li, L., Zhang, Y., & Bhatti, U. A. (2018). A clinical decision support framework for heterogeneous data sources. *IEEE Journal of Biomedical and Health Informatics, 22*(6), 1824–1833. DOI: 10.1109/JBHI.2018.2846626 PMID: 29994279

Humayed, A., Lin, J., Li, F., & Luo, B. (2017). Cyber-physical systems security—A survey. *IEEE Internet of Things Journal, 4*(6), 1802–1831. DOI: 10.1109/JIOT.2017.2703172

Islam, T., Akter, A., Islam, M. N., Zafir, E. I., Hasib, S. A., Sarker, S. K., & Bhatti, U. A. (2025). A novel explainable deep generative model-aided transfer learning CNN for pelvis fracture detection. *Biomedical Signal Processing and Control, 110*, 107987. DOI: 10.1016/j.bspc.2025.107987

Jagielski, M., Carlini, N., Berthelot, D., Kurakin, A., & Papernot, N. (2020). High accuracy and high fidelity extraction of neural networks. In *29th USENIX security symposium (USENIX Security 20)* (pp. 1345-1362).

Kairouz, P., & McMahan, H. B. (2021). Advances and open problems in federated learning. *Foundations and Trends in Machine Learning, 14*(1-2), 1–210. DOI: 10.1561/2200000083

Karimireddy, S. P., Kale, S., Mohri, M., Reddi, S. J., Stich, S. U., & Suresh, A. T. (2020). SCAFFOLD: Stochastic Controlled Averaging for Federated Learning. *37th International Conference on Machine Learning, ICML 2020, PartF16814*, 5088–5099.

Khan, W. Z. (2020). UAV communication networks: Architecture, protocols, and applications. *Journal of Network and Computer Applications, 134*, 34–58.

Khezri, R., Steen, D., & Tuan, L. A. (2022). Vehicle to Everything (V2X) - A Survey on Standards and Operational Strategies. *2022 IEEE International Conference on Environment and Electrical Engineering and 2022 IEEE Industrial and Commercial Power Systems Europe, EEEIC / I and CPS Europe 2022, June*. DOI: 10.1109/EEEIC/ICPSEurope54979.2022.9854561

Khraisat, A., Alazab, A., Singh, S., Jan, T., & Gomez, A. (2024). Survey on Federated Learning for Intrusion Detection System: Concept, Architectures, Aggregation Strategies, Challenges, and Future Directions. *ACM Computing Surveys, 57*(1). Advance online publication. DOI: 10.1145/3687124

Knorst, T., Jordan, M., Korol, G., Rutzig, M. B., & Beck, A. C. S. (2025). Adaptive model switching for dynamic inference serving in the IoT-edge-cloud continuum. *Proceedings of the 15th Brazilian Embedded Systems Seminar*, 11288829. DOI: 10.1109/SBESC68008.2025.11288829

Konečný, J., McMahan, H. B., Yu, F. X., Richtárik, P., Suresh, A. T., & Bacon, D. (2017). *Federated Learning: Strategies for Improving Communication Efficiency*. 1–10. https://arxiv.org/abs/1610.05492

Kong, L.. (2022). Edge intelligence: A survey on edge computing and AI integration. *IEEE Internet of Things Journal*. Advance online publication. DOI: 10.1109/JIOT.2022.3200431

Konsta, A. M., Lafuente, A. L., & Dragoni, N. (2023). A Survey of Trust Management for Internet of Things. *IEEE Access : Practical Innovations, Open Solutions*, *11*, 122175–122204. DOI: 10.1109/ACCESS.2023.3327335

Laiu, P., Li, M., Nichols, J. A., Huettel, M., Sikkema, I., & Mathur, M. (2026). Designing resilient IoT and edge computing with federated TinyML. *Journal of Systems Architecture*, *174*, 103709. DOI: 10.1016/j.sysarc.2026.103709

LeCun, Y., Bengio, Y., & Hinton, G. (2015). Deep learning. *Nature*, *521*(7553), 436–444. DOI: 10.1038/nature14539 PMID: 26017442

Lee, J., & Na, W. (2022). A survey on mobile edge computing architectures for deep learning models. *IEEE International Conference on ICT Convergence*, 9952954. DOI: 10.1109/ICTC55196.2022.9952954

Lee, J., Bagheri, B., & Kao, H. A. (2018). A cyber-physical systems architecture for Industry 4.0-based manufacturing systems. *Manufacturing Letters*, *3*, 18–23. DOI: 10.1016/j.mfglet.2014.12.001

Li, J., Bhatti, U. A., Nawaz, S. A., Huang, M., Ahmad, R. M., & Ghadi, Y. Y. (2024). Remote-sensing image classification: A comprehensive review and applications. In *Deep Learning for Multimedia Processing Applications* (pp. 18–47).

Li, B., Fei, Z., & Zhang, Y. (2018). UAV communications for 5G and beyond. *IEEE Wireless Communications*, *26*(1), 10–16. DOI: 10.1109/MWC.2016.7422399

Li, E., Zeng, L., Zhou, Z., & Chen, X. (2019). Edge AI: On-demand accelerating deep neural network inference via edge computing. *IEEE Transactions on Wireless Communications*, *19*(1), 447–457. DOI: 10.1109/TWC.2019.2946140

Li, H., Ge, L., & Tian, L. (2024). Survey: Federated learning data security and privacy-preserving in edge-Internet of Things. *Artificial Intelligence Review*, *57*(5), 130. DOI: 10.1007/s10462-024-10774-7

Li, H., Kadav, A., Durdanovic, I., Samet, H., & Graf, H. P. (2017). Pruning filters for efficient convnets. *Proceedings of the International Conference on Learning Representations*.

Lilhore, U., Simaiya, S., Sharma, Y. K., Rai, A. K., Padmaja, S. M., Nabilal, K. V., Kumar, V., Alroobaea, R., & Alsufyani, H. (2025). Cloud-edge hybrid deep learning framework for scalable IoT resource optimization. *Journal of Cloud Computing (Heidelberg, Germany)*, *10*(1), 729. DOI: 10.1186/s13677-025-00729-w

Lin, X., Yajnanarayana, V., Muruganathan, S. D., Gao, S., Asplund, H., Maattanen, H. L., Bergstrom, M., Euler, S., & Wang, Y. P. E. (2018). The sky is not the limit: LTE for unmanned aerial vehicles. *IEEE Communications Magazine*, *56*(4), 204–210. DOI: 10.1109/MCOM.2018.1700643

Li, Q., Wen, Z., Wu, Z., Hu, S., Wang, N., Li, Y., Liu, X., & He, B. (2023). A Survey on Federated Learning Systems: Vision, Hype and Reality for Data Privacy and Protection. *IEEE Transactions on Knowledge and Data Engineering*, *35*(4), 3347–3366. DOI: 10.1109/TKDE.2021.3124599

Li, S., Xu, L. D., & Zhao, S. (2018). The internet of things: A survey. *Information Systems Frontiers*, *17*(2), 243–259. DOI: 10.1007/s10796-014-9492-7

Li, T., Sahu, A. K., Talwalkar, A., & Smith, V. (2020). Federated Learning: Challenges, Methods, and Future Directions. *IEEE Signal Processing Magazine*, *37*(3), 50–60. DOI: 10.1109/MSP.2020.2975749

Liu, C. F., Bennis, M., Debbah, M., & Poor, H. V. (2018). Dynamic task offloading and resource allocation for ultra-reliable low-latency edge computing. *IEEE Transactions on Communications*, *67*(6), 4132–4150. DOI: 10.1109/TCOMM.2019.2898573

Liu, J., Du, Y., Yang, K., Wu, J., Wang, Y., Hu, X., Wang, Z., Liu, Y., Sun, P., Boukerche, A., & Leung, V. C. M. (2025). Edge-cloud collaborative computing on distributed intelligence and model optimization: A survey. *IEEE Communications Surveys and Tutorials*, *28*(2), 3669216. DOI: 10.1109/COMST.2026.3669216

Liu, Y. (2019). Secure data transmission in UAV-assisted networks. *IEEE Transactions on Wireless Communications*, *18*(5), 2732–2746.

Liu, Y., Chen, M., Zhang, Y., & Dou, W. (2020). Real-time IoT analytics: Edge-based deep learning models and applications. *Future Generation Computer Systems*, *108*, 102–117.

Li, X. (2019). Privacy-preserving data aggregation in UAV networks. *IEEE Internet of Things Journal*, *6*(2), 2943–2954.

Li, X., Li, H., Li, H., & Li, K. C. (2019). Real-time anomaly detection for IoT networks based on deep learning. *IEEE Access : Practical Innovations, Open Solutions*, *7*, 127961–127970.

Li, Y., Li, J., Shao, C., Bhatti, U. A., & Ma, J. (2022). Intelligent multimedia security using deep feature extraction. *International Conference on Cyber Security Proceedings.*

Mach, P., & Becvar, Z. (2017). Mobile edge computing: A survey on architecture and computation offloading. *IEEE Communications Surveys and Tutorials*, *19*(3), 1628–1656. DOI: 10.1109/COMST.2017.2682318

Mao, Y., You, C., Zhang, J., Huang, K., & Letaief, K. B. (2017). A survey on mobile edge computing. *IEEE Communications Surveys and Tutorials*, *19*(4), 2322–2358. DOI: 10.1109/COMST.2017.2745201

Mao, Y., Zhang, J., & Letaief, K. B. (2016). Dynamic computation offloading for mobile-edge computing. *IEEE Journal on Selected Areas in Communications*, *34*(12), 3590–3605. DOI: 10.1109/JSAC.2016.2611964

Matam, P. (2025). Smart crop monitoring and disease prediction using IoT sensors and deep learning models deployed on edge-cloud architecture. *IEEE International Conference on Advanced Computing, Robotics, and Sensors*, 11324361. DOI: 10.1109/ICACRS67045.2025.11324361

McMahan, B., Moore, E., Ramage, D., Hampson, S., & Arcas, B. A. (2017, April). Communication-efficient learning of deep networks from decentralized data. In *Artificial intelligence and statistics* (pp. 1273–1282). Pmlr.

Moghaddasi, K., Rajabi, S., Gharehchopogh, F. S., & Ghaffari, A. (2024). An advanced deep reinforcement learning algorithm for three-layer D2D-edge-cloud computing architecture for efficient task offloading in the Internet of Things. *Sustainable Computing : Informatics and Systems*, *44*, 100992. DOI: 10.1016/j.suscom.2024.100992

Mozaffari, M., Saad, W., Bennis, M., & Debbah, M. (2019). A tutorial on UAVs for wireless networks. *IEEE Communications Surveys and Tutorials*, *21*(3), 2334–2360. DOI: 10.1109/COMST.2019.2902862

Myakala, P. K. (2025). Distributed data intelligence in the edge-to-cloud continuum: A survey of architectures, models, and applications. *IEEE International Conference on Data Intelligence and Communications*, 11135068. DOI: 10.1109/ICDICI66477.2025.11135068

Myakala, P. K., Naayini, P., & Kamatala, S. (2025). A survey on federated learning for TinyML: Challenges, techniques, and future directions. *Partners Universal International Innovation Journal*, *3*(2), 97–114.

Nawaz, S. A., Li, J., Shoukat, M. U., Bhatti, U. A., & Ahmad, M. R. (2023). Hybrid watermarking framework for secure medical image management. *Computers & Electrical Engineering*.

Nguyen, D. C., Ding, M., Pathirana, P. N., Seneviratne, A., Li, J., & Poor, H. V. (2021). Federated learning for Internet of Things: A comprehensive survey. *IEEE Communications Surveys and Tutorials*, *23*(3), 1622–1658. DOI: 10.1109/COMST.2021.3075439

Nieto, G., Iglesia, I. D. L., López-Novoa, U., & Perfecto, C. (2024). Deep reinforcement learning techniques for dynamic task offloading in the 5G edge-cloud continuum. *Journal of Cloud Computing (Heidelberg, Germany)*, *24*(1), 658. DOI: 10.1186/s13677-024-00658-0

Nizamani, A. H., Chen, Z., & Bhatti, U. A. (2026). Deep-Fusion: A lightweight feature fusion model with Cross-Stream Attention and Attention Prediction Head for brain tumor diagnosis. *Biomedical Signal Processing and Control*, *111*, 108305. DOI: 10.1016/j.bspc.2025.108305

Oteafy, S. M. A., & Hassanein, H. S. (2017). Resilient IoT Architectures over Dynamic Sensor Networks with Adaptive Components. *IEEE Internet of Things Journal*, *4*(2), 474–483. DOI: 10.1109/JIOT.2016.2621998

Papernot, N., Goodfellow, I., Abadi, M., Talwar, K., & Erlingsson, Ú. (2017). Semi-supervised knowledge transfer for deep learning from private training data. *5th International Conference on Learning Representations, ICLR 2017 - Conference Track Proceedings, 2015*, 1–16.

Peng, M., Liu, Y., Khan, A., Ahmed, B., Sarker, S. K., Ghadi, Y. Y., Bhatti, U. A., Al-Razgan, M., & Ali, Y. A. (2024). Crop monitoring using remote sensing land use and land change data: Comparative analysis of deep learning methods using pre-trained CNN models. *Big Data Research*, *36*, 100448. DOI: 10.1016/j.bdr.2024.100448

Petrakis, K., Agorogiannis, E., Antonopoulos, G., Anagnostopoulos, T., Grigoropoulos, N., Veroni, E., Berne, A., Azaiez, S., Benomar, Z., Kakoulidis, H., Prasinos, M., Sotiriades, P., Mavrothalassitis, P., & Alexopoulos, K. (2025). Enhancing DevOps practices in the IoT–edge–cloud continuum: Architecture, integration, and software orchestration demonstrated in the COGNIFOG framework. *Software*, *4*(2), 10. DOI: 10.3390/software4020010

Qu, Y., Yu, S., Gao, L., Sood, K., & Xiang, Y. (2024). Blockchained dual-asynchronous federated learning services for digital twin empowered edge-cloud continuum. *IEEE Transactions on Services Computing*, *17*(3), 3382952. DOI: 10.1109/TSC.2024.3382952

Reddy, C. K., Rajesh, P., Chellammal, S., Muthuselvan, E. M., & Swathi, A. (2025). Real-time embedded system optimization using edge computing and lightweight deep learning architectures for data efficiency. *Proceedings of ICSOFT 2025*, 13870900004919. DOI: 10.5220/0013870900004919

Rieke, N., Hancox, J., Li, W., Milletarì, F., Roth, H. R., Albarqouni, S., Bakas, S., Galtier, M. N., Landman, B. A., Maier-Hein, K., Ourselin, S., Sheller, M., Summers, R. M., Trask, A., Xu, D., Baust, M., & Cardoso, M. J. (2020). The future of digital health with federated learning. *npj. Digital Medicine*, *3*(119), 119. Advance online publication. DOI: 10.1038/s41746-020-00323-1 PMID: 33015372

Roman, R., Lopez, J., & Mambo, M. (2018). Mobile edge computing, fog computing, and IoT security. *Future Generation Computer Systems*, *78*, 680–698. DOI: 10.1016/j.future.2016.11.009

Roman, R., Zhou, J., & Lopez, J. (2013). On the features and challenges of security and privacy in distributed IoT. *Computer Networks*, *57*(10), 2266–2279. DOI: 10.1016/j.comnet.2012.12.018

Sabt, M., Achemlal, M., & Bouabdallah, A. (2015). Trusted execution environment: What it is, and what it is not. *Proceedings - 14th IEEE International Conference on Trust, Security and Privacy in Computing and Communications, TrustCom 2015*, *1*, 57–64. DOI: 10.1109/Trustcom.2015.357

Sadeghi, A. R., Wachsmann, C., & Waidner, M. (2015, June). Security and privacy challenges in industrial internet of things. In *Proceedings of the 52nd annual design automation conference* (pp. 1-6). DOI: 10.1145/2744769.2747942

Sardellitti, S., Scutari, G., & Barbarossa, S. (2015). Joint optimization of radio and computational resources. *IEEE Transactions on Signal and Information Processing Over Networks*, *1*(2), 89–103. DOI: 10.1109/TSIPN.2015.2448520

Satyanarayanan, M. (2017). The emergence of edge computing. *Computer*, *50*(1), 30–39. DOI: 10.1109/MC.2017.9

Shamsoshoara, A., Korenda, A., Afghah, F., & Zeadally, S. (2020, September). A survey on physical unclonable function (PUF)-based security solutions for Internet of Things. *Computer Networks*, *183*, 107593. Advance online publication. DOI: 10.1016/j.comnet.2020.107593

Sharma, P. K., Chen, M. Y., & Park, J. H. (2017). A blockchain-based secure framework for UAV systems. *Journal of Network and Computer Applications*, *94*, 48–57.

Sharma, V., You, I., & Atiquzzaman, M. (2016). Secure and efficient protocol for UAV communication. *IEEE Transactions on Vehicular Technology*, *65*(12), 10229–10239.

Shi, W., Cao, J., Zhang, Q., Li, Y., & Xu, L. (2016). Edge computing: Vision and challenges. *IEEE Internet of Things Journal, 3*(5), 637–646. DOI: 10.1109/JIOT.2016.2579198

Shuvo, M. M. H., Islam, S. K., Cheng, J., & Morshed, B. I. (2022). Efficient acceleration of deep learning inference on resource-constrained edge devices: A review. *Proceedings of the IEEE, 110*(12), 3226481. DOI: 10.1109/JPROC.2022.3226481

Sıcakyüz, Ç., Asaad, R. R., Almufti, S. M., & Rustamova, N. R. (2024). Adaptive deep learning architectures for real-time data streams in edge-computing environments. *Quarterly Technical Journal, 3*(2), 25. DOI: 10.48161/qtj.v3n2a25

Sicari, S., Rizzardi, A., Grieco, L. A., & Coen-Porisini, A. (2015). Security, privacy and trust in Internet of Things: The road ahead. *Computer Networks, 76*, 146–164. DOI: 10.1016/j.comnet.2014.11.008

Singh, K. (2020). Intrusion detection systems in UAV networks. *IEEE Communications Surveys and Tutorials, 22*(2), 1407–1434.

Sivasankaran, S., Al-Safarini, M. Y., Vaishnavi, V., Bhavana, M., & Dinesh, M. (2025, November). Application of Edge-Based Deep Learning in Industrial IoT: Employing the Compact Neural Networks for Local Industrial Monitoring. In *2025 International Conference on Digital Innovations for Sustainable Solutions (ICDISS)* (pp. 1-7). IEEE.

Sze, V., Chen, Y. H., Yang, T. J., & Emer, J. S. (2017). Efficient processing of deep neural networks: A tutorial and survey. *Proceedings of the IEEE, 105*(12), 2295–2329. DOI: 10.1109/JPROC.2017.2761740

Taleb, T., Samdanis, K., Mada, B., Flinck, H., Dutta, S., & Sabella, D. (2017). On multi-access edge computing: A survey of the emerging 5G network edge cloud architecture. *IEEE Communications Surveys and Tutorials, 19*(3), 1657–1681. DOI: 10.1109/COMST.2017.2705720

Tang, H., Cheng, M., Bhatti, U. A., Xu, B., Zhou, N., Guo, R., & Wei, B. (2025). Digital twin-driven reinforcement learning-based operational management for customized manufacturing. *Engineering Applications of Artificial Intelligence, 159*, 111754. DOI: 10.1016/j.engappai.2025.111754

Teerapittayanon, S., McDanel, B., & Kung, H. T. (2017). Distributed deep neural networks over the cloud, edge, and end devices. *IEEE International Conference on Distributed Computing Systems*, 328–339. DOI: 10.1109/ICDCS.2017.226

Tramèr, F., Zhang, F., Juels, A., Reiter, M. K., & Ristenpart, T. (2016). Stealing machine learning models via prediction {APIs}. In *25th USENIX security symposium (USENIX Security 16)* (pp. 601-618).

Turnip, T. N., Andersen, B., & Vargas-Rosales, C. (2026). Toward 6G Authentication and Key Agreement Protocol: A Survey on Hybrid Post Quantum Cryptography. *IEEE Communications Surveys and Tutorials*, *28*, 3311–3345. DOI: 10.1109/COMST.2025.3567439

Vashisth, S., & Goyal, A. (2025). A Survey of Federated Learning for IoT: Addressing Resource Constraints and Heterogeneous Challenges. *Informatica (Slovenia)*, *49*(17), 1–10. DOI: 10.31449/inf.v49i17.7707

Wang, Z., Tan, H., Tan-Y, N., Duy-Dong, L., Thai-Thinh, D., & Khoa, T. A. (2025). Latency-aware split learning optimization via genetic algorithms. *ACM Proceedings of the 31st Annual Symposium on Parallelism in Algorithms and Architectures*, 3734433. DOI: 10.1145/3733566.3734433

Wang, S., Tuor, T., Salonidis, T., Leung, K. K., Makaya, C., He, T., & Chan, K. (2019). Adaptive federated learning in resource-constrained edge computing systems. *IEEE Journal on Selected Areas in Communications*, *37*(6), 1205–1221. DOI: 10.1109/JSAC.2019.2904348

Wang, W. (2019). Secure communication in UAV networks: A survey. *IEEE Access : Practical Innovations, Open Solutions*, *7*, 48668–48683.

Xiao, L. (2016). UAV relay in wireless networks: Security and performance. *IEEE Communications Letters*, *20*(10), 2067–2070.

Xu, B., Bhatti, U. A., Tang, H., Yan, J., Wu, S., Sarhan, N., Awwad, E. M., Syam, S. M. S., & Ghadi, Y. Y. (2024). Towards explainability for AI-based edge wireless signal automatic modulation classification. *Journal of Cloud Computing (Heidelberg, Germany)*, *13*(1), 10. DOI: 10.1186/s13677-024-00590-3

Xu, B., Wang, S., Bhatti, U. A., Zhang, X., & Tang, H. (2025). Explainability Analysis Based on Attribution Features for Optimizing Automatic Modulation Classification. *Computer Networks*, *272*, 111696. DOI: 10.1016/j.comnet.2025.111696

Xu, X., Li, Y., Huang, T., Xue, Y., Peng, K., Qi, L., & Dou, W. (2018). An energy-aware computation offloading method. *Future Generation Computer Systems*, *85*, 1–14.

Yang, Z., Chen, M., Wong, K. K., Poor, H. V., & Cui, S. (2022). Federated Learning for 6G: Applications, Challenges, and Opportunities. *Engineering (Beijing)*, *8*, 33–41. DOI: 10.1016/j.eng.2021.12.002

Yanmaz, E. (2012). Connectivity versus area coverage in unmanned aerial vehicle networks. *IEEE International Conference on Communications*, 719–723. DOI: 10.1109/ICC.2012.6364585

Yan, Z. (2020). Privacy protection techniques in UAV systems. *IEEE Network, 34*(5), 162–168.

Yan, Z., Zhang, P., & Vasilakos, A. V. (2014). A survey on trust management for Internet of Things. *Journal of Network and Computer Applications, 42*, 120–134. DOI: 10.1016/j.jnca.2014.01.014

Yao, A. C. (1982). Protocols for Secure Computations. *Annual Symposium on Foundations of Computer Science - Proceedings*, 160–164. DOI: 10.1109/SFCS.1982.38

Yi, D., Liu, J., Li, J., Zhou, J., Bhatti, U. A., Fang, Y., & Nawaz, S. A. (2020). Multimedia security framework based on machine learning techniques. *International Conference on Computer Security Proceedings.*

You, C., Huang, K., Chae, H., & Kim, B. H. (2017). Energy-efficient resource allocation for mobile-edge computation offloading. *IEEE Transactions on Wireless Communications, 16*(3), 1397–1411. DOI: 10.1109/TWC.2016.2633522

Yu, W., Liang, F., He, X., Hatcher, W. G., Lu, C., Lin, J., & Yang, X. (2018). A survey on the edge computing for the Internet of Things. *IEEE Access : Practical Innovations, Open Solutions, 6*, 6900–6919. DOI: 10.1109/ACCESS.2017.2778504

Zaharia, M., Chowdhury, M., Franklin, M. J., Shenker, S., & Stoica, I. (2010). Spark: Cluster computing with working sets. *Proceedings of the USENIX Conference on Hot Topics in Cloud Computing*.

Zanella, A., Bui, N., Castellani, A., Vangelista, L., & Zorzi, M. (2014). Internet of Things for smart cities. *IEEE Internet of Things Journal, 1*(1), 22–32. DOI: 10.1109/JIOT.2014.2306328

Zeng, Y., Zhang, R., & Lim, T. J. (2016). Wireless communications with UAVs: Opportunities and challenges. *IEEE Communications Magazine, 54*(5), 36–42. DOI: 10.1109/MCOM.2016.7470933

Zhang, J., Wang, Y., Cai, Y., Bi, B., Chen, Q., & Zhang, Y. (2025). A low power spiking neural network accelerator on FPGA for real-time edge computing. *IEEE International Conference on AI and IoT Infrastructure Systems*, 11051374. DOI: 10.1109/ICAISISAS64483.2025.11051374

Zhang, C., Aamir, M., Guan, Y., Al-Razgan, M., Awwad, E. M., Ullah, R., Bhatti, U. A., & Ghadi, Y. Y. (2024). Enhancing lung cancer diagnosis with data fusion and mobile edge computing using DenseNet and CNN. *Journal of Cloud Computing (Heidelberg, Germany)*, *13*(1), 91. DOI: 10.1186/s13677-024-00597-w

Zhang, C., Aamir, M., Guan, Y., Al-Razgan, M., Awwad, E., Ullah, R., Bhatti, U. A., & Ghadi, Y. Y. (2024). Intelligent cloud-based systems for geospatial analytics. *Journal of Cloud Computing (Heidelberg, Germany)*.

Zhang, F., Zhang, C., Guan, J., Zhou, Q., Chen, K., Zhang, X., He, B., Zhai, J., & Du, X. (2025). Breaking the edge: Enabling efficient neural network inference on integrated edge devices. *IEEE Transactions on Cloud Computing*, *13*(2), 3559346. DOI: 10.1109/TCC.2025.3559346

Zhang, Q., Chen, M., Yang, L. T., & Zhang, Z. (2018). Deep learning for sensor-based activity recognition: A survey. *IEEE Communications Surveys and Tutorials*, *21*(1), 1–31.

Zhang, Q., Chen, M., Zhao, L., & Wu, J. (2018). Deep learning for edge computing: A survey. *Proceedings of the IEEE*, *107*(8), 1655–1674.

Zhang, T., Jia, F., & Chen, L. (2025). Blockchain adoption in supply chains: Implications for sustainability. *Production Planning and Control*, *36*(5), 699–722. DOI: 10.1080/09537287.2023.2296669

Zhang, Y. (2019). Secure UAV communication with physical layer security. *IEEE Wireless Communications*, *26*(5), 12–18. DOI: 10.1109/MWC.001.1900050

Zhang, Y., Zhang, W., & Zhao, K. (2021). Heterogeneous IoT data analytics with deep learning: Techniques and applications. *Sensors (Basel)*, *21*(8), 2765. PMID: 33919861

Zhantileuov, E., Idrees, A. K., & Schuster, R. (2025). DNNPaS: Deep neural network partitioning strategy for optimizing end-to-end latency in dynamic mobile edge computing. *IEEE International Conference on Cloud Computing*, 00015. DOI: 10.1109/FiCloud66139.2025.00015

Zhou, L., Chen, X., Li, Z., & Li, W. (2020). Edge intelligence: Challenges and opportunities. *Proceedings of the IEEE*, *108*(11), 1821–1841.

Zhou, R. G., Yu, H., Cheng, Y., & Li, F. X. (2019). Quantum image edge extraction based on improved Prewitt operator. *Quantum Information Processing*, *18*(9), 261. DOI: 10.1007/s11128-019-2376-5

Zhou, Z., Chen, X., Li, E., Zeng, L., Luo, K., & Zhang, J. (2019). Edge intelligence: Paving the last mile of artificial intelligence with edge computing. *Proceedings of the IEEE, 107*(8), 1738–1762. DOI: 10.1109/JPROC.2019.2918951

About the Contributors

Uzair Bhatti (Senior Member, IEEE) was born in 1986. He received his Ph.D. degree in Information and Communication Engineering from Hainan University, Haikou, China. In 2021, he completed his postdoctoral research in Earth Observation and Remote Sensing at Nanjing, China. He is currently serving as an Associate Professor in the School of Information and Communication Engineering, Hainan University. Dr. Bhatti has published more than 300 research papers in internationally recognized journals and conferences. In addition, he is the inventor of 22 patents and has served as both Principal Investigator (PI) and participant in several national and provincial research-funded projects in China. He has also edited eight books and conference proceedings published by Springer Nature, Taylor & Francis, and IGI Global. His research interests include Artificial Intelligence, Intelligent Systems, Remote Sensing, Medical Image Analysis, Geographic Information Systems (GIS), and Machine Learning. He has served as a Session Chair at numerous IEEE conferences, including PRAI, DLCV, and IEEE FIT, and has also acted as an Editor and Guest Editor for several SCI- and EI-indexed journals

Yonis Gulzar obtained his Ph.D. in Computer Science in 2018 from International Islamic University Malaysia. He received best Ph.D. Student award from Kulliyyah of Information and Communication Technology (KICT) in the 34th IIUM convocation ceremony held from in Nov'18 His research interests include preference queries, skyline queries, probabilistic and uncertain databases, query processing and optimisation and management of incomplete data, data integration, location-based social networks (LBSN), recommendation systems, and data management in cloud computing.

***

Muinat Adedokun is a Data Scientist with an MSc in Data Science with Distinction from the University of Salford, experienced in healthcare, research, and commercial analytics. She is skilled in Python, SQL, R, cloud platforms (AWS & Azure), ETL development, and data visualization (Power BI, Tableau). Muinat has a proven ability to build scalable data pipelines, deliver predictive insights, and transform complex datasets into actionable results. A strong collaborator with expertise in data governance, automation, and evidence-based decision-making, she is passionate about using data to drive innovation and improve outcomes.

Anorgul Ashirova is working as an Associate Professor at the Department of General Professional Sciences, Mamun University, Khiva, Uzbekistan

Ulugbek Bobamuratov is a faculty member in the Department of Information Technology and Exact Sciences at Termez University of Economics and Service, Termez, Uzbekistan. He is engaged in teaching and academic activities in information technology and exact sciences, with interests in applied computing, data-driven problem solving, and technology-enhanced education. His work focuses on strengthening students' analytical and technical competencies through contemporary pedagogical approaches, and he contributes to curriculum development and academic initiatives supporting innovation and quality education in higher education.

Itohowo Charles is a technology, AI, and data professional . He has built his career at the intersection of business, technology, and digital transformation, with experience delivering data-driven and technology-enabled solutions across regulated industries, particularly financial services. His work spans artificial intelligence, data engineering, enterprise systems, and digital product delivery, with a strong interest in how emerging technologies can be implemented securely, responsibly, and at scale. He has contributed to initiatives involving analytics, automation, cloud-based platforms, and complex system integration, bringing a practical industry perspective to the challenges of security, privacy, and trust in intelligent systems. His professional interests include applied AI, edge intelligence, AI governance, and the design of resilient digital solutions that balance innovation with operational and regulatory demands.

Anorgul I. Ashirova is working in the Department of General Professional Sciences at Mamun University, Khiva, Uzbekistan.

Meletius Igbokwe is a cybersecurity-focused Modern Workplace Engineer with a strong passion for protecting organizational data and identities in today's cloud-driven world. With expertise spanning cloud security, infrastructure, and automation, he is dedicated to helping organizations adopt modern technologies while maintaining a strong security posture. A professional member of BCS, The Chartered Institute for IT, and a holder of a Master's degree in Cloud and Network Security from the University of Bolton, Meletius is deeply invested in advancing cybersecurity through research, innovation, and real-world application. His interests include the intersection of AI and cybersecurity, digital forensics, identity security, and securing enterprise environments using industry best practices.

Vijayakumar K is an Assistant Professor in Department of Computer Science and Engineering, Madras Engineering College, Chennai, Tamilnadu.

Erkin Kholiyarov is working in the Department of Information Technology and Exact Sciences at Termez University of Economics and Service, Termez, Uzbekistan.

Nosir Khurramov is a faculty member in the Department of Information Technology and Exact Sciences at Termez University of Economics and Service, Termez, Uzbekistan. His academic interests include information systems, computational methods, data analysis, and their applications in solving real-world economic and scientific problems. He is actively involved in teaching technology-driven courses, guiding student research, and contributing to departmental academic initiatives. His work focuses on fostering technical proficiency, analytical thinking, and innovation to equip students for emerging opportunities in the digital and knowledge-based economy.

Odilbek Kosimov is working in the Department of Information Technology and Exact Sciences at Termez University of Economics and Service, Termez, Uzbekistan.

Obinna Obi-Akwari is a Lawyer and Software Developer, currently working as a Front-End Developer. He specializes in Javascript, TypeScript, React, and Node. js, building scalable, user-friendly applications. Passionate about technology and innovation, he is a future founder driven to create impactful software solutions. He is also an avid researcher in software development and AI, exploring advancements in automation, machine learning,and software testing. With extensive experience in API integrations, full-stack development, and quality assurance, he strives to enhance performance, efficiencyy, and user experience in dynamic environments. His interdisciplinary background in law and technology enables him to approach problem-solving with a unique perspective.

Oluwafemi Olawoyin (Femi) is a Specialist Data Engineer at Somerset NHS Foundation Trust (UK), where he designs secure, scalable data platforms aligned with NHS Information Governance and GDPR standards. He holds an MSc in Data Science (Distinction) from the University of Salford and certifications in AI

Security & Governance and AI Management Systems (ISO/IEC 42001). His research and publications span AI-driven education, ICT policy for sustainability, and deep learning in medical diagnostics. He is a member of the BCS, The Chartered Institute for IT Beyond his professional engineering work, Femi's independent research explores the intersection of AI ethics, attention protection, and human sovereignty in an era of abundant machine intelligence - advocating for responsible AI development centered on human well-being and interpretability.

Ananya Pandey is a Research Scholar in School of Law at Christ University, Bangalore. She has her research interests in the field of Constitutional Law, Environment Law, Human Rights, Food Security, Intellectual Property Law and Jurisprudence.

Khurramov Ruslan is affiliated with the Department of Information Technology and Exact Sciences, Termez University of Economics and Service, Termez, Uzbekistan. His academic interests span information technology, applied computing, and exact sciences, with a focus on developing analytical and technology-driven solutions for contemporary educational and socio-economic challenges. He is actively involved in teaching, research, and academic development initiatives within the university.

Mukimov Askar Shukhratovich is an Associate Professor in the Department of Digital Technologies at Alfraganus University, Tashkent, Uzbekistan. His academic and research interests focus on digital technologies, information systems, data analytics, and the application of modern computing solutions in education and industry. He is actively involved in teaching and scholarly activities that promote the development of students' technical skills in programming, information technology, and digital innovation. His work emphasizes the integration of advanced digital tools, emerging technologies, and data-driven approaches to address contemporary technological challenges. Mukimov Askar Shukhratovich also contributes to academic discussions related to digital transformation, information technology management, and the advancement of technology-based education. Through his teaching and research engagement, he aims to support the development of skilled professionals capable of contributing to modern digital ecosystems and technological innovation.

Akbar Toyirov is working in the Department of Information Technology and Exact Sciences at Termez University of Economics and Service, Termez, Uzbekistan.

Index

A

C

D

E

F

H

I

M

N

P

R

S

T

U

www.ingramcontent.com/pod-product-compliance
Lightning Source LLC
LaVergne TN
LVHW081520300926
849161LV00006B/1236